The International
Airline Industry

Books published under the Transport Research Program

Wilfred Owen
Strategy for Mobility

Gary Fromm, Editor
Transport Investment and Economic Development

Edwin T. Haefele and Eleanor B. Steinberg
Government Controls on Transport: An African Case

George W. Wilson, Barbara R. Bergman, Leon V. Hirsch, and Martin S. Klein
The Impact of Highway Investment on Development

Robert T. Brown
Transport and the Economic Integration of South America

Holland Hunter
Soviet Transport Experience: Its Lessons for Other Countries

Wilfred Owen
Distance and Development: Transport and Communications in India

Edwin T. Haefele, Editor
Transport and National Goals

Mahlon R. Straszheim
The International Airline Industry

The International Airline Industry

MAHLON R. STRASZHEIM

The Brookings Institution

TRANSPORT RESEARCH PROGRAM

Washington, D.C.

Foreword

THE INTERNATIONAL AIRLINE industry has developed at a spectacular rate since World War II and is now one of the fastest growing and most technologically advanced of all world industries. It provides a wide network of air service with high safety standards and reasonably convenient schedules. When judged by criteria of economic efficiency, however, its performance has been mixed. In this book, the ninth in the Brookings Transport Research Program series, Mahlon R. Straszheim analyzes the structure of the industry, points out the problems which inhibit maximum economic efficiency, and suggests policies which would improve the operation of the industry and promote the best interests of the traveling public.

Most industries present difficult problems of analysis because of continual changes in the structure of the market and the performance of individual firms. This is certainly so in the case of the international airline industry, owing to rapidly growing demand and frequent changes in aircraft technology. On the other hand, the institutional framework, policy environment, and decision-making processes have not changed as quickly as might be supposed. The inertia that characterizes cartel-dominated and highly regulated industries simplifies the task of the analyst.

Most of the author's empirical analysis was conducted in 1965. The production and cost data are for 1962 and 1964. Because many firms were making the transition from piston to jet equipment in 1962, inferences about the performance of individual firms must be made with great caution. But since periods of equipment change are a fact of life in the airline industry, a transition period is not necessarily an inappropriate time to analyze performance.

The author conducted the original research for this study as a graduate student at Harvard University, which has participated in the Transport Research Program since its beginning in 1962. The Program is financed through a research grant to Brookings from the U.S. Agency for International Development. It is directed by Wilfred Owen and is conducted as part of the Brookings Economic Studies Program, headed by Joseph A. Pechman.

In addition to the four members of the reading committee—James R. Nelson, Merton J. Peck, Allen R. Ferguson, and Franz B. Wolf—the author wishes to express his gratitude to John R. Meyer, his adviser at Harvard, for his invaluable suggestions and criticisms during the preparation of his thesis, and Richard E. Caves, whose book *Air Transport and Its Regulators* (1962) served as a model for the present study. He also wishes to thank Edwin T. Haefele and Wilfred Owen for their helpful comments when he was revising the manuscript for publication, and Evelyn P. Fisher for her careful checking of the statistical material. The manuscript was edited by Eleanor B. Steinberg and Mary E. Baker, and the index was prepared by Florence Robinson.

Opinions expressed by the author do not necessarily represent the views of the U.S. Agency for International Development, the reading committee for the study, or the trustees, officers, or staff members of the Brookings Institution.

KERMIT GORDON
President

May 1969
Washington, D.C.

Contents

Text Tables

Text Tables *continued*

Text Figures

Appendix Tables

Appendix Tables *continued*

Appendix Figure

CHAPTER I

Introduction

THE INTERNATIONAL AIRLINE INDUSTRY has developed at a spectacular rate, especially since World War II, and it is now one of the fastest growing and most technologically advanced of all international industries.[1] The network of air service has so expanded that it is now possible to reach virtually any national capital or almost any other major city of the world in less than a day. Reductions in both travel time and costs have been large. The results include increased economic, social, and diplomatic contact among all nations, the creation and facilitation of investment and trade opportunities, and the stimulation of tourist travel.

The industry is not, however, without problems. In recent years a large number of new carriers have entered the industry; many of them

[1] This book excludes from discussion the airlines of the Soviet Union, Eastern Europe, and mainland China and the aircraft manufacturers of the Soviet Union. Carriers of these countries are not members of the International Civil Aviation Organization, and data are largely unavailable. In addition, these carriers are not major participants in international air service outside their political boundaries. The Soviet Union has produced a variety of turboprop and jet equipment, which generally has been adapted from bomber aircraft and has not proved commercially viable relative to comparable aircraft produced in the United States and Western Europe. The Soviet Union has sold little of this equipment to non-Communist countries; hence the influence of Russian equipment has been confined largely to the U.S.S.R. Nevertheless Aeroflot, the Soviet state-owned carrier (equipped with Soviet aircraft), by virtue of its extensive and rapidly growing domestic network, is the largest in the world. See R. E. G. Davies, *A History of the World's Airlines* (London: Oxford University Press, 1964), pp. 499–500.

1

are not efficient operators and thus often sustain large losses. The entire industry has suffered considerable losses in some periods—most recently in the early 1960s, during the transition from piston aircraft to jets. Given prevailing management difficulties and pricing practices, capacity increased faster than it could be utilized profitably.

There have also been other problems. The success of charter operators and non-regulated carriers offering lower-priced and less luxury-oriented service suggests that the industry may be overemphasizing service and that it might be more profitable to lower air fares. A high level of service on international flights is still commonplace despite the lack of evidence that consumer preferences lie in this direction. With regard to individual city-pair markets, there are many instances of questionable performance. Excess entry and excess capacity often exist, and prices frequently bear little relation to cost because of a rather extensive system of value-of-service pricing.

This mixed industry performance is the result of an industry structure which in many respects is unique, which has both economic and political characteristics, and which includes a substantial amount of public participation. Many airlines are state-owned and subsidized, and for many carriers decisions on entry, pricing, and choice of aircraft are made at the governmental level. In the market structure of most other industries these types of decisions are normally left to the firm or are made in the marketplace. Industry participants therefore cannot be considered as profit-maximizing firms in the customary sense, but rather represent a mix of public and private interests. The industry is also affected at least indirectly by issues and problems which occur in diplomatic negotiations at the intergovernmental level.

The basis for public interest in the airline industry is not the traditional one of an industry which requires economic regulation as a natural monopoly. It will be argued in this book that the converse is true; a competitive market environment probably would create the best industry performance. The motive behind public interest lies in the many external effects, some more valid than others (and all certainly substantially exaggerated), that accrue to industry participants. These external effects include balance of payments effects, the attraction of trade, tourism, and investment, and the political prestige of showing the flag.

Nations generally have been unwilling to risk the fortunes of their flag airlines in a competitive environment because of the real or assumed importance of these non-market considerations. Most nations have chosen to create an environment of restricted and regulated competition in which they can protect their own interests. Entry is decided in bilateral agreements between governments, and prices are set by an international conference procedure subject to approval by each government. Pooling agreements and capacity restrictions prevail in many markets; international aviation policies pursued in this context reflect an interesting blend of economics and applied diplomacy. Finally, nations have been willing to pay substantial subsidies to their flag carriers to cover losses incurred as a consequence of these non-economic considerations. This commitment to subsidy is perhaps the most important single factor conditioning the behavior of individual firms in the industry; it unfortunately insulates them from competitive pressures which usually improve performance in a market context.

The mixed nature of industry performance to date raises important questions regarding the future role of public participation and regulation. The international airline industry, with an available technology more or less comparable to that of the U.S. domestic trunklines, has not been able to achieve a comparable level of performance. There is a strong suggestion that public influence and regulation in the international industry could be altered to improve performance from an economic point of view. The major focus of this book is on explaining and evaluating the economic performance of the industry and on recommending changes to improve it.

The criterion which will be used to evaluate industry performance and the aim to which policy prescriptions will be directed is economic efficiency—that is, production at least cost and extension of output until price equals marginal cost. This study attempts to specify an efficient or rational industry configuration and to describe the nature of the production function and scale economies. An entry pattern which reflects participation in the industry by least-cost carriers only is suggested, along with the nature of the product which consumers will buy at prices equal to costs of efficient operations.

Efficiency as an objective is one which some nations will find unacceptable, particularly those countries in which the flag carriers would suffer if the airline industry approached rationality. These carriers are usually poorly financed, equipped, and managed. Profit maximization in a competitive market is clearly an uncomfortably narrow objective for such countries. Unfortunately, no overall industry objective exists which will be universally acceptable. Political decisions are necessarily involved and must be reconciled in international negotiations.

Efficiency is examined in this study for two reasons. First, it is an objective which will be of interest to many nations. (The United States, for example, has indicated that efficiency is its policy objective.) Second, the description of a rational industry configuration is useful in assessing alternative politically motivated decisions, such as different entry patterns and pricing standards. The economic costs of these alternatives will be important in policy decisions which weigh economic objectives in terms of political and social consequences. Objectives other than economic efficiency will be neither formulated nor judged in this study, although alternative policy objectives will be evident in the detailed discussion of the industry. In the last analysis, each nation must itself weigh the various potential and economic consequences of decisions affecting the industry.

Chapters I through VII examine the structure of the industry, showing the relationships between the underlying economic patterns, the regulatory environment, the political interests of governments, and market performance. Chapters VIII and IX develop a theoretical model of economic efficiency and evaluate performance on this basis. Chapters X through XII consider various structural changes in the regulatory environment and in the nature of governmental participation, and prescribe policies aimed at improving performance.

The description of the industry structure involves, first, an examination of the role of state interests in the industry: the effects governments have on the decision process of participant carriers and the restrictions which they have imposed on the market. This political and institutional framework is examined in Chapter II, which describes the motives for state intervention and the direct means by which governments influence their own carriers' decisions through ownership and subsidy, and in Chapter III, which describes the entry process and national attitudes with respect to entry. Most countries have strongly protected their entry rights, granting entry in bilateral agreements with other countries; restrictions on plane type, schedule frequency, and schedule times are often matters of negotiation at the governmental level in the process of working out these bilateral agreements. This restricted entry environment has resulted in a costly inflexibility in the industry. (The governmental role in pricing policies in the industry is discussed in Chapter VII.)

The underlying production and cost relationships in the industry structure are examined in detail. Chapter IV describes the production function for the industry, including differences across national boundaries and determines the extent to which these differences or differences in factor prices affect the efficiency of various producers of international airline service. This description of the underlying technological and cost relationships will be useful in determining an efficient pattern of entry. Chapter V is a study of the structure of airline costs as they relate to route structure; this will be useful in prescribing a price structure related to the costs of providing service. Chapter VI develops the characteristics of demand in the airline industry, in order to assess consumer preferences for type of service, schedule frequency, and price. Judgments about pricing policies in the industry will rest on analysis of the demand function and the cost structure.

The pricing environment is described in Chapter VII. A conference of airlines—the International Air Transport Association (IATA)—has governmental sanction to determine rates, subject to approval by the countries involved. Governments have only loosely supervised this process. The U.S. Civil Aeronautics Board (CAB) has continually tried, with only moderate success, to exert influence on the rate-setting procedure. The CAB and the privately owned U.S. carriers often have divergent interests. Since the carriers participate in IATA proceedings, the CAB influence is an indirect one. The attitudes of other governments vary widely—some countries show little interest, while other governments actively support their carriers in the bargaining sessions. The result is a rather loosely supervised private cartel of airlines, which sets prices based primarily on a complex value-of-service pricing structure with a variety of implicit transfers among travelers and countries.

This environment of state participation and the concomitant market restriction have produced various effects on the performance of the market as a whole. The effects of this political environment and the variety of publicly and privately motivated decisions are not easily assessed. Public and private decision-making are interdependent; moreover, these policies are superimposed on an economic structure which has been changing rapidly as a result of the growth in market demand and technological advances in aircraft equipment. The impact of this changing technology has itself been conditioned by the market environment. To understand causation of particular dimensions of market performance or to assess the effects of particular regulatory policies requires analysis beginning with the market structure itself. The nature of underlying production, cost, and demand functions are important to this analysis. The relationship of the market structure to performance is shown so that the causal structure can be developed. (This will be the basis for the assessment of costs of alternative policies and the policy prescriptions made in the last part of this study.)

In the part of the book that evaluates industry performance, Chapter VIII develops the theoretical framework. The Law of Comparative Advantage is necessary in evaluating an industry in an international setting. The conditions under which cost comparisons can be used to discern the countries with comparative advantages in producing international airline service are spelled out. In addition to specifying entry criteria, Chapter VIII also develops criteria for capacity and pricing decisions which have certain welfare properties. The evaluation of the industry based on these standards is summarized in Chapter IX. The performance of particular carriers, many of which have incurred substantial financial deficits, is also reviewed there.

Finally, the third part of the study assesses the role of public regulation and suggests changes which would promote a more economically efficient industry. The changes which are recommended require a more responsible attitude by all governments. Given the considerable motives for government interest and participation in the industry, progress necessarily lies in a more enlightened perception of these responsibilities. In addition, the recommendations imply a greater reliance on competition and freer markets. The alternative of placing greater reliance on regulatory processes is reviewed but generally rejected. The major thrust of Chapter X is that while the motives for the public role are strong and represent a structural dimension of the industry which the analyst must accept as given, there appears to be considerable scope for improved performance within the confines of feasible changes in public policy.

Chapter XI spells out specific recommendations for the United States which should help promote the objective of industry rationality. These remarks are in large part applicable to other countries with similar objectives.

There is even perhaps some reason for optimism. In some countries besides the United States, there appears to be a trend in favor of a more economically efficient industry organization. There are a number of reasons why economic rationalization of the industry as an objective may become more important in the future. These reasons, although by no means compelling for all nations, are important to many. The prospects are sketched in the concluding chapter, and the challenge of the future is outlined.

CHAPTER II

Government Influence in the Industry

WITH THE EXPANSION of international air travel and the
proliferation of independent countries in the world, various noneconomic benefits have increasingly influenced the decision of a country
to establish its own international airline service. The prestige attached
to operating an international jet carrier is one example. Serving routes
to former colonies for political reasons is another. These and other external benefits of industry participation are highly valued in many
countries and have produced considerable interest at the state or government level. One result of this is that countries have generally been
motivated to assume a very protective attitude with regard to their
own flag carriers. In addition, governments have exerted an influence
in many decisions which normally would be left in the hands of the
airlines.

Motives for State Interest

An international flag carrier typically accounts for a very small share
(usually less than one-half of one percent) of national income or of
employment. In contrast, the balance of payments effects are quite important and usually represent one of the chief reasons for having a flag
carrier. A flag carrier earns balance of payments receipts in the form of
passenger fares and thus can save potential foreign exchange losses by
accommodating its nation's traveling public. In advanced countries

8

such as the United States, whose citizens travel a great deal, this saving is generally the most important balance of payments consideration.

Balance of Payments Considerations

The magnitude of foreign exchange costs depends on the choice of aircraft, the scheduling of that equipment, the nature of the route system, and the extent of subcontracting and external assistance required. International carriers of the United States spend slightly less than 25 percent of total fare receipts at each foreign port for landing charges, fuel and taxes, terminal rental, wages and support of foreign-based personnel, crew expenses while in port, and a variety of indirect expenses such as passenger food and services.[1]

Foreign carriers probably spend somewhat less proportionally on port expenses in the United States. The relatively high American labor costs account for the greater port expenses of U.S. carriers. The foreign exchange consequence for the United States (net of direct input purchases) of creating a flag carrier to carry a single passenger previously carried by a foreign carrier to or from the United States would be a change in the balance of payments accounts of about 50 percent of the fare. This is the fare net of necessary port expenses abroad by the U.S. carrier less the foregone port receipts which the United States would have received from the foreign carrier. (For the United States and the United Kingdom, both of which use primarily domestic equipment and financing, this calculation essentially reflects the total foreign exchange result of a flag carrier's operation.)

In addition to port charges, most foreign carriers require foreign exchange for aircraft and spare parts, since about 90 percent of the industry's equipment is imported from the United States. The foreign exchange cost of imported equipment depends on the choice of aircraft and its utilization. Aircraft and spare parts depreciation charges for a Boeing 727 amount to about 15 percent of total available ton-mile costs. Thin route densities or poor aircraft scheduling which result in lower utilization increase these costs—in some instances by as much as 50 percent. By contrast, depreciation expenses for a used DC-6 are only about 5 percent of total costs.

The smaller and newer carriers, especially those of the developing

[1] Civil Aeronautics Board, *The Impact on the Balance of Payments of the Air Transport and Aircraft Industries* (1965), pp. 14–15.

TABLE II–1. *Air Transportation Accounts and Total Travel Accounts, U.S. Balance of Payments, 1952–63*
(In millions of U. S. dollars)

Type of Account	1952	1953	1954	1955	1956	1957	1958	1959	1960	1961	1962	1963
U. S. receipts from other countries												
Air export freight	24	28	26	33	36	41	44	49	55	46	51	53
Air passenger fares	88	86	88	98	101	124	132	145	126ª	174	181	195
Port expenditures of foreign airlines in the U. S.	32	36	40	53	65	77	95	118	147	163	175	187
U. S. payments to other countries												
Air import freight	3	4	5	7	9	12	13	19	22	22	26	26
Air passenger fares	42	48	56	68	87	131	157	205	301ª	291	341	390
Port expenditures of U. S. airlines abroad	87	91	92	108	119	127	151	161	181	168	169	178
Net totals for U. S. air transport												
Freight	21	24	21	26	27	29	31	30	33	24	25	27
Passenger fares	46	38	32	30	14	−7	−25	−60	−175	−117	−160	−195
Port expenditures	−55	−55	−52	−55	−54	−50	−56	−43	−34	−5	6	9
Total	12	7	1	1	−13	−28	−50	−73	−176	−98	−129	−159
U. S. overall travel account												
U. S. expenditures abroad	−840	−929	−1,009	−1,158	−1,275	−1,372	−1,460	−1,610	−1,745	−1,747	−1,892	−2,070
Foreign expenditures in the U. S.	550	574	595	654	705	785	825	902	875	885	870	934

Sources: U. S. Department of Commerce, Office of Business Economics, *Balance of Payments Statistical Supplement, Revised Edition*, a supplement to *Survey of Current Business* (1963), pp. 134 and 140; *Survey of Current Business*, various issues; U.S. Bureau of the Census, *Statistical Abstract of the United States* (1966), p. 599.
ª New series.

countries, incur some additional foreign exchange costs since they often subcontract much of their maintenance and externally finance much of their capital investment. Maintenance for a Boeing 727 is about 18 percent of total costs; for the DC-6, it is nearly 23 percent. Some of the smaller carriers contract more than half of this work to larger foreign carriers. The interest cost of external financing for a Boeing 727 is about 15 percent of total costs and for a DC-6, about 4 percent. In addition, technical assistance costs, such as jet pilot training, can also be substantial. (Depreciation, maintenance, and overhead expenses are shown in Table IV-4. Typical utilization rates appear in Table A-1.)

EFFECTS ON U.S. BALANCE OF PAYMENTS. The United States, using its own aircraft and serving the largest traveling public in the world, enjoys a greater foreign exchange gain from its carriers than does any other country.[2] The total travel account and air transport items in the United States balance of payments are shown in Table II-1. The air transport accounts are, of course, only part of the total travel account, with air fares accounting for almost half of the total budget of American travelers. The magnitude of the total travel account is largely governed by the number of a nation's citizens who travel abroad. The overall travel account for the United States has assumed a larger deficit over time as more Americans travel abroad relative to the number of foreign nationals visiting the United States. The air transport account portion has shown a steadily increasing deficit, partly because of more travel abroad by American citizens, and also because U.S. carriers have been earning a progressively smaller share of total fares to and from the United States. The data in Table II-2 reflect this trend. U.S. airlines carried 66.4 percent of all travel to and from the United States in 1954, 50.1 percent in 1959, and only 49.8 percent in 1964.[3]

[2] Data on the balance of payments consequences of U.S. travel and U.S. carriers' operations are not readily available. The distribution of total U.S. travel abroad by country of origin and destination and the percentage share using U.S. carriers are not accurately known. For a discussion of the data problem, see Review Committee for Balance of Payments Statistics, *The Balance of Payments Statistics of the United States*, Report to the Bureau of the Budget (Government Printing Office, 1965). Data for other countries are also scarce. Occasionally air travel data are given in the International Monetary Fund, *Balance of Payments Yearbook*, and sometimes the annual reports of various carriers contain such data.

[3] U.S. Department of Justice, Immigration and Naturalization Service, *Report of Passenger Travel between the United States and Foreign Countries* (1964).

TABLE II–2. *Value of Air Travel to and from the United States, Selected Years, 1950–60*

(In millions of U. S. dollars)

Type of Payment	1950	1952	1954	1956	1958	1960
U. S. residents to						
U. S. carriers	75	111	145	229	275	358
Foreign carriers	26	42	56	87	157	251
Foreign visitors to						
U. S. carriers	35	50	46	49	79	106
Foreign carriers	21	28	32	42	96	178
Total						
U. S. carriers	110	161	191	278	354	464
Foreign carriers	47	70	88	129	253	429

Source: U. S. Department of Commerce, Office of Business Economics, *Balance of Payments Statistical Supplement, Revised Edition,* a supplement to *Survey of Current Business* (1963), p. 141.

An estimate from these data can be made of the effect of U.S. flag carriers on the balance of payments. In 1960, U.S. international carriers earned approximately $625 million in revenues, including $464 million on traffic to and from the United States and $161 million on "fifth freedom traffic" (travelers moving between two foreign countries). Reported port expenses of $181 million arose from charges in a single port or in both ports of entry for U.S.-based and fifth freedom traffic, respectively. Relating these port charges to total revenue of U.S. carriers shows that 23 percent of fares on the average is spent on port expenses for each foreign port. Thus, if the United States had given up its flag carriers in 1960, the net balance of payments effects in lost revenue less port charges would have been an increased foreign exchange deficit of $342 million or an amount greater than one-third of the total travel account deficit. This constitutes a substantial motive for U.S. interest in the industry and in its flag carriers.

BALANCE OF PAYMENTS CONSEQUENCES IN OTHER DEVELOPED COUNTRIES. The major carriers in other developed countries have reported similar results, although the amounts are smaller in absolute terms. For example, Italian carriers in 1963 earned $96 million in passenger fare receipts from foreign nationals and received $83 million in fares paid by Italian citizens. Foreign port expenses amounted to $29 million, and approximately $40 million was spent on equipment (the average of Alitalia's equipment purchases over recent years).[4] The total positive effect

⁴ Alitalia annual reports, and International Monetary Fund, *Balance of Payments Yearbook,* Vol. 18 (March 1967), Italy, Table C.

of Italy's possession of a flag carrier, both in net foreign exchange receipts and in net savings of fare payments which Italian travelers would otherwise pay to foreign carriers, was about $75 million in 1963. British European Airways (BEA) in fiscal 1963–64 earned a net foreign exchange saving of $34 million out of a total revenue of $168 million.[5] Added savings resulted from carrying British citizens abroad.

KLM Royal Dutch Airlines has reported an even more impressive result. Company officials estimated that in 1960 KLM earned a net of $65 million in foreign exchange from foreign travelers and saved $72 million in foreign exchange by carrying Netherlands' nationals abroad. Aircraft purchases abroad left a net plus of $25 million—almost 8 percent of the Netherlands' net goods and services foreign exchange balance.[6] During the period 1946 to 1961, inclusive, KLM earned a net $30–35 million per year or about 10 percent of the nation's net surplus.[7] The Netherlands has enjoyed these high foreign exchange earnings because of KLM's strategic location in the lucrative North Atlantic market and because the country itself is a prominent tourist attraction.

In short, countries whose citizens travel abroad a great deal see a potential gain in foreign exchange (or reduced loss) as an important justification for supporting a flag carrier. Well managed jet operations may earn 25 percent or more of total revenue from foreign travelers even when aircraft and spare parts must be imported. The effects of a flag carrier on a nation's total balance of payments is therefore not insignificant for most developed countries in North America and Europe.

UNDERDEVELOPED COUNTRIES: FOREIGN EXCHANGE LOSSES. In many of the less developed countries, by contrast, foreign exchange losses are often incurred because of necessary reliance on external financing and technical assistance, because of the problems of achieving high levels of scheduling equipment and personnel, and because of the unprofitable route structures which these countries often serve. The combination of thin route densities and poor scheduling is the most important cause of

---

[5] "BEA Expects Smaller Profit This Year," *International Aviation,* Supplement to *Aviation Daily,* Vol. 154 (September 8, 1964), p. 102; BEA annual report, 1964.

[6] International Monetary Fund, *Balance of Payments Yearbook,* Vol. 15 (July 1964), Netherlands, Table 1, and KLM annual reports.

[7] Civil Aeronautics Board, Docket No. 12063, "Rebuttal Exhibits of KLM Royal Dutch Airlines," November 22, 1961, p. 1. This is part of "Direct Testimony of James C. Buckley appearing as a witness for KLM Royal Dutch Airlines and Sabena Belgian World Airlines."

losses. Many carriers of less developed countries have sustained a foreign exchange deficit when they entered the jet market or have been forced to make large entry concessions to carriers of the developed countries in order to obtain special foreign exchange arrangements. The exceptions are a few carriers favorably situated on dense international routes. The implications of such foreign exchange losses depend among other things upon the opportunity cost of foreign exchange. The high cost of foreign exchange to many of these countries implies that they must (or should) value the external effects of industry participation very highly.

External Effects for Developed Nations

A variety of external effects—economic, political, and military—which result from the possession of an international flag carrier have produced interest at the national government level. The impact and evaluation of these external effects vary greatly between developed and less developed nations. The external effects most important to a developed nation are serving its own citizens; promoting trade, investment, and tourism from other countries; and serving political routes. The United States, for example, is interested in providing safe, reliable service over a wide network and at a reasonable price for its traveling citizens. Other nations wish to encourage American investment or to earn a share of the American tourist dollar; they may do this by providing frequent scheduling to and from the major cities along the international routes. A flag carrier also simplifies the provision of route systems to present or former colonies or the provision of any other services on politically oriented routes which are not profitable.

A flag carrier may also support domestic aircraft manufacturers. Development costs of new aircraft are high, and unit production costs decrease greatly as more aircraft are sold. Therefore, a new type of plane is unlikely to be commercially profitable unless the sales level reaches at least 100. These rising development costs and the marketing uncertainty facing the manufacturer of new aircraft have produced many financial failures of smaller companies and mergers with larger firms. The sale of a new model to flag carriers clearly is an important form of support of domestic manufacturers.

Aircraft purchases and sales are an important balance of payments consideration for the few countries which make up the industry; this is especially true for the United States, whose aircraft exports are a sizable portion of total net export sales. U.S. manufacturers dominate the international aircraft industry. This dominance favorably affects the U.S. balance on current account and is a basic motivation for the U.S. objective of promoting an expanding and efficient international airline sector.

Finally, there is a military motive for supporting a flag carrier which can act as a ready reserve. A carrier provides a fleet of planes, supporting equipment, and a staff of trained personnel which can be used in flying men and materiel to a combat theater. American carriers in World War II and in the Korean War served such a role, and in one Berlin crisis carried cargo to West Germany, whence Air Force planes took it to Berlin. In Great Britain almost all private airlines were used in the British share of the Berlin airlift. The British government subsequently realized the value of a civilian transport reserve and made efforts to aid the development of private carriers, largely through sizable troop contracts.[8] In recent years British Eagle, an independent airline, has flown troops to Malaysia to deal with crises there.[9]

External Effects for Developing Nations

As seen from the point of view of the developing countries, the benefits of possessing an international airline are (1) that it aids in the development process and (2) that it enhances the national image. The latter, seemingly the less important of the two, has probably been the most important motivating force in the last decade.

The economic rationale for investment in international airlines by less developed countries includes the effects of decreases in travel time and costs and of improved communications on trade, investment, and tourism. Air travel has done much to make the developing countries far more accessible. Investment, technical and economic cooperation, and the importation of advisory personnel have also been facilitated. Tourist travel, facilitated by the development of international air routes, could become an increasingly important source of revenue to the less developed countries as more and more tourists look beyond Europe

[8] Stephen Wheatcroft, *Air Transport Policy* (London: Michael Joseph, Ltd., 1964), pp. 33–35.

[9] *Aeroplane and Commercial Aviation News*, Vol. 109 (January 7, 1965), p. 30.

and the Mediterranean.[10] In general, the less developed nations have been brought more into the "world of nations" by air travel.

These benefits, however, could accrue to the developing countries regardless of what airline provided international air service; hence in and of themselves they do not justify having a flag carrier. Furthermore, there is no apparent lack of entrants into the long-haul markets to provide service to the less developed countries. Regional air service, on the other hand, may not be profitable initially and hence a developing nation may find it desirable to provide service connecting its cities with its neighbor countries and with major international airports.

The political benefit that apparently has assumed overriding importance in the decision-making of the developing countries is the boost to national image of a flag carrier, and especially of an international jet operation. A jet carrier has become a major status symbol of the developing countries. In the last decade dozens of new national carriers have appeared, all of which are anxious to show the flag. One motivation for this behavior lies in the intense desire of these nations for rapid growth and a highly urbanized and technologically advanced society. Also, the unstable political environment which often prevails may have led the government in power in some less developed countries to undertake projects with a short time horizon. New jet airports and aircraft are flashy symbols of progress.

However, while the possession of a flag carrier does serve as a status symbol and a means of advertising abroad, the positive effects on outside trade and investment decisions appear to be only marginal. As will be shown subsequently, most of the underdeveloped-country entrants into the long-haul markets have incurred losses. These nations' carriers are entering markets in which they do not have a comparative advantage, in which competition is at times intense, and in which there is often sufficient capacity already.

Defining Governmental Objectives

The various market and nonmarket consequences of international air service include impacts on the traveling public, airline owners and

[10] Jacques Jordeau, "Reflections on the Role of Air Transport in the Harmonious Evolution of Underdeveloped Countries" (The RAND Corporation, November 1962), RAND Memo 3165, pp. 12–14.

management, suppliers of aircraft and other commodities, and governments and their constituent taxpayers. The formulation of an objective function which reflects these effects is a complex task involving a variety of economic and political issues. It is a task, moreover, which nations themselves have found difficult. More often than not, objectives have been vaguely defined and policies poorly conceived.

No single generalization would adequately represent what each nation considers an acceptable synthesis of the various consequences of participation in the industry. Most would agree that a broad network which offers fast and dependable service and incorporates the latest technology is required (although the latter will not be acceptable to everyone when the supersonic transport appears with its sonic boom). Little agreement can be found on who should provide the service, what should constitute the service, how much should be provided, or how it should be priced.

Broadly defined political and social issues loom large over the economics of much decision-making in the airlines industry. Nations differ on the proportion of economic costs which should be allocated to these political considerations, although all pay at least some attention to them. Viewing policy formulation in its broadest perspective, the fact that international air transport decisions are arrived at through international negotiation implies that questions of foreign policy are introduced. A close identification of international air transport policy as one instrument in these broader negotiations considerably complicates the formulation of policy objectives.

Various nations differ in their attitudes with regard to international air transport objectives; this can be explained in part by fundamental differences in social and economic institutions and ideologies. Objectives of the United States are generally consistent with its historic advocacy of free world trade and unrestricted capital markets. Similarly, American reliance on private ownership without government regulation, and the American dislike for pooling arrangements and other nonmarket procedures for deciding on the allocation of resources, are important in the formulation of U.S. objectives in the industry. At the same time, many other countries have very different inclinations. European nations, for example, appear more likely to permit restrictions in their markets, and European firms seem more anxious to form pools and divide the existing market than to enter into competition, which might well expand the market for all.

The underlying objectives of each nation are not always easily ascertained. Probably the most important single indication of a nation's objectives is the role it wishes to reserve for its own flag carrier. This sometimes is only imperfectly mirrored in policies pursued. If the flag carrier is economically inefficient, the government's evaluation of the importance of participation in the international industry can be measured by the extent to which it tries to induce concessions or changes in the more efficient industry configuration. Many governments apparently are willing to incur large subsidy costs and to impose costs on other nations' carriers and travelers by protective policies in order to assure or to improve the position of their carriers. On the other hand, when a flag carrier is economically efficient, the role its government envisons for it is not so obvious. A favorable competitive position usually exists because of previous economic development, location in important air markets, or both. Advocating competitive markets in these circumstances is quite consistent with concern over the fortunes of one's own flag carrier.

Indeed, the relative competitive position of a country's carrier is probably the most important rationale behind that country's support of free competition and industry rationalization as opposed to restricted international air markets. For example, prices set at the level of marginal costs of U.S. carriers would force heavy losses on many carriers, especially some of the younger carriers of developing areas. The "infant industries" rationale for higher prices is a familiar argument frequently given; more realistically, most of the protected carriers have no hope of ever belonging in the industry on economic grounds and use the price protection to reduce the subsidy cost of their operations. This sort of very practical consideration of national interests is the major basis for the opposition to efficiency as an objective.

The remainder of this chapter will consider the means which nations have used to exert influence over their own flag carriers. Chapters III and VII will describe government policies with regard to entry and pricing.

Governmental Influence over Flag Carriers

The particular institutional arrangements through which public financial support is provided and the public sector is represented in carrier management decision-making varies considerably among countries. The kinds of decisions being influenced are, however, strikingly similar. Indeed, government influence over international airlines through public ownership and subsidy has been quite pervasive throughout the industry, with governments having influenced the decisions concerning aircraft and route choice of virtually every carrier in one instance or another.

"Chosen Instruments"

One important means governments have used to exert influence has been the creation of "chosen instruments," or flag carriers owned and subsidized by the state. This has become the predominant form of ownership in the industry. In the pre-World War II years, many European governments bought out private carriers to create these chosen instruments. The creation of chosen instruments was accelerated after World War II as small private companies were merged and nationalized. Many newly independent countries have created their own flag carriers, usually by acquiring local carriers that had previously been subsidiaries of large foreign airlines.

Detailed information on airline ownership has been presented by Davies.[11] Almost all European airlines are now state owned. In Latin America, there has been a pattern of consolidation and nationalization similar to that which took place in Europe, with state ownership in many instances replacing foreign ownership. Foreign companies once predominated in Latin America, largely by ownership of subsidiary companies. Pan American Airways (PAA), with minority shares in many of the local carriers, was the dominant Latin American carrier. Great Britain and the Netherlands, motivated by existing or former colonial ties, were also important outside owners of airlines serving Latin America. In the period since World War II, these foreign interests have gradually been bought out and the carriers nationalized. In 1954, only three of the ten largest carriers in Latin America were free from foreign sponsorship. By 1960, only three were still partially owned by outside interests—PAA continued to hold minority shares in Compania Mexicana de Aviacion, Avianca, and Panair do Brasil. Most Latin American nations now have flag carriers which they strongly support with restrictionist policies.

[11] R. E. G. Davies, *A History of the World's Airlines* (London: Oxford University Press, 1964).

In the Middle and Far East, and more recently in Africa, many new carriers, usually state-owned, have appeared. In many instances, these carriers were initiated through the help of outside financing by European or American carriers, only to be nationalized later. State ownership now predominates in the Middle and Far East, although there is still considerable outside control in Africa.

The details of airline ownership are complicated by a variety of means of state control and a variety of parent-subsidiary relationships. A summary of government participation is given in Table II-3, which shows the percentage of state ownership in most of the major carriers.[12] The U.S. carriers, privately owned, are the most important exception to this predominant pattern of state ownership. It will be shown subsequently that the United States faces some special problems because of differences between the objectives of private ownership and what the government might define as the public interest. This problem is unique to the United States and to those nations that have encouraged private ownership.

Choice of Plane

State ownership has been accompanied by state influence over decisions at the firm level. One area of influence has been that of plane choice. Since aircraft manufacture is important for national security reasons to a few countries and aircraft export sales are important in balance of payments accounts, plane choice has been subjected at times to considerable political pressure.

While immediately after World War II U.S. planes were about the only aircraft available, the subsequent rebuilding of British and French aircraft industries has made flag carrier support of domestic manufacturers a very real question. Though British and French manufacturers would protest, it appears that U.S. planes have been more economical to operate.[13] The economic superiority of American aircraft leaves no problem for the United States, although there have been a few cases where pressure has been exerted on U.S. carriers not to buy abroad. A former U.S. domestic carrier, Capital Airlines, was able to acquire the

---

[12] For a detailed survey, see "World Airline Ownership and Control," *Aviation Report Supplement* (London: Aviation Studies International, Ltd., September 1963), No. 130, pp. 3–31; see also "World Airline Survey," *Flight International*, Vol. 87 (April 15, 1965), pp. 562–608.

[13] See Chapter V, p. 88, and Appendix B, Table B-4.

TABLE II-3. *Percentage Share of Government Ownership in International Airlines, Selected Countries and Carriers, 1960*

Country and Carrier	Percentage	Country and Carrier	Percentage
Africa		Scandinavian Airlines System	
Air Afrique	66	(SAS)	50
Air Algerie	51	Swissair	30
Air Congo	65	Transportes Aéreos Portugueses	0
Central African Airways	100	Union de Transports Aériens	0
East African Airways	100		
Ethiopian Airlines	100	*Latin America*	
Ghana Airways	100	Aerolineas Argentinas	100
Royal Air Maroc	55	Aerovias Venezolanas	0
		Avianca Airlines	0
Asia		Linea Aeropostal Venezolana	100
Air Ceylon	100	Panair do Brasil	0
Air-India	100	Transportes Aereos Nacionales	
Indian Airlines	100	(TAN-Honduras)	0
Pakistan International Airlines	65	Venezuelan International	
Royal Nepal Airline	100	Airways	55
Union of Burma Airways	100	Viacao Aerea Rio Grandense	0
		Viacao Aerea São Paulo	100
Australia			
Qantas Empire Airways	100	*Middle East*	
Tasman Empire Airways	100	Aden Airways (by BOAC)	0
		El Al Israel Airlines	61
Europe		Iranian Airways	51
Aer Lingus	95	Iraqi Airways	100
Aerlinte Eireann	100	Jordan National Airways	25
Air France	100	Kuwait Airways	0
Alitalia Airlines	84	Middle East Airlines	0
Austrian Airlines (AUA)	70	Saudi Arabian Airlines	100
Aviacion y Comercio		United Arab Airlines (UAA)	100
(Aviaco)	100		
British European Airways		*North America*	
(BEA)	100	Air Canada	100
British Overseas Airways		Canadian Pacific Airlines	0
Corporation (BOAC)	100	U. S. carriers	0
Cunard-Eagle Airways	0		
Cyprus Airways	51	*Orient, Pacific*	
Finnair	0	Air Laos	50
Flugfelag Islands H.F.	50	Air Vietnam	75
Iberia Airlines of Spain	100	Borneo Airways	51
Icelandic Airlines	0	Civil Air Transport (Formosa)	0
Lufthansa German Airlines	50	Garuda Indonesian Airways	100
Olympic Airways	0	Japan Air Lines	75
KLM Royal Dutch Airlines	70	Korean National Airlines	100
Sabena Belgian World Airlines	65	Philippine Air Lines	54
		Thai International	70

Source "World Airline Ownership and Control," *Aviation Report Supplement* (London: Aviation Studies International, Ltd., September 1963), No. 130.
Note: This table lists most of the major international carriers. It overstates the predominance of state ownership in that most of the medium- and smaller-sized carriers are privately owned.

British-built Viscount only after considerable public pressure of this sort. The real dilemma faces the British and French carriers with regard to aircraft manufactured in those countries.

The British have probably been most disadvantaged by nationally oriented or politically inspired equipment policies. The one bright spot occurred in the middle 1950s: the Viscount, the first turboprop, proved to be a reliable, economic, and profitable aircraft and was very important to British European Airways (BEA) in expanding its route system. Recently BEA placed an order for the American built DC-9, a short-haul jet, only to have the decision subsequently reversed and the British-built BAC-111 ordered. It remains to be seen how these two aircraft will compare in terms of efficiency.

British Overseas Airways Corporation (BOAC), however, has fared worse than BEA, having been forced to rely on British-built planes in long-haul markets, where the competitive disadvantage of British planes as compared with their American counterparts has been greatest. BOAC enjoyed a brief moment of glory when the first jet aircraft, the Comet 1, was introduced, but its subsequent structural failure converted this temporary advantage into a $7.8 million capital loss. This cost was small, however, compared to BOAC's difficulties with the transition to jets. BOAC's initial decision was to purchase the British-produced turboprop, the Britannia, scheduled for delivery in 1956. Because of production delays, a fleet of DC-7s had to be purchased as a stop-gap. The introduction of jets soon thereafter placed both the DC-7C (the last long-range piston plane produced) and the Britannia at a huge cost and marketing disadvantage. BOAC thus found itself with two undesirable fleets in 1961 and 1962.[14] Both the Britannias and the DC-7Cs were expensive to operate and therefore sold at sizable capital losses. Comet 4, Britain's competition to the Boeing and Douglas jets and the British replacement for the Britannia and DC-7, was quickly surpassed in performance by the American jets. The difference in operating costs favored the American planes by an amount between 5 and 10 percent. The total capital losses which BOAC incurred from the sale of aircraft by March, 1964, amounted to $122,640,000. This included, by plane type, Comet 4, $13 million; Britannia, $63 million; Comet 1, $8 million; DC-7C, $13 million.[15]

[14] Wheatcroft, op. cit., pp. 114–15.
[15] "Details of BOAC's $253.4 Million Deficit," International Aviation, Supplement to Aviation Daily, Vol. 155 (November 16, 1964), p. 131.

The VC-10, Britain's subsequent long-haul jet aircraft, is an example of a more recent unfortunate experience. The VC-10 was designed to operate on shorter runways than the 707 or the DC-8. By the time the VC-10 was completed, airports had been expanded all over the world to such an extent that runway length was an insignificant constraint. The VC-10 airfield capability and greater cruise speed was not attained, however, without cost. Early estimates of the operating costs of the VC-10 place them at a level between 10 and 15 percent above the 707.[16] BOAC purchased the VC-10 and later placed orders for thirty of its successor, the Super VC-10. The performance of the VC-10, however, estimated to have cost BOAC $10 million in excess costs in 1964,[17] left the company less than anxious to receive its successor. Though reputedly cheaper to operate, the excessive annual cost of the Super VC-10 fleet was estimated variously at twice the $10 million figure.[18] Accordingly, BOAC attempts to reduce its second order caused a considerable stir in Britain. The question essentially became whether BOAC should subsidize British aircraft manufacturers and, if so, by what amount.

BOAC's record, involving some substantial operating losses, was scrutinized again and again by various public officials.[19] The result of the investigations seems to indicate that the British Ministry of Aviation and BOAC never agreed on the extent to which the corporation should disregard commercial considerations. A directive to BOAC to act on commercial grounds is inconsistent with support of the VC-10, for example, or with maintenance of certain political routes. BOAC subsequently went ahead with its purchase of Super VC-10s, though in smaller quantity than originally announced. It is clear that BOAC's plane choice was not based on economic considerations alone.

Choice of Route Systems

Route systems chosen by airlines are another type of decision affected by political considerations. Many state-owned carriers have over-

[16] "BOAC and the VC-10," *Aeroplane and Commercial Aviation News*, Vol. 107 (May 14, 1964), pp. 8–10.
[17] "The BOAC Crisis," *Flight International*, Vol. 86 (July 9, 1964), p. 39.
[18] "BOAC and the VC-10," pp. 8–10.
[19] "Parliament Investigates BOAC," *Flight International*, Vol. 86 (July 2, 1964), p. 4.

extended route systems. One common situation is a domestic route system operated at a loss or at very low profits. Scandinavian Airlines System (SAS) and Alitalia, for example, serve uneconomic domestic systems. BEA serves the Scottish Highlands and Islands at a loss. (The United States, of course, explicitly subsidizes local service carriers to provide this type of service.) The politically motivated international routes can be explained primarily by the need to link former and present colonies. This goes back to the period prior to World War II when British, French, Belgian, Italian, and Dutch airlines extended routes to their colonies. Many of these former colonial routes are still operated at a loss (for example, KLM in the Caribbean).

A prominent case concerns BOAC's route along the east coast of South America. This route was cancelled in 1954 because the Comet 1 failure left BOAC short of capacity and because of low load factors.[20] However, pressure was exerted by British traders to re-establish the service, on the grounds that cancellation was looked upon as an indication that Britain had "lost interest" in the area; service was therefore restored in 1960. BOAC again had difficulty with the route. Argentina and Brazil continued to be very restrictive in their bilateral agreements, which severely limited the frequency of flights and prohibited the use of 707 aircraft. With load factors of approximately 40 percent, BOAC petitioned to cancel the route, claiming it cost the company $3.5 million a year.[21] After much discussion with the South American governments BOAC was permitted to cancel. The corporation, however, still serves a number of uneconomic routes to present and former British colonies.[22]

State Subsidy

To sustain politically motivated operations, governments have been willing to pay a price in the form of subsidy, initiated in the industry's early years when the industry was nowhere near commercial viability. The subsidy has also paid for the existence of clearly inefficient opera-

[20] See Wheatcroft, op. cit., p. 186.

[21] "Adios BOAC," Flight International, Vol. 86 (September 10, 1964), pp. 446–47.

[22] "The Corporation's Uneconomic Routes," Flight International, Vol. 86 (August 13, 1964), p. 242.

tors and the incremental costs of political decisions concerning routes or aircraft. The subsidy bill has been substantial.

In the decade after World War II all nations paid subsidies because even efficient carriers could not earn sufficient revenues. However, by 1955 or 1956, increased demand and technological advances were such that efficient operators could exist without subsidy. U.S. carriers went off subsidy in 1958. Nevertheless, the commitment to subsidy persists, in order to pay for losses resulting from a combination of high fares, poor management, and inappropriate entry. Subsidy has taken many forms: government provision of equity capital, government loans and guarantee of loans, government transfers of foreign aid loans, tax exemptions, mail subsidy, provision of equipment, and direct cash payments to meet operating losses. There are also disguised subsidies, such as aid to flight and technical training and diversion of traffic to the national carrier by such means as limiting the availability of foreign exchange to citizens for airline tickets. In addition, there are a number of implicit subsidies that accrue on more or less an equitable basis to both national and foreign flag carriers alike through government provision of airports and navigational aids.

Measurement of the extent of these subsidies is difficult since data are sketchy and since some subsidies are not easily quantifiable. The Civil Aeronautics Board (CAB) reports a payment of $271 million to U.S. international carriers for 1946–58, or roughly 6.3 percent of total revenue. PAA received $193 million of these payments (7.7 percent of its total revenue during the period).[23] These amounts do not include any interest costs. The other international carriers also received payments. The International Civil Aviation Organization (ICAO) statistics, however, should be used with caution for estimation purposes since most of the carriers' subsidies take the form of capital grants or absorption of operating losses. These appear, usually only implicitly, in the owner equity accounts, which are complicated by partial or complete state ownership and financing.[24]

[23] Civil Aeronautics Board, *Handbook of Airline Statistics,* various years; and *Separation of Air Mail Pay from Subsidy,* Hearings before the Senate Committee on Interstate and Foreign Commerce, 82 Cong. 1 sess. (1951), pp. 235–36.
[24] The BOAC record is a good example. BOAC aggregate losses as of March 31, 1964, were $253 million; capital and development losses on aircraft, $157 million; interest, $113 million; losses of associated companies, $41 million; less accumulated operating surplus, $58 million (these figures are from BOAC's 1964 annual report). These losses appear not as a subsidy in the BOAC accounts but

An approximate measure of the amounts of subsidies involved can be obtained from the overall operating results over the last decade. The rate of return for all ICAO firms on operating revenues for the years 1955–63 was 0.94 percent.[25] Capital-output ratios vary widely, with 0.80 an approximate industry median. This implies an operating return on capital of 1.1 percent over a fourteen-year span, as against a normal return on private industrial investments of perhaps 6 to 8 percent or even more. The difference has been provided as a "subsidy" in some form by bondholders and shareholders or governments. Bondholders in the world capital market have for the most part been paid. Governments, as majority owners and as payers of public subsidy, have therefore carried the majority of the bill.

An examination of operating results for specific carriers provides an approximate indication of which nations have borne the larger subsidy burden. The annual subsidy cost was defined for present purposes as 8 percent of operating revenue less reported operating profits. The subsidy cost for a number of countries is listed in Table II-4, with the average operating subsidy for the years 1957–62 expressed as a percentage of 1958 gross domestic product. A number of countries were omitted because data were incomplete.[26] The nations paying the largest relative subsidy appear to be certain Latin American and African nations, and a group of European nations supporting large well-established carriers which have proved to be rather inefficient operators. As indicated earlier, a major motivation for these subsidies has been the desire to attract capital investment and tourist travel. In general, the subsidy bill in the period 1957–62 appears to be spread fairly evenly among the developed and less developed countries.[27]

---

rather as a liability item in the balance sheet, "Unappropriated Balance of Profit or Loss." They include interest costs, which are a poor approximation of the real cost of capital in Britain over the relevant period.

[25] Details on this estimate can be found in Chapter IX.

[26] These figures are only an approximation of the operating subsidy incurred by the major international carriers (both public and private) of the listed countries. The total subsidy should include any subsidy of airports, navigational aids, and training; subsidies via mail payments or other direct transfers to firms; any absorption of operating costs not reflected in ICAO data; and the operating results of flag carriers which have not reported data to ICAO.

[27] This comparison of operating results should not be used as an indication of which airlines are efficient operators, since the route structure and operating procedures generating these results have not been considered.

TABLE II-4. *Operating Deficit for International Airlines, 1957–62, as a Percentage of 1958 Gross Domestic Product, Selected Countries*

Country	Percentage	Country	Percentage
Netherlands	17.8	Turkey	3.4
Rhodesia, Zambia, Malawi	17.2	Kenya, Uganda, Tanzania	3.2
Venezuela	12.8	Finland	2.4
Ireland	12.0	Tunisia	2.3
Belgium	8.4	Australia	1.9
Argentina	7.4	Italy	1.3
Sweden, Norway, Denmark	6.7	Spain	1.3
Switzerland	5.4	India	1.2
Colombia	5.4	Japan	0.7
Canada	5.0	Union of South Africa	0.6
France	4.7	New Zealand	0.6
China (Formosa)	4.1	United States	0.5
West Germany	3.9	Indonesia	−1.1[a]
United Kingdom	3.5	Ethiopia	−5.9[a]

Sources: 1957–62 operating costs: Chapter IX. Gross domestic product, 1958, at factor cost: United Nations, *Yearbook of National Accounts Statistics* (1964), Table 6a, pp. 383–88.
[a] A negative figure denotes a greater than 8 percent annual return on operating revenue.

Foreign Aid in International Aviation

State influence of a somewhat different sort exists where foreign aid has been an important source of capital for many carriers in the less developed countries.[28] This aid, from the United Nations and from various governments and airlines (through investments in subsidiaries) has helped shape the existing industry and, in particular, has provided a stimulus to the development of long-haul jet service. Aid from ICAO, the administrator of United Nations funds, has been only about $1.5 million per year. The World Bank has made loans only very infrequently and in each case for the purchase of aircraft.

At the national level, however, the amounts are far more significant. The United States has been predominant, providing almost $300 million in capital assistance from 1956 to 1961. Of this, $136 million was in the form of Export-Import Bank loans for the purchase of U.S. aircraft. These Export-Import loans are not markedly different from financing in the private capital market; they carry a 5¾ percent interest rate for seven years and are available only to countries judged able to

[28] Hans Heymann, Jr., "Civil Aviation and U.S. Foreign Aid: Purposes, Pitfalls, and Problems for United States Policy," R424-RC (The RAND Corporation, January 1964).

handle the dollar debt-service burden. In many cases the recipients could have received financing in the private capital market. Additional aid has been made available by the Agency for International Development, through such devices as loans at long maturities with low rates of interest.[29]

One of the important motives behind this American aid has been to promote the development of international aviation by the construction of jet airports and navigation systems around the world. This amounts to a subsidy to the major long-haul jet carriers, and also facilitates the creation of regional carriers which would serve as feeder lines to the long-haul routes. American aid has also been motivated by political considerations, as a means of countering Soviet aid. The economy of the less developed country is often little affected by the investment in jet airports; in view of the difficulties these countries' carriers have in participating in the long-haul jet market, the net effect of these public investments on the economic development process has tended to be relatively limited.[30]

Grants made directly by other governments have been much smaller and on a less systematic basis. West Germany has provided pilot training to the Somali government.[31] The United Kingdom has provided training to a number of underdeveloped countries.[32] Most of the aid of other countries that are aviation powers has been in the form of investments made by their own carriers in subsidiaries. Carriers in the United Kingdom, France, Netherlands, the Scandinavian countries, and the United States have invested in a number of carriers in the less developed areas. These investments sometimes are in the form of capital and eventually lead to partial ownership. In other cases, the investments are in the form of technical assistance or leasing of aircraft, pilots, and other personnel.[33]

[29] Ibid., pp. 5–12.

[30] Ibid., pp. 16–19.

[31] United Nations Economic and Social Council, Economic Commission for Africa, Report on Joint Activities with the ICAO towards the Development of Air Transport in Africa (February 19–March 3, 1964), pp. 16–18.

[32] Keith Granville, "The United Kingdom's Part in the Development of Air Transport of Other Nations," Journal of the Institute of Transport (May 1962).

[33] For example, Air France holds these minority shares: Tunis-Air, 49 percent; Air Algerie, 17.7 percent; Royal Air Maroc, 21.05 percent; Air Madagascar, 38.36 percent; Air Vietnam, 20.5 percent; Royal Air Cambodge, 24 percent; and Middle East Airlines, 30 percent. BOAC owns these percentages of the following: Aden

Carriers have undertaken these commercial ventures in less developed countries for a number of reasons. One has been to develop regional carriers to feed the parent line's long-haul routes. Another has been to develop these new carriers as a market for used aircraft of the parent company. In some instances, development of subsidiaries has served as means of entry to new routes. PAA and BOAC in the years immediately after World War II helped to start a number of new companies, which they soon annexed into the parent organization.[34] In other instances, the capital investment has been traded for route grants to the parent. BEA, for example, originally held 40 percent ownership in Alitalia and also shares in Olympic and Aer Lingus. In each case BEA was able to obtain favorable bilateral agreements as a result.[35] An additional reason for investment in subsidiaries was the expectation that the investments would be profitable ventures; capital, crews, and technical equipment leased to subsidiaries can be a paying proposition.

The international airline industry clearly has benefited from this aid. The close ties fostered through parent-subsidiary relationships have helped disseminate technical information and create homogeneity in production techniques. Cost-saving cooperation in spares pools and in subletting arrangements has been facilitated. Most importantly, a large portion of fixed capital in the form of airports and navigational aids has been provided; the political and economic incentives for jet airport construction have produced a good network of modern airports. Expansion of jet service has been furthered by the availability of foreign aid financing.

Aviation aid, however, has not made any significant direct contribution to the developing countries and in many cases has been a stimulus to their entering the long-haul jet market, which is undoubtedly irrational. In some cases the generosity of aid grants has stimulated these irrational investments. The underlying cause of the irrationality, however, is the high value which many nations have placed on the external

---

Airways, 100 percent; Bahamas Airways, 20 percent; British West Indies Airlines, 10 percent; Cathay Pacific, 15 percent; Fiji Airways, 33 percent. PAA holds 38 percent of Avianca and 30 percent of Aerovias Venezolanas.

[34] Davies, *op. cit.*, pp. 333–36.

[35] E. A. G. Verploeg, *The Road Towards a European Common Air Market* (Utrecht: Uitgeverij Kemink en Zn. N.V., 1963), p. 97.

effects attached to flag carriers, with the availability of foreign aid financing merely helping to activate the desire for participation.

State Interests Versus Economic Efficiency

The state's role in the international airline industry is substantial, arising from the external effects of having a flag carrier. Though somewhat intangible, these external effects are highly valued. Many countries own their own carriers, subsidize their operations, and may dictate any number of decisions which are highly politically motivated. The industry is not a profit-maximizing one in the customary sense. Many countries have created a restricted market environment in which the various flag carriers' fortunes are best promoted. Subsequent chapters will indicate the very substantial extent to which political interests affect entry and pricing decisions. This context of state interest poses a considerable challenge in terms of rationalizing the industry and eliminating some of the very obvious shortcomings of existing performance. State interest, moreover, is unlikely to decline in the foreseeable future.

CHAPTER III

Entry Conditions

THE INTERNATIONAL AIRLINES INDUSTRY is not characterized by high economic barriers to entry, but noneconomic considerations have greatly complicated the entry process. The right to enter can be obtained only through intergovernmental negotiations, which are typically influenced by political considerations. Bilateral agreements resulting from these negotiations determine the city-pairs to be served and in some cases determine the amount of capacity, schedule frequency, type of equipment, and departure times. This chapter develops the economic basis for the bilateral negotiation process and a rationale for the kind of bargaining and agreements which are reached.

The Bilateral Entry Process

The bilateral bargaining process, like any other bargaining at the governmental level, involves a complicated gamesmanship that cannot be simply or briefly unraveled or described. The motives and positions of interested nations are not common knowledge. The discussion here of the bargaining process and the positions of particular nations is developed from fragmentary evidence in trade journals, occasional press reports about the bargaining, and similar informal sources.

Historical Setting

The bilateral entry process developed because of national attitudes toward airline entry that were different from attitudes toward any

31

other means of international transportation. For example, unlike the free and unrestricted access of steamships to ports around the world, commercial air service is carried on only by consent of the governments involved. The nations participating in the Paris Conference in 1919 agreed that each was to have sovereign control over its air space in order to protect national security and to promote a reasonable operating safety level.[1]

In 1944, representatives of fifty-four nations met in Chicago to discuss the increase in air traffic expected after World War II and to develop an entry procedure that would allow healthy growth in the industry. The various nations represented wished to promote increased international air traffic.[2] One achievement at Chicago was the multilateral International Air Services Transit Agreement, which allowed carriers to fly through sovereign air space and to land for fuel or technical reasons. Also, the International Civil Aviation Organization (ICAO) was created; it became the central organization for coordination in the industry and later became a part of the United Nations. The Chicago participants did not, however, agree to a multilateral exchange of traffic rights.

The debate at Chicago has been extensively considered in the literature. The United States advocated multilateral free entry, as did Sweden and the Netherlands. Most other nations wanted some form of government determination of capacity and also control over routes and fares. The United Kingdom wanted an international authority created to determine routes and capacities for all carriers. Canada supported this proposal. Australia and New Zealand favored the creation of an international organization which would own the aircraft and manage their operation on long-haul international routes. France backed this scheme. The opinions on how both national and public interests should be protected were so diverse that no compromise was reached.[3] The basic fear which conditioned the attitudes of all participants except the United States was that well equipped and experienced U.S. carriers, backed by U.S. government subsidy where necessary, would dominate the industry.

[1] Peter Sand, *An Historical Survey of the Law of Flight* (Montreal: McGill University, Institute of Air and Space Law, 1961), pp. 1–21.

[2] *Proceedings of the International Civil Aviation Conference*, Chicago, Illinois, November 1–December 7, 1944, U.S. Department of State Publication 2820 (2 vols.; 1948, 1949).

[3] H. A. Wassenbergh, *Post-War Civil Aviation Policy and the Law of the Air* (The Hague: Martinus Nijhoff, 1962), pp. 75–77.

THE BERMUDA AGREEMENT. The United States and the United Kingdom, the two countries with the greatest stake in achieving a solution, signed a compromise agreement in Bermuda in February 1946. In the compromise, the United States (a supporter of free airlines markets) agreed to accept fares set by carrier agreement through the International Air Transport Association (IATA), subject to government approval, and the United Kingdom (an advocate of strict regulation) agreed to yield its position that capacity be limited strictly. The two countries exchanged traffic rights between certain listed city-pairs, and each nation's carriers then were permitted to provide capacity (based on specific criteria) in these city-pair markets.

The Bermuda Agreement can be interpreted in terms of five "freedoms" of the air: (1) to fly across territory of a foreign nation without landing; (2) to land for purposes other than traffic; (3) to set down in a foreign country traffic coming from the country of the airline's nationality; (4) to pick up in a foreign country traffic destined for the country of the airline's nationality; (5) to carry traffic from a point of origin in one foreign country to a point of destination in another foreign country. The first two freedoms were agreed upon at Chicago. The heart of the Bermuda compromise concerning traffic rights involved the last three. According to the agreement, capacity is to be provided with the primary objective of serving traffic between the airline's country and the country of ultimate destination—that is, third and fourth freedom traffic. There is no restriction on the frequency of service which may be supplied to serve third and fourth freedom traffic. A carrier is also allowed to accept "fill-up" traffic from other countries on intermediate stops—fifth freedom traffic. The specific terms of the agreement regarding capacity for third, fourth, and fifth freedom traffic is contained in the following rather imprecise language:[4]

. . . it is the understanding of both Governments that services provided by a designated air carrier under the Agreement and its Annex shall retain as their primary objective the provision of capacity adequate to the traffic demands between the country of which such air carrier is a national and the country of ultimate destination of the traffic. The right to embark or disembark on such services [for] international traffic destined for and coming from third countries at a point or points on the routes specified in the Annex to the Agreement shall be applied in accordance with the general principles

[4] "Air Services Agreement and Final Act of the Civil Aviation Conference, held at Bermuda January 15 to February 11, 1946," *Treaties and Other International Acts Series,* No. 1507 (1946), pp. 18–19; hereinafter referred to as the Bermuda Agreement.

of orderly development to which both Governments subscribe and shall be subject to the general principle that capacity should be related:

    (a) to traffic requirements between the country of origin and the countries of destination;

    (b) to the requirements of through airline operation; and

    (c) to the traffic requirements of the area through which the airline passes after taking account of local and regional services.

For example, on one route—New York/Rome/Cairo/Karachi—U.S. carriers are allowed to offer capacity on each leg of the route sufficient to carry passengers from the United States bound for the country concerned, and vice versa. This is third and fourth freedom traffic. Fifth freedom traffic involves U.S. carriers flying passengers on an intermediate leg (for example, from Rome to Cairo) whose trips neither originate in the U.S. nor are destined for the United States. Similarly, traffic on intermediate segments of this same route, but with origin in New York and destination in Karachi, is fifth freedom traffic to any except a U.S. or Pakistani carrier.

This general criterion for providing passenger capacity has become known as the "Bermuda principle." The language of the agreement was relatively imprecise, in the hope that informal agreement could be reached on the interpretation of third, fourth, and fifth freedom traffic and on whether capacity was being provided consistent with the agreement. In practice, however, the interpretation of the freedom classification and the right to provide capacity has been a source of considerable dispute. In particular, clause (c), concerning fifth freedom traffic, in the Bermuda Agreement is sufficiently ambiguous so that either expansion or restriction of such traffic could be allowed. The intention of the clause was to exclude unfair and destructive competition, especially that of subsidized carriers. In fact, it has generally been interpreted in a restrictive sense—"taking account of local and regional services" is usually interpreted by nations located at intermediate stops as a justification for limiting fifth freedom service by carriers from other nations.

The Bermuda Agreement initiated bilateral agreements and served as a model for many subsequent agreements. The United States and major European nations quickly contracted a large number of bilaterals granting them access to a network of cities. Nations have continued to make such agreements, as entry is needed. The resultant contracts range all the way from the Bermuda type to those in which strict capacity controls are included. The route exchanges have ranged from a detailed listing of each city-pair, along with intermediate stops, to general route descriptions that merely indicate that traffic is to be carried between two countries via some pattern of intermediate stops. A small amount of service is provided on the basis of a temporary agreement or permit when two countries are unable to reach a formal bilateral agreement.

FAILURE AT GENEVA. A period in which there was still hope for a multilateral free entry solution followed. Meetings held in Geneva in November 1947 came closest to such a solution, but the basic problem of conflicting interests could not be resolved. Proposals ranged from multilateral free entry to various means of government determination of routes, capacity, and fares.[5] In essence, international airline markets have seen the triumph of absolute state sovereignty, with entry determined by bilateral or unilateral permits and fares, although set by IATA, subject to unanimous approval by all governments.

Economics of Bilateral Entry

The political processes of bilateral negotiation have led to an inefficient entry pattern. Contracting nations in a bilateral agreement receive the right of entry, even though perhaps one or both may not belong in the industry on economic grounds. Efficient carriers are often excluded. The bilateral negotiation process is based largely on political rather than economic considerations, and nations in many cases exchange air rights for diplomatic reasons. The bilateral process also frequently results in two carriers entering a market which can support only one.

Moreover, the division of traffic into third, fourth, and fifth freedoms causes difficulties when used as a criterion for how much capacity a carrier should provide. The problem is particularly evident when the carrier serves widely separated cities where traffic is thin and intermediate stops are necessary. Fifth freedom traffic as fill-up is permitted under Bermuda-type agreements as described in clause (c). In practice, this requires negotiation with intermediate countries. Such negotiation is usually difficult and rarely produces the desired result as described in the Bermuda Agreement. Intervening countries may re-

---

[5] Stephen Wheatcroft, *Air Transport Policy* (London: Michael Joseph, Ltd., 1964), pp. 71–72.

strict fifth freedom traffic by specifying the number of flights or times of departure permitted. In extreme cases the insistence of an intervening country on claiming all third and fourth freedom traffic has meant that no fill-up traffic is available. Many long-haul routes require intermediate traffic if they are to be profitable; the fact that no nation has a sufficient demand from its own citizens bound for a distant country may result in no carrier being permitted to offer the service, though service on the route might be justified if no distinction were made between third, fourth, and fifth freedom traffic.

In short, insistence by all nations on their own third and fourth freedom traffic would mean, at best, that a carrier would supply progressively less and less capacity farther from home as traffic originating in or destined for its country decreased. Passengers taking long trips would be forced to continually switch carriers as they passed out of the area in which a carrier could justify operations on third and fourth freedom traffic. At worst, cases could arise where no carrier could justify service economically on the basis of terminal traffic alone. The freedom classification is an arbitrary division of traffic from an economic point of view, independent of rational decisions concerning entry or capacity.

Bilateral Entry Agreements in Practice

National attitudes toward route grants and bilateral bargaining can be explained by a consideration of the vested interests of each country. National policies and resultant negotiations reflect a continual struggle between the "haves" and "have-nots." The early post-war years were characterized by liberal bargaining, with Bermuda principles predominant, since traffic seemed adequate for all and little regard was paid to possible competitive losses. However, established carriers with profitable routes have faced continual pressure from newer carriers desiring entry. State subsidized carriers, especially of the less developed countries, have been eager entrants. The result has been a competitive loss of traffic by many existing carriers. This competition has led to protective efforts, both by young carriers and by established carriers hoping to protect their market share. Attitudes with regard to route awards have become very conservative, with entry closely guarded and agreements very individualistic and detailed in their specification.[6]

---

[6] An excellent book on the details of bilateral negotiation is Bin Cheng's, *The Law of International Air Transport* (London: Stevens and Sons, Ltd., 1962).

EUROPEAN ATTITUDES TOWARD ENTRY. The attitudes of European nations, ranging from very restrictive to non-restrictive positions with regard to entry, reflect this sort of consideration of national interests. The general trend in Europe is toward more protection. The Netherlands, Sweden, Norway, and Denmark—free traders who have always supported multilateralism and whose bilateral agreements are non-restrictive in nature—represent one pole. The reason is the obvious one of reliance on fifth freedom traffic; these countries themselves generate relatively small amounts of traffic compared to the fifth freedom traffic in the North Atlantic available because of their strategic locations.

The attitude of the United Kingdom has evolved from an advocacy of strict regulation prior to 1946 to what is best characterized as a pragmatic mix of Bermuda principles and restriction. While the United Kingdom has entered into many Bermuda-type agreements, it has generally been cautious in route grants and has been mindful of potential competitive traffic losses. For example, along with France, Britain has closely guarded the prized London-Paris route, permitting no other entrants that would be significant competition. The British recently held negotiations with KLM Royal Dutch Airlines and Scandinavian Airlines System (SAS) over fifth freedom traffic in the North Atlantic, in which they tried to limit the capacity of KLM and SAS leaving Prestwick for the North Atlantic; similarly Britain has tried to limit Sabena's capacity at Manchester departing for North America.[7]

West Germany has entered into both Bermuda agreements and more restrictive bilaterals which specify flight frequencies. France has generally resorted to a strict division of traffic in its markets, either by pooling agreements or explicitly in its bilaterals, with the exception of its Bermuda bilaterals with the Netherlands and the United States. Italy has favored policies similar to those of France; the two countries have agreed on traffic allocation on their principal routes and periodically review the passengers carried in order to preserve the agreed distribution. The Franco-Italian Committee and the Franco-British Committee both review the results on pooled routes.[8] Belgium, Ireland, Austria,

---

[7] "Bilateralism in the Light of Recent IATA Developments: Part II," *ITA Bulletin*, No. 36 (Paris: Institut du Transport Aérien, October 12, 1964), pp. 939–42; and "Air Transport Policy (April-October, 1964)," *ITA Bulletin*, No. 38 (October 26, 1964), pp. 1007–12.

[8] "Bilateralism in the Light . . . Part I," *ITA Bulletin*, No. 35 (October 5, 1964), pp. 911–12.

and Greece also favor predetermination and include restrictions in their bilaterals.

Spain and Portugal are perhaps the most extreme restrictionists. All traffic between these two countries is shared in agreed proportions. All outside bilaterals are restrictive in nature, with capacity clauses and stipulations regarding the percentage of fifth freedom traffic which foreign carriers may carry. Compensation has even been requested from outside carriers when excessive fifth freedom traffic has allegedly been carried.

European countries have generally taken a quite pragmatic approach to their route grants. Most of Europe opposed multilateral traffic rights and free competition after World War II, but as their airlines became equipped and experienced, these countries evolved into free traders in the North Atlantic. These countries have not been free traders everywhere, however; many have faced the same pressure for entry by the developing nations' carriers as has the United States. Access to the major European gateways is not easily obtained by carriers of the developing countries. Most European countries have included specific capacity restrictions in their bilaterals or have granted access subject to participation in pooling arrangements. The United States, with its liberal route grants up until the late 1950s, gave the European carriers far longer to rationalize their operations than the latter appear willing to grant now to the carriers of many of the developing countries desiring access to Europe.

LATIN AMERICAN ATTITUDES TOWARD ENTRY. In Latin America, there are two policy extremes. Many small, newly organized non-IATA carriers are supported by governments with very restrictive policies. These carriers are poorly equipped and managed, and their public reputation for dependability (and sometimes safety) is such that they cannot compete with the large American and European carriers. Carriers from Argentina, Brazil, Chile, Ecuador, Paraguay, Peru, Honduras, and Uraguay make up part of this group of non-IATA firms. Some of the bilaterals entered into by the governments of these carriers include capacity restrictions. In some instances, capacity restrictions have been made in violation of Bermuda agreements (notably with the United States) previously entered into by the governments in question.[9]

---

[9] *Foreign Air Transportation*, Hearing before a Subcommittee of the House Committee on Interstate and Foreign Commerce, 87 Cong. 2 sess. (1962).

All bargaining in Latin America occurs in the context of a highly protectionist attitude.[10] Latin American countries have generally stood together in their opposition to and restriction of foreign flag carriers. A number of agreements have been reached, including one which restricted fifth freedom traffic on outside carriers to one-third of the market. Argentina and Brazil have used this sort of formula. Bilateral negotiations between the U.S. and either of these countries have been difficult.

The second category of Latin American carriers includes the IATA members, generally larger and more efficient operators. These carriers also are backed by governments which often advocate restrictive policies; however, some of this group (for example, Avianca) have gradually realized that an overly rigid and determined set of controls in the industry could seriously hamper efficient operations on the continent. In some cases, carriers have appeared to become more liberal as their operations have become more efficient. The appearance of this more liberal viewpoint within the group of Latin American carriers has hampered the efforts toward common pools and regional cooperation which are continually initiated by the small protectionist firms.[11]

THE U.S. POSITION. The U.S. position, along with that of the British, has been a major influence on policy throughout the world.[12] The United States has generally followed the Bermuda principle and was especially lenient in its route concessions in the years immediately following World War II, when it was securing its own route network. A number of reasons can be given for this leniency. U.S. superiority in providing air service in 1945 was so great that serious competition from abroad seemed very distant. Liberal U.S. concessions were judged useful in that the relative improvement of European carriers vis-à-vis the U.S. carriers would encourage a freer, more competitive, and less restrictive environment. Also, the United States made liberal concessions as part of its aid program of rebuilding the western world—economically as

[10] "The Difficulties of International Air Transport As Seen in Relations between the U.S.A. and Latin America," *ITA Bulletin*, No. 33 (September 21, 1964), pp. 861–63.

[11] "South American Carriers Continually Search for Common Policy," *ITA Bulletin*, No. 38 (October 21, 1963), pp. 1047-48.

[12] International air agreements entered into by the United States appear in *Air Laws and Treaties of the World* (Government Printing Office, 1965), Vol. 3. This was prepared at the request of Senator Warren G. Magnuson, Chairman of the Senate Committee on Commerce.

part of the dollar shortage cure and politically as a part of its efforts to unite the West.

In the next decade, more and more carriers began to implement the access rights they had been granted, and the U.S. saw its share of world air markets decline. Gradually, more attention was given to route grants. The first serious negotiation the United States conducted was with SAS in 1952–54, over the polar route to the West Coast. The second was the bilateral agreement with West Germany in 1955, which caused such a protest from U.S. carriers that the bargaining process was reviewed by a congressional subcommittee. The agreement gave Lufthansa access from New York to the Caribbean and all points in South America in exchange for some fifth freedom rights to U.S. carriers on routes beyond West Germany. U.S. carriers immediately objected that the exchange was far too generous. Some twelve years later, it is difficult to determine how bad the exchange was. The Smathers investigation,[13] however, revealed a number of features of U.S. bilateral diplomacy. First, the concession was made in part to encourage West Germany to steer clear of restriction. It also appears that no real effort was made by the State Department or the Civil Aeronautics Board, which acted as advisors, to calculate the benefits or costs of proposed bilateral agreements. This lack of an overall estimate of the costs involved in terms of traffic lost is in itself part of the explanation of U.S. generosity in its entry negotiations.

In recent years, the United States has become more cautious in its bargaining, largely as a result of the loss of traffic to fifth freedom operations. There is reluctance to grant access to internal points, to allow transcontinental traffic carriage, or to permit Canada excessive fifth freedom rights from U.S. ports to the Caribbean, for example. Access to the West Coast by KLM, Alitalia, and SAS was denied in the period 1960–62 because of the fear of fifth freedom traffic losses. U.S. policy with regard to route grants at present appears to reflect a careful weighing of benefits and costs of any proposed entry, on a case by case basis. The traffic involved is an important consideration.

European observers[14] have labeled these U.S. actions as restriction-

[13] *International Air Agreements,* Report of the Senate Committee on Interstate and Foreign Commerce, 84 Cong. 2 sess. (1956).

[14] "U.S. International Aviation Policy—Its Basis and Trends in the World Air Transport Context Since June, 1945," *ITA Studies 62/17* (Paris: Institut du Transport Aérien, May 1962).

ist. While the U.S. has tried to protect its own carriers' competitive position, it has not resorted to capacity controls. More importantly, it has tried to use its route grants to encourage the industry trend toward rationality, refusing entry when the entrance leads to overcapacity or when the entrant cannot manage an efficient operation. Consistent with these two objectives of promoting industry rationality and protecting U.S. carriers from excessive abuse of fifth freedom rights, the United States has recently refused Egypt, Austria, and Poland access to the North Atlantic. Political considerations sometimes have an impact, however. Air Afrique and Nigerian Airways have been granted access to New York in exchange for additional route grants to Pan American Airways (PAA) in Africa.[15] These agreements were recommended by the White House as consistent with the United States aid program to Africa, despite CAB opposition.

One of the most pressing current-day issues in bilateral negotiations for the United States has been the situation in the Pacific. Japan Air Lines has sought a transcontinental and transatlantic route to complete its around-the-world flight since 1960, but the United States until only recently denied these rights because of the fear that Japan would carry too much fifth freedom traffic in these markets. Diplomatic relations were strained in this period of denial. At one point Japan claimed that it had reduced tourist restrictions and had joined the Organization for Economic Cooperation and Development—gestures which it felt should be rewarded. In July 1964, the United States offered a compromise: the Japanese carrier could serve New York if it gave up its service to San Francisco. At that time Japan Air Lines had eleven flights a week to the West Coast—six to Los Angeles and five to San Francisco. Japan refused.[16]

This bilateral dispute was recently resolved when the United States granted the Japanese carrier access to New York and the Atlantic in exchange for U.S. landing rights in Osaka, plus some additional flying rights beyond Tokyo (which added flexibility to the PAA Pacific cargo operations).[17]

[15] "Air Transport Policy (April-October, 1964)," *ITA Bulletin*, No. 38 (October 26, 1964), p. 1008.
[16] "Problems and Prospects in the Pacific in the Light of Recent Aeronautical Negotiations," *ITA Bulletin*, No. 43 (November 30, 1964), pp. 1127–29; and *American Aviation*, Vol. 28 (September 1964), p. 12, and Vol. 28 (November 1964), p. 12.
[17] "Japanese Flight Around World Set," *New York Times*, December 29, 1965.

In summary, national attitudes with regard to route grants reflect a compromise of economic and political motives and mercantilist ideas of protecting carriers under the national flag. Action based on political motives has ranged far and wide, including, for example, route grants as part of foreign aid in the context of the East-West cold war. Perhaps the most extreme circumstance concerning route grant decisions based on political considerations was the denial of landing and overflying rights to South African Airways by a coalition of newly formed African states in 1963.[18] This denial, stimulated by the intense nationalism of the newly independent countries, increased the length of South African Airways flights from London to Johannesburg by 1,500 kilometers—forcing the airline to advertise "get a full night's sleep."[19]

The Decline in Bermuda Principles

The increasing use of capacity restrictions in bilateral agreements has occurred because of the difficulties of applying Bermuda concepts to situations where one nation has far more to gain in the way of fifth freedom traffic than the other. Unequal bargaining positions of this sort were not a problem at Bermuda, where the two largest traffic-generating nations were negotiating, but more and more bargaining situations have since arisen in which the two parties involved are in vastly different circumstances. While Bermuda agreements include limitations on fifth freedom traffic, in practice it has been difficult for nations to control the carrying of fifth freedom traffic by third-country carriers once access is granted.

The Bermuda agreements suggested that an ex post facto review of traffic be conducted and consultation undertaken to reach agreement on interpretation of the capacity clauses. No formal procedure, however, was specified. Agreement has not been reached or the conceptual definition or empirical determination of the freedom classification of traffic, and procedures for the settlement of differences have not been devised. Charges that a carrier is taking excessive fifth freedom traffic —so called "sixth freedom traffic"—have been commonplace. The in-

---

[18] Frank G. McGuire, "Inside Story of African Walkout and IATA Crisis," *American Aviation*, Vol. 27 (December 1963), pp. 55–60.

[19] "SAA Promotes New Route to Europe," *International Aviation*, Supplement to *Aviation Daily*, Vol. 149 (December 2, 1963), p. 146.

terpretation of the freedom classification has, therefore, been a major issue in implementing Bermuda agreements.[20]

Multilateral free entry, of course, would pose no such problems. However, since nations exchange rights bilaterally, some right to carry fifth freedom traffic is necessary for a viable system. The efforts of all airlines to carry as much fifth freedom traffic as possible, in the context of the Bermuda-type bilateral system, necessarily cause difficulties in interpretation. The Bermuda system of exchanging traffic rights is based on equivalent "legal" rights of the bargainers, even though the economic stakes involved are often very different. This difference in economic stakes and the difficulty of applying Bermuda principles more than anything else have led to the declining use of those principles.

The Fifth Freedom Problem for the United States

The problem for the United States has been to protect its share of the Atlantic and other predominantly American tourist routes. The denser, long-haul routes have generally been the most profitable and have been the entry objective of the new carriers. What is essentially an internal subsidy results from the value-of-service pricing procedures, discussed in Chapter VII. The North Atlantic—often referred to as the "dollar route" of the industry—has long been a source of high profits. U.S. negotiations in the 1950s were a continual struggle between additional carriers hoping to enter the North Atlantic market and the U.S. carriers, which wished to expand their route systems without having to make such concessions. The structure of the industry led to a common strategy for many carriers: enter the North Atlantic market with as much capacity as possible and use profits from this route to subsidize politically motivated operations elsewhere.

The United States has continually objected to KLM and SAS operations in the North Atlantic; most of the traffic carried via Amsterdam or Copenhagen originates in New York with ultimate destination points beyond the Netherlands or Denmark. KLM and SAS claim that their stops make a New York-Amsterdam-Paris passenger, for example, their legitimate third and fourth freedom traffic. No agreement, however,

[20] To implement the Bermuda provisions on fifth freedom traffic, a set of origin-destination data is needed. In 1958 the United States asked that carriers be required to report such data to the ICAO or that a study be made, but neither suggestion has been carried out.

has been reached on the definition of stop-over traffic. The United States has attempted to define stops of less than 72 hours as "through traffic," but this definition has never received total acceptance. The location of particular countries and the relative amounts of through versus originating traffic (however defined) make the bargaining positions of the United States vis-à-vis Europe on this question obvious. Other countries have taken positions favoring more liberal or strict definitions of stopovers, depending on the location of their flag carrier. Greece, for example, has usually argued that a 48-hour stop is sufficient to make passengers landing at Athens their legitimate third and fourth freedom traffic.[21]

The United States has probably been in a less favorable bargaining position in obtaining fifth freedom traffic from European countries than vice-versa. The trade-off with Europe has roughly involved granting European carriers an opportunity for fifth freedom traffic in the North Atlantic in exchange for permission for U.S. airlines to carry fifth freedom traffic within and beyond Europe. The North Atlantic is the more profitable opportunity because of its long stage length and high traffic density and the prevailing fare structure. Europe over the years has taken a common stand against the proposed U.S. interpretation of fifth freedom traffic (with the exception of the recent British concern over KLM and SAS).

Direct Capacity Restrictions

The most important consequence of the difficulties in handling the problems of fifth freedom rights is that more and more agreements contain capacity restrictions. An entry system of pre-arranged capacities solves such problems at the bilateral bargaining stage. This predominance of capacity restrictions in bilateral agreements is the major reason the sixth freedom issue has received less public attention of late. (A less important reason is that jets have made more nonstop service economical. This reduces the need for frequent intermediate stops, with the inevitable concomitant introduction of local carriers which want to protect their own traffic or which want a share of through traffic. Sixth freedom problems in the Atlantic have been somewhat reduced since jets have made it feasible to operate nonstop from the United States to more of the major European cities.)

[21] "Stopover Regulation and Practice," *ITA Documents 63/10-E* (Paris: Institut du Transport Aérien, 1963), pp. 21–25.

Capacity restrictions, however, can introduce rigidities and inflexibility in scheduling and may hamper equipment utilization rates. They also may make it difficult to adjust to changes in demand or service requirements since renegotiation of the bilateral agreement must take place. Furthermore, these restrictions hamper any marketing innovation which might take the form of equipment or schedule choice.

Direct capacity restrictions have taken a number of forms. In some cases a restriction is placed on the type of equipment to be used, in order to protect a flag carrier less well equipped. Italy for some time would not permit Trans World Airlines (TWA) to operate all-cargo jet service in and out of Rome;[22] cargo could be carried only in DC-7Fs or in the holds of passenger jets. The British Overseas Airways Corporation's (BOAC) eastern route in South America faced a similar problem, with Brazil and Argentina limiting BOAC service to two Comet 4 flights per week and prohibiting the introduction of Boeing 707s.[23] An important consideration in BOAC's abandonment of the route was the British government's inability to renegotiate a bilateral agreement permitting the use of jet equipment. British United Airways was subsequently allowed to take over the route, using VC-10s, which, however, it was forced to schedule at odd hours to keep from hurting local carriers.[24] To cite another example, Brazil in 1961 cancelled its bilateral with SAS when the latter introduced jet service.

The other major form of restriction is a simple one on flight frequencies. Latin American countries tend to make such restrictions. Argentina and Venezuela, for example, restrict flight frequencies of PAA.[25] European countries have shown a similar tendency; West Germany restricts SAS capacity through its country and forces SAS to alter its departure times if they are too near those of Deutsche Lufthansa (DLH).[26] Many intercontinental routes are affected in the same way.

The United States represents the major countervailing force against this trend toward detailed capacity specification and has remained loyal to Bermuda principles. In 1962, however, thirty-two countries exercised control over U.S. carriers, by either requiring traffic data, re-

[22] *Flight International*, Vol. 85 (April 16, 1964), p. 602.

[23] "Adios BOAC," *Flight International*, Vol. 86 (September 10, 1964), pp. 446–47.

[24] *Interavia Air Letter*, No. 5560 (January 1, 1965), p. 1.

[25] "The Difficulties of International Air Transport As Seen in the Relation Between the U.S.A. and Latin America," *ITA Bulletin*, No. 33 (September 21, 1964), pp. 861–63.

[26] *Airlift*, Vol. 25 (May 1961), p. 45.

quiring that schedules be approved, or controlling capacity.[27] Nine of these countries had no bilaterals with the United States, and operations were conducted under temporary permit. While twenty-two countries have bilateral agreements with the United States, their governments have "illegally" imposed capacity restrictions. The U.S. government has protested unsuccessfully.[28] Markets so restricted comprise only a small percentage of the total market in which U.S. carriers participate. Only in the case of India are capacity restrictions part of the bilateral agreement with the United States. The Indian government claimed that PAA and TWA carriage of fifth freedom traffic in and out of India warranted capacity restrictions. In January 1955 India denounced the existing bilateral agreement, and operations continued on a temporary basis. A new agreement was reached on February 3, 1956, in which the United States was forced to make considerable concessions. PAA and TWA flight frequencies were specified and could be changed only by consent of the Indian government. India argued, of course, that the primary traffic between the United States and India was only a small percentage of all traffic.[29]

Pooling Agreements

Market-sharing pools are another method that countries have devised for controlling capacity. Pooling arrangements, stemming from excess entry problems created by reciprocal granting of access rights, predominate in the major European markets. Europe's political boundaries have created the problem of many governments desiring entry into city-pairs which are often so close together that economic operation is difficult unless the scale of operation is high. In addition, World War II retarded the development of European air markets substantially. Partly in response to these problems, many pools were formed in the early 1950s. The trend has continued to the present, with a pool

[27] The countries were Argentina, Austria, Brazil, Chile, Costa Rica, El Salvador, Finland, Ghana, Guatemala, Honduras, Greece, India, Indonesia, Iran, Iraq, Japan, Korea, Lebanon, Mexico, New Zealand, Nicaragua, Nigeria, Pakistan, Paraguay, Philippines, Portugal, Spain, Switzerland, Thailand, Turkey, Uruguay, and Venezuela.

[28] *Foreign Air Transportation*, Hearings before a Subcommittee of the House Committee on Interstate and Foreign Commerce, 87 Cong. 2 sess. (1962), pp. 47–48.

[29] *Air Laws and Treaties of the World*, Vol. 3, pp. 3665–80.

arranged as soon as a market becomes sufficiently large. Little is publicly known about the terms of these pools. They customarily involve a coordination of schedules and selling staff and a sharing of traffic revenue according to determined market quotas. The quotas may or may not be periodically reviewed. A carrier generally does not earn revenue above its quota even though it may attract proportionately more traffic to the coordinated schedule that the pool operates. The ability to attract extra traffic is usually not taken into account when shares are renegotiated. These pools obviously do not generally encourage competitive incentives. While the coordinated schedules often raise load factors, this is frequently accomplished by inconveniencing peak-hour users.

In Europe the short-haul pools are generally between the two nations of origin and destination and are aimed at third and fourth freedom traffic. Long-haul service, outside the pool, may be provided as well; however, it is generally not a significant check on the pool operation since the short-haul traveler usually finds the long-haul schedules less convenient.

The important pools on the intercontinental routes generally are the result of influence by European carriers. Two European pools have operated parallel service from Europe to South America. A number of the major Europe-to-Africa routes are also run by pools, and BOAC and Qantas Empire Airways have had a long-standing pool on long-haul routes through the Far East. These pooling arrangements deny entry to outsiders and also negate the advantages of existing entry. Their restrictive tendencies represent a potentially serious trend in the industry.

The Effect of Entry Restrictions on Seller Concentration

The determination of states to have their own flag carriers and their protection of these carriers by entry restrictions have resulted in a low seller concentration in the industry. The international airline industry is much less concentrated, for example, than the U.S. domestic airline industry.

Table III-1 indicates the international market share, for three postwar years, of all firms reporting to the International Air Transport Association. The share of output produced by the largest firms has decreased as follows (in percentages):

	1951	1957	1965
Top four	55.0	47.1	37.8
Top ten	77.1	71.3	62.3

The most significant change in the relative importance of particular firms is the appearance of Japan Air Lines and Lufthansa in the top fifteen in 1965; they were absent in 1951. Another important change is the increase in numbers and importance of a set of new carriers which entered during the 1950s, many of which represent less developed countries. In 1951 the twenty-nine smallest firms in the industry accounted for 9.66 percent of output. By 1965 the nineteen firms in this group that still reported to IATA had been joined by twenty-nine new carriers. Although this group of smallest carriers now accounted for only 6.66 percent of output, the trend of new carriers entering the market is likely to continue because of the prestige which developing nations attach to a flag carrier.

The data in Table III-1 do not indicate the seller concentration in particular markets. While there is some tendency for new carriers to appear in areas that are developing new markets, there has been a definite reduction in seller concentration in many markets.

The Nonscheduled Market

In examining concentration in particular markets, two broad classifications should be considered—scheduled and nonscheduled service. Scheduled service, as defined by ICAO, is service open to the public at a fixed price and according to a published timetable or at sufficiently regular times as to constitute a recognizable systematic series. Nonscheduled service is all other service—in effect, all charter operations.

The traditional form of charter involves a contract between an airline and people belonging to a particular group. Such charter flights are booked *in toto* and are therefore not open to the public. Two types of buyers are eligible for charter flights which are not part of an inclusive tour: a firm that provides seats for its employees, and organizations or clubs. (These must be formed for some purpose other than that of obtaining reduced air fares and must "not be so large as to be in effect a substantial section of the public.") IATA has customarily limited the

TABLE III-1. *Percentage Distribution of International Air Market, by Carrier, in 1951, 1957, and 1965*[a]

Carrier	1951	1957	1965
Pan American Airways (PAA)	25.32	20.00	16.17
British Overseas Airways Corporation (BOAC)	13.27	10.13	8.89
Air France	6.89	7.65	6.98
Trans World Airlines (TWA)	5.87	4.95	5.80
KLM Royal Dutch Airlines	9.49	9.34	5.27
Lufthansa German Airlines	—	1.93	4.92
Alitalia Airlines	0.39	1.42	4.13
Scandinavian Airlines System (SAS)	5.59	6.26	3.66
Qantas Empire Airways	2.74	3.14	3.51
Swissair	1.78	3.72	2.95
Japan Air Lines	—	1.17	2.71
British European Airways (BEA)	3.35	3.94	2.68
Air Canada	1.49	1.55	2.42
Sabena Belgian World Airlines	1.57	2.17	2.13
Northwest Airlines	2.69	1.50	1.66
Iberia Airlines of Spain	0.78	0.80	1.59
Air-India	1.07	1.73	1.57
El Al Israel Airlines	0.72	0.57	1.54
Canadian Pacific Airlines	0.27	1.47	1.35
Union de Transports Aériens (UTA)[b]	—	0.90	1.32
Eastern Air Lines	—	0.69	1.28
Varig Airlines	0.02	0.32	1.21
Seaboard World Airlines	—	0.59	1.02
South African Airways	1.15	0.98	0.88
Air Afrique	—	—	0.82
Pan American–Grace Airways	1.92	1.28	0.66
British United Airlines[c]	—	0.17	0.61
Aerlinte Eireann	—	—	0.60
United Arab Airlines[d]	0.30	0.24	0.58
Aerolineas Argentinas	1.43	0.90	0.57
Middle East Airline Airliban[e]	0.09	0.71	0.53
Ceskoslovenske Aerolinie	—	0.18	0.49
Avianca Airlines	0.39	0.67	0.49
Venezuelan International Airways	—	—	0.48
Aeronaves de Mexico	—	—	0.48
Pakistan International Airlines	—	0.25	0.48
Braniff International	0.90	0.60	0.47
Tasman Empire Airways	0.85	0.52	0.44
29 others[f]	9.66	6.57	3.57
13 new carriers[g]	—	—	0.85
16 new carriers[h]	—	—	2.24
Total[i,j]	100.00	100.00	100.00

Sources: International Air Transport Association, *IATA Bulletin*, No. 15 (1952); *World Air Transport Statistics*, No. 2 (1957), No. 10 (1965).

[a] Percentage shares are of revenue tonne-kilometres performed by IATA members.

[b] Union de Transports Aériens (UTA) was formed in 1963 by a merger of Compagnie de Transports Aériens Intercontinentaux and Union Aeromaritime de Transport. Data for 1957 are for the two parents of UTA.

[c] British United Airlines was formed by a merger of Hunting-Clan Air Transport and Airwork Limited. Data for 1957 are for Hunting-Clan, which operated internationally at the time.

[d] United Arab Airlines was formed on January 1, 1961, by a merger of Syrian Airways and Misrair. Only Misrair operated internationally in 1951 and 1957.

[e] Middle East Airline Airliban was formed by a merger of Middle East Airlines and Air Liban on October 1, 1965. Figures for 1951 and 1957 combine the percentages for the individual carriers.

[f] Twenty-nine carriers operating scheduled international service in 1951 that are not listed individually above. By 1957 this set of firms numbered 23, and by 1965, only 19, as a result of firms having resigned from IATA during this period.

[g] Thirteen carriers operating scheduled international service in 1957 that are not listed individually above and were not operating internationally in 1951. By 1965, 2 of these had resigned from IATA.

[h] Sixteen carriers that are not listed individually above and were not operating internationally in 1951 or in 1957.

[i] In 1951, 9 carriers did not report statistics. IATA estimated that they represented 1 percent of total traffic (*IATA Bulletin*, No. 15, p. 115). A 1 percent addition was made to the estimate of the total traffic carried by the reporting carriers in 1951.

[j] Columns will not necessarily add to 100 because of rounding.

size of eligible groups to 20,000 members.[30] There are no controls on the price to be offered for charter operations, and entry permission is generally obtained on a case-by-case basis from the governments at the origin and destination.

This sort of charter service was initiated in the early 1950s by U.S. flag and supplemental carriers in the North Atlantic and has subsequently spread to other markets. A more recent form of charter service is the "inclusive tour," a combination package of transport and hotel accommodations sold by travel agents for a single price. The customary rules defining a group are not applicable in booking inclusive tours. The rate at which the agent books the airline space is negotiated by the agent and the airline. This is a far more flexible charter arrangement. It began in Europe, where the competitive rewards for charter service were greatest and recently has been spreading to other markets.

The economic rationale for charter operations is that they provide a means for carriers to provide service to people who otherwise could not afford to travel, on equipment which would otherwise stand idle. Charter rates are related to the level of regular fares and to the economics of jet operation. The ability of charter operators to offer lower fares is dependent on their ability to achieve high load factors and high utilization of equipment. The scheduling of equipment imposes the greatest limit on the level at which charter services can be sold. Charter operations almost always face a directional imbalance due to seasonal traffic, and hence the empty back haul poses a serious scheduling problem. Markets with small passenger density can make these problems acute.

However, the marketing advantages enjoyed by charter operators are obviously increased by high fares for scheduled service, in this case IATA fares. In addition, luxurious IATA service levels have provided charter operators with an opportunity to cut fares by reducing passenger amenities. This marketing environment which IATA has maintained has provided the opportunity for charter entrants, an opportunity which more and more airlines have seized upon. Whereas initially most of the charter operations were conducted in the off season with otherwise idle equipment, in recent years carriers have switched to a competitive struggle for travelers at the low end of the price spectrum

---

[30] *International Civil Aviation Organization, Document 7278–C/941,* May 10, 1952. For a detailed discussion of the classification and growth of nonscheduled services, see "Non-Scheduled Transport and International Aviation Policy," *ITA Studies 65/1-E* (1965).

in the peak tourist seasons. The European flag carriers have led this change in the North Atlantic.

Data describing nonscheduled operations in 1963 appear in Table III-2. The 79 firms of IATA surveyed here produced 1.1 billion tonne-kilometers of nonscheduled service that year, or roughly 8 percent of their total service. The nonscheduled market is still very concentrated, with the largest four operators accounting for 52.8 percent of the total, and the top ten firms producing 73.8 percent of total service. Four of the seven largest operators are essentially independent charter operators; two are U.S. cargo carriers and two are British independents. The remainder of the top twenty firms are passenger carriers which primarily offer scheduled service, but which have recently also entered the charter market.[31] This market is quickly becoming less concentrated, a change which can have only favorable results.

Market Shares in the North Atlantic and Europe

Tables III-3 and III-4 give relative shares in two important markets, the intra-European and the North Atlantic. The intra-European market had essentially the same firms in 1962 as in 1957, but the size distribution changed considerably. The growth in Lufthansa and Alitalia is noteworthy. The most important change in Europe has been the increase in inclusive tour charters from a level of 560,000 passengers in 1960 to 1,850,000 passengers in 1964.[32] The primary cause was the high fares on scheduled service, which had suppressed a latent tourist demand growing with European income levels. This market was eventually exploited by small charter operators using DC-7s and other piston planes they were able to acquire at very low prices. In many cases these equipment purchases from the major airlines included a subcontract of traffic from the larger flag carrier (which had sold the aircraft) and a gradual period of debt repayment. Now, however, all of the European airlines are engaging in a competitive struggle in the charter market. In some of the tourist routes inclusive tour service is one-half of the total market.

The North Atlantic has experienced new entry and reduced seller concentration. The number of carriers offering scheduled service nearly

[31] "Non-Scheduled Transport and International Aviation Policy," *ITA Documents* 65/1-E (1965), Appendix 5.

[32] J. Mercier, "Differential Fares for Differentiated Air Services," *ITA Documents* 66/6-E (1966), p. 33.

TABLE III-2. *Nonscheduled Service of International Airlines, by Carrier, 1963*

Carrier	Nonscheduled Traffic (thousands of tonne-kilometers)[a]	Nonscheduled as a Percentage of Scheduled Traffic	Percentage of All Nonscheduled Service
Flying Tiger Line	189,413	166.7	17.1
Pan American Airways (PAA)	166,554	11.2	15.0
British Overseas Airways Corporation (BOAC)	116,590	19.6	10.5
British United Airways	112,954	422.5	10.2
Seaboard World Airlines	68,600	64.1	6.2
KLM Royal Dutch Airlines	42,935	11.5	3.9
British Eagle International Airlines	39,376	816.6	3.5
Northwest Airlines	30,301	7.3	2.7
Air Canada	27,060	5.9	2.4
Air France	24,509	4.1	2.2
Trans World Airlines (TWA)	21,708	1.7	1.9
Scandinavian Airlines System (SAS)	21,310	6.8	1.9
United Air Lines	17,185	1.1	1.5
Canadian Pacific Airlines	16,649	12.5	1.5
Qantas Empire Airways	16,086	7.2	1.5
Sabena Belgian World Airlines	14,481	8.1	1.3
Air Congo	11,907	58.8	1.1
Lufthansa German Airlines	11,174	3.2	1.0
Ceskoslovenske Aerolinie	10,737	15.5	1.0
Alitalia Airlines	9,874	2.8	0.9
Middle East Airlines	9,548	28.4	0.8
Aerlinte Eireann	8,934	27.5	0.8
Skyways	8,256	230.6	0.7
American Airlines	7,296	0.6	0.7
Pakistan International Airlines	6,367	6.7	0.6
Air Algerie	4,854	14.1	0.4
Olympic Airways	4,688	11.2	0.4
Aviacion y Comercio (Aviaco)	4,599	19.5	0.4
Aer Lingus	4,333	13.2	0.4
Varig Airlines	4,275	3.7	0.4
El Al Israel Airlines	4,247	4.3	0.4
United Arab Airlines	4,150	9.9	0.4
Japan Air Lines	4,088	1.7	0.4
Turk Hara Yollari	3,352	2.5	0.3
Trans-Australia Airlines	3,288	2.9	0.3
44 others	57,666	—	5.2
Total	1,109,344	7.7	100.0

Source: "Non-Scheduled Transport Aviation and International Aviation Policy," *ITA Studies 65/1-E* (Paris: Institut du Transport Aérien, 1965), Appendix 5.
[a] Here and throughout this book "tonne" denotes the metric ton (2,240 lbs.).

TABLE III-3. *Percentage Distribution of Intra-European Air Market, by Carrier, 1957 and 1962*

Carrier	1957	1962
British European Airways (BEA)	25.9	23.1
Air France	19.6	14.5
Scandinavian Airlines System (SAS)	13.2	10.7
Alitalia Airlines	4.6	9.3
Swissair	10.7	9.1
Lufthansa German Airlines	3.7	7.1
KLM Royal Dutch Airlines	8.3	6.3
Sabena Belgian World Airlines	5.2	5.1
Aer Lingus	3.9	3.6
Olympic Airways	0.7	3.5
Iberia Airlines of Spain	1.8	3.0
Finnair	1.6	1.9
British Overseas Airways Corporation (BOAC)	0.0	1.4
Transportes Aéreos Portugueses	0.0	0.8
Flugfelag Islands H. F.	0.8	0.6
Total	100.0	100.0

Source: Air Research Bureau, Brussels.
Note: Intra-Europe is traffic on routes originating and terminating within the geographical area covered by the European continent and countries bordering the Mediterranean (North Africa, Madeira, Canary Islands, the Near East up to the Persian Gulf, and Cyprus). (Intra-Europe data exclude domestic flights, intercontinental routes through the area, and traffic of non-European Air Research Bureau members.)

doubled in fifteen years, and the share of this market accounted for by the United States and other leading carriers has fallen. The charter market in the Atlantic has also grown considerably, and faster than scheduled service. (Charter passengers were 6.3 percent of scheduled passengers in 1956, 13.4 percent in 1961, and 15.9 percent in 1964.) Charter operations increased dramatically in 1961, when the increase of jet capacity left piston aircraft available for charter operations. This increase in charter operations has come primarily from scheduled operators, although recently U.S. supplemental carriers and even a few non-IATA foreign carriers have expanded operations.

Finally, one important non-IATA firm in the North Atlantic, Loftleidir (commonly known as Icelandic) accounts for about 2 percent of the total market. Icelandic obtained a bilateral agreement with the United States in 1946 of the Chicago type, and therefore Icelandic is not subject to IATA fares. This airline has chosen to offer service on older piston and turboprop equipment at rates 10 to 15 percent below IATA fares and has earned large profits. European carriers and their governments (with the exception of Luxembourg) have raised protests

TABLE III-4. *Percentage Distribution of North Atlantic Air Market, by Destination and Carrier, Selected Years, 1954–64*

Destination and Carrier	Scheduled Service					Nonscheduled Service	
	Number of Passengers in 1964	Percentage of Market				Number of Passengers in 1964	Percentage of Market, 1964
		1954	1958	1962	1964		
Europe to U.S.							
Pan American Airways (PAA)	675,397	28.3	26.4	22.6	24.3	15,928	4.3
Trans World Airlines (TWA)	488,161	24.2	15.2	13.9	17.5	5,298	1.4
British Overseas Airways Corporation (BOAC)	294,701	9.5	11.4	10.4	10.6	51,903	14.0
Air France	209,127	8.3	8.2	9.8	7.5	45,851	12.3
Lufthansa German Airlines	198,322	—	5.2	7.2	7.1	61,491	16.5
Alitalia Airlines	168,181	2.3	2.5	6.1	6.0	20,940	5.6
Scandinavian Airlines System (SAS)	163,931	9.1	9.8	6.5	5.9	16,538	4.4
KLM Royal Dutch Airlines	158,089	8.6	7.4	6.3	5.7	41,137	11.1
Swissair	111,486	4.0	4.2	4.0	4.0	19,901	5.4
Aerlinte Eireann	87,094	—	0.9	2.8	3.1	33,005	8.9
Sabena Belgian World Airlines	72,327	3.9	5.6	4.3	2.6	32,064	8.6
El Al Israel Airlines	64,670	1.5	1.8	2.8	2.3	11,621	3.1
Iberia Airlines of Spain	43,132	0.3	0.9	0.8	1.6	3,157	0.8
Air-India	32,282	—	—	1.3	1.2	11,970	3.2
Qantas Empire Airways	15,308	—	0.5	0.6	0.6	1,126	0.3
Pakistan International Airlines	0	—	—	0.4	0	0	0
Total	2,782,208	100.0	100.0	100.0	100.0	371,930	100.0
Europe to Canada							
Air Canada	145,160	—	45.4	39.1	50.6	58,645	51.1
BOAC	72,192	—	20.8	31.4	25.2	22,812	19.8
Canadian Pacific Airlines	47,403	—	16.5	14.2	16.5	28,002	24.4
KLM	15,281	—	17.3	15.3	5.3	4,201	3.7
Air France	6,934	—	—	—	2.4	1,074	1.0
Total	286,970	—	100.0	100.0	100.0	114,734	100.0

Source: *American Aviation*, various issues.

concerning these fares and have required that Icelandic charge IATA rates from Iceland to most points on the continent. Furthermore, when Icelandic began introducing the CL-44 (a large turboprop plane with 160 seats) on its routes in 1964, European governments generally prohibited its use. The motive behind this prohibition was to keep Icelandic from using the lower costs of the CL-44 to sustain its prices below IATA levels. Icelandic therefore uses its CL-44s from New York to Iceland and then switches to DC-6Bs for the trip to the continent. Icelandic remains free to substantially lower the rate from the United States to Iceland. Luxembourg, however, encourages Icelandic, presumably as a means of tourist promotion. Icelandic flies directly from New York to Luxembourg. A variety of pressures, from U.S. carriers, the CAB, and the U.S. government to have the bilateral agreement revoked have not been successful. The value of U.S. air bases in Iceland continues to be an important and overriding consideration in favor of allowing Iceland to retain the existing arrangement. It will subsequently be argued that Icelandic's fare cutting has been a useful stimulus in the overall structure of the market.

If a detailed examination were made of individual city-pair markets, the sort of reduction in seller concentration noted above would generally be observed. Generally, the important major city-pairs are served by several carriers rather than one or two. On the whole, the industry probably suffers from excess entry rather than excessive concentration. However, as shown in Chapter IX, the losses associated with excess entry have been needlessly multiplied by inefficient firms.

CHAPTER IV

Input Markets
and the Production Function

DIFFERENCES AMONG NATIONS in the availability of capital, skilled labor, and other inputs, differences in the ease with which technology is implemented, and differences in relative factor prices are translated into cost differences, which determine the relative competitive position of particular carriers. These cost differences indicate which airlines are efficient producers of service and, therefore, what constitutes an efficient pattern of entry. These differences also influence the conduct of market participants.

The Production Function

The production function for airline service is reasonably homogeneous among firms that, in a broad sense, are drawing on roughly similar inputs and using them in a similar fashion, despite a wide range of relative factor prices among countries. The nature of aircraft technology is the principal explanation for this homogeneity. The dominant aircraft technology generally has been quite evident to both aircraft manufacturer and airline alike. Military aircraft research as an important source of commercial aircraft technology has been a substantial force in creating homogeneity in capital equipment. In addition, the aircraft manufacturing industry has been relatively highly concentrated, with firms drawing on an essentially common pool of technical information and with new ideas quickly disseminated. Commercial planes are produced by a small number of manufacturers located principally in the United States, United Kingdom, France, and Canada. While there are some 80 types of planes being used in the industry, most service is provided by less than two dozen plane types, and of this two dozen there are many with very similar operating characteristics and costs. There is relatively little difference in potential efficiency (costs per available ton-mile) between the Boeing 707 and the Douglas DC-8, for example, in providing long-range jet service.

Similarity of Technology

Aircraft technology is such that there is considerable similarity among firms in many factor inputs used, and certain input relationships are relatively fixed. Any specific aircraft will produce nearly the same number of ton-miles (depending on utilization rates and stage lengths), require the same type and amount of fuel per hour flown, and require roughly similar amounts of maintenance work in the hands of any airline. The number of pilots and co-pilots required per flight is the same for all. There is considerable similarity in the quality of the pilots and other skilled personnel employed, due largely to the need for careful and highly specific training. The U.S. carriers and a few European ones provide most of this training. Certain terminal facilities for servicing passengers and their baggage also must be provided. Even many of the terminal operations are performed in roughly similar fashion. Heterogeneity among firms is found chiefly in the quality and use of lesser skilled labor, and in management, as will be seen below.

Variations in Scheduling

While the operations of all carriers appear similar, characterized by similar technological coefficients, there is one important difference—the ability with which firms schedule the use of their inputs. Daily utilization rates of a particular plane type vary considerably among firms, independently of effects of the route structure. Firms also record different capabilities in scheduling their pilots and co-pilots. Explicit measures of firms' abilities to schedule aircraft, flight crew, and other personnel are summarized here, based on a model developed in Appendix A.

AIRCRAFT SCHEDULING. Aircraft scheduling as reflected in daily utilization rates has perhaps the most important effect on a firm's costs. A number of components of direct operating costs depend upon aircraft utilization rates since they are overhead charges incurred each day regardless of the number of plane-hours flown. Aircraft depreciation, a function of time rather than of physical use, is one such component. Physically, aircraft wear out only very slowly; if it has had excellent maintenance, a plane ten years old often performs better than when it was new. Aircraft become obsolete due to the very rapid technological changes in the industry and consumer preference for new aircraft. A certain portion of maintenance facilities also depends upon utilization rates, since a staff and inventory of parts and equipment must be maintained regardless of the amount of use.

Since these costs are related largely to time rather than to aircraft use, firms have an obvious incentive to maximize equipment utilization rates. (At some point, of course, increased utilization should be sacrificed if it is achieved only by scheduling planes at very inconvenient departure times.) Daily aircraft utilization rates are therefore useful in providing a measure of scheduling ability.

Each firm's fleet productivity was compared with the industry average. (See Appendix A.) Adjustments in the comparisons were made for the effect of stage length (average distances between cities served). Shorter stage lengths obviously make scheduling inherently more difficult. The use of scheduling comparable to the industry average as a benchmark provides only a relative measure of scheduling ability. Average daily utilization rates for the international industry are not high. For example, in 1964, utilization rates (measured in hours per day) for the following aircraft were: 707, 9.52 hours; Caravelle, 6.08 hours; Electra, 6.83 hours. These rates are lower than the average realized by U.S. domestic carriers. Large variation exists among firms; for example, the international industry's average utilization rate in 1964 for DC-6Bs was only 5.78 hours per day, while Icelandic Airlines' utilization rate for the DC-6B was 8.38 hours per day.

Explanations for differences in scheduling ability were not readily apparent. There is no evidence that firm size has any effect, nor is there any correlation with scheduling of flight crews or other personnel. There is some tendency for firms paying higher wages, and hence having relatively cheaper capital costs and using more capital, to be superior schedulers of jet aircraft. These scheduling differences do affect costs, as will be seen below.

CREW SCHEDULING. Scheduling differences are also important in determining flight crew needs. There are minimum crew sizes prescribed for each plane type. In addition, many carriers and their pilots have agreed to a maximum number of hours a pilot can serve in a month (usually eighty). A firm's incentives are to schedule personnel so as to achieve the greatest output per man within these constraints. Relative scheduling ability of flight crews (pilots, co-pilots, navigators, and radio operators, but not stewardesses) can be measured by a comparison of the output of these personnel (flying hours per man) for each firm with the overall industry average. Calculations for crew scheduling appear in Appendix A.

There is even more variation in this phase of scheduling than in aircraft utilization. There was no correlation between crew scheduling and stage length or route density. The primary conclusion was that high-wage firms are better pilot schedulers, as indicated by the correlation of crew scheduling with pilot wages. Crew scheduling was also correlated with the scheduling of "all other labor." No correlation with firm size was observable.

SCHEDULING OF OTHER PERSONNEL. The final measures of scheduling involve "all other labor" (all labor excluding the flight crew). The extent of a firm's requirement for other labor depends upon many factors, including its plane choice, route system, and relative factor prices. It will be shown below that jet planes reduce labor requirements and increase output-labor ratios. Longer stage lengths and denser routes also increase the productivity of supporting personnel, both by increasing efficiency of those hired and by permitting the use of larger aircraft which conserve labor. Finally, relative factor prices affect the requirements for labor since it is possible to substitute relatively cheap for relatively expensive inputs in the production function.

Using cross-section data, an equation for labor requirements (per seat-mile) was estimated, with independent variables which reflected plane choice, route system, and the wage level. Firms were classified according to whether they employed more or less labor than would be indicated by this equation representing "average" behavior—those employing more labor were labeled poor at labor utilization or scheduling, and vice versa. There were large differences in the relative performance of various firms on these grounds. Ability at labor scheduling was not correlated with capital scheduling, but was correlated with pilot scheduling.

The scheduling measures for particular firms for the years 1962 and 1964 are presented in Appendix A. These scheduling differences can be summarized as follows: higher-wage firms do a significantly better job of scheduling flight crews and other labor and are somewhat superior in scheduling aircraft. This seems to be a likely result in view of the relative factor prices involved.

The Production Implications of Pooling Agreements

Cost reduction is one of the primary motivations behind pooling and related types of carrier agreements.[1] Agreements of this type involve airline cooperation on the technological side and generally are concerned with eliminating the duplication of certain overhead costs. These agreements have important implications for the nature of the production function, since they reduce heterogeneity among firms and have somewhat alleviated the problems of small size.

Spare Parts Pools

The most important type of agreement pertains to the pooling of spare parts. The first such pool was formed in 1954 for the Lockheed 749 and 1049. The Beneswiss Agreement among KLM, Sabena, and Swissair (later joined by SAS and Air France) was another early agreement. This agreement involved common maintenance service, mechanics, workshops, and spare parts for the DC-3, DC-4, Convair 240, and DC-6.[2] Many such spare parts pools providing service for a particular plane type have since been established, including pools for the Comet 4, DC-8, and 707.[3] Many but not all carriers using such equipment participate in these pools, which essentially allow participants to draw on

[1] Another type of pooling arrangement—market sharing agreements—is discussed in Chapter III, pp. 37–38.

[2] E. A. G. Verploeg, *The Road Towards a European Common Air Market* (Utrecht: Uitgeverij Kemink en Zn., N.V., 1963), pp. 78–79.

[3] The DC-8 pool, for example, involving Alitalia, Japan Air Lines, KLM, PAA, SAS, and Swissair covers 25 stations in which these carriers land DC-8s. KLM, with operations at 16 of these stations, had to keep spare parts at only six. KLM estimated the average cost per station of spares for the DC-8 at $87,000, as contrasted with $31,000 for the DC-7C. See "Airline Commercial Agreements, Pacts, and Consortiums," *Aviation Report Supplement,* No. 141 (London: Aviation Studies International, Ltd., August 1964), pp. 17–18.

a common inventory of spare parts. For example, the Boeing pool involves member carriers paying an "availability charge" annually for the right to draw parts when needed, with repair and replacement in the inventory of any borrowed piece to be made as soon as possible.[4]

These spares pools have produced considerable cost savings. Air France has estimated that its savings from the Boeing pool amount to 70 percent of the firm's spare parts expense for this type of aircraft.[5] The potential cost saving of pools has grown considerably since the advent of the jets with their higher fixed costs. The latter have provided considerable impetus to pooling arrangements.

Maintenance Pools

Cooperation of a bilateral nature also exists, as exemplified by the many subcontracting and leasing arrangements made among firms. Reduction in maintenance expense has been a major objective. The most notable example is the agreement between SAS and Swissair. All aircraft of a single type in the fleets of both companies are ordered according to agreed specifications for interior and cockpit configuration. Fleet maintenance is then divided between the carriers, with Swissair servicing the Convair 880s and 990s while SAS tends to the Caravelles and DC-8s.

A large number of these maintenance agreements exist, generally involving small carriers subcontracting maintenance work to larger ones. The smaller carriers save on fixed costs and reduce capital requirements, while the larger firms earn additional revenue by employing their fixed inputs more effectively. The British European Airways-Olympic consortium signed in 1959 is an excellent example. BEA maintains the Comet 4 fleet for Olympic and further guarantees that two aircraft will always be available for Olympic's use. (In addition, these two carriers engage in a joint sales and advertising program.) Without the service agreement, Olympic would have required one additional Comet at a cost of almost $3 million, in order to introduce jets onto its Mediterranean routes, and also would have needed a jet

[4] "BOAC Reports on Savings from Spares Pooling," *International Aviation*, supplement to *Aviation Daily*, Vol. 141 (August 6, 1952), p. 95.

[5] Stanford Research Institute, *Air Transport Development and Coordination in Latin America: A Study of Economic Factors* (SRI for the Organization of American States, 1961), pp. 33–43.

overhaul base at Athens at a cost of about $2 million. Olympic also saves an estimated $850,000 in annual operating expenses. BEA has received in exchange the right of entry into Greece's routes in the Mediterranean.[6] (Greece's very protectionist attitude historically in its air markets makes this entry consideration a very important motivation for BEA.)

In maintenance subcontracting agreements of this general type, one party is often a smaller carrier of a less developed nation. Philippine Air Lines was able to begin jet service with one DC-8 because of a pooling arrangement with KLM; KLM agreed to maintain the Philippine Air Lines' DC-8 and to further guarantee that one plane would always be available.[7] Without such an agreement this small airline would not have been able to enter jet service.

Equipment Pools

A third type of pooling arrangement involves the leasing of equipment. Leasing often is one component of a wider intercarrier agreement. For example, a new subsidiary carrier may lease equipment from its parent company until it can afford its own. This is an effective means of circumventing capital constraints and is often used by developing countries. Crews and other technical personnel may or may not be included in the lease arrangement, although technical advisory service almost always is. For example, SAS has chartered DC-6Bs to Thai International airline and has also provided financing and technical and administrative assistance. The motivation for SAS has been to dispose of its surplus piston fleet and to gain access to routes which would otherwise be unavailable. SAS has also agreed to accept a share of the profits or losses, a decision which has so far been expensive.[8]

Space Leasing Arrangements

Another recent form of cooperation is block space leasing. Under this type of arrangement one carrier leases space on another carrier's planes, sells the space in its own name, and pays for it irrespective of

[6] *Ibid.*, pp. 36–37.

[7] Stephen Wheatcroft, *Air Transport Policy* (London: Michael Joseph, Ltd., 1964), p. 105.

[8] SAS annual reports, various years.

use. Air Afrique has leased seats from PAA on flights from New York to the eleven African member nations of Air Afrique. For the Africans, this is a means of circumventing a capital constraint, while PAA has accepted the arrangement since it serves as a means of entry to certain African cities. This kind of cooperation will probably not become very important in the future because the lessee tends to lose his "airline identity" too quickly, and passengers then approach the other carrier directly. Block space leasing may continue, however, to be a means of entry.

Other Types of Intercarrier Cooperation

There are some additional forms of cooperation not easily categorized. Sharing or leasing training responsibilities is one practice. Jets have raised training costs considerably because of requirements such as the electronic flight simulator necessary for jet pilot training. Collective purchasing is another means of reducing costs. The major European carriers have a standing organization for such cooperation.[9] Management subcontracting arrangements are another form of cooperation. For example, TWA has managed Ethiopian Airlines under three-year contracts. Finally, many carriers directly share or jointly employ personnel, especially sales and station personnel. Aer Lingus and Aerlinte, the Irish carriers, have an arrangement whereby Aer Lingus personnel work for both firms.

This technical cooperation has had several effects. It has helped produce greater homogeneity among firms in production techniques. It has also produced a considerable cost saving, which has done much to reduce the cost disadvantage of small-scale operations, including jet operations. In light of the possibilities for subcontracting, the old assumption that six or seven planes of one type were necessary for efficient operations is no longer considered valid. Many carriers are able to operate jet fleets of three planes quite effectively (for example, Avianca and El Al Israel Airlines in 1962). While large numbers of a single plane type would produce lower costs, the difference does not appear great, and certainly not beyond what many governments are willing to pay for jet operations. In short, these pooling arrangements have helped create a production function of essentially constant returns to scale and hence somewhat reduce any scale or size barriers to entry.

[9] Wheatcroft, *op. cit.*, p. 106.

Input Markets

Most inputs for international airline operations are purchased in worldwide markets, with input sellers providing services to carriers of many countries. Fuel, landing facilities, new and used aircraft, spare parts, ground equipment, and capital are such inputs. Some of these markets are competitive, while others are not. For example, sometimes government policies in support of their flag carriers result in low-cost provision of capital or discrimination in airport user charges. Labor is the one input purchased in a national rather than a worldwide market; widely differing labor prices thus reflect the availability of labor in particular countries. Capital, though often acquired in a worldwide market, is also available at varying opportunity cost levels for different countries. These latter sources of variation in the opportunity cost of factors must be considered in determining which airlines are efficient producers of service.

The following discussion of input markets focuses on two questions: First, what are the effects of different relative factor prices on the factor mix chosen and on the costs incurred by various nations' carriers? Second, how closely do market prices reflect real costs? Answers to these questions are useful in determining the relative efficiency of various producers of airline service and in determining the source of comparative cost differences.

Fuel Market

Fuel is sold at almost uniform and generally nondiscriminatory prices by a few huge companies. Aircraft fuel is therefore a prime example of inputs which are sold in markets where input price variation among international carriers in any given regional market is small.

Landing Facilities Market

International airports and terminal facilities, on the other hand, are made available at prices which vary regionally and may reflect discrimination in favor of flag carriers. These facilities have generally been publicly provided, in much the same fashion as U.S. airports; such public provision obviously removes a huge fixed cost burden from the airlines. A wide variety of user charges exist: a basic landing charge, a night surcharge, parking fees, hangar rentals, air navigation and tele-communications charges for overflying and landing, passenger taxes, and fuel taxes[10]—any or all of which may be present at a given international airport. Table IV-1 lists the basic landing charge, which is the most important of all airport-user charges. The low levels in North and South America are noteworthy. Africa and the Far East have levels twice as high. Among European countries, the United Kingdom and Ireland have very high charges.

Aircraft Markets

The markets for both new and used aircraft are nearly perfect, worldwide. The new aircraft market is characterized by individual bargaining because transactions are large and infrequent for any one carrier and because there are relatively few sellers. However, intense competition exists among aircraft manufacturers, and any order is gratefully received; this competition eliminates most price discrimination. The discrimination which does exist probably favors the large carriers at the expense of smaller ones and takes on disguised forms such as earlier delivery times or higher trade-in allowances on older equipment. Published information on the sale prices of aircraft shows little variation for each plane type, other than that accounted for by the different amounts of spare equipment and the different interiors involved.

The used aircraft market is no less perfect, with transactions being made at prices established in a fairly extensive worldwide market. The advent of the jet is most responsible for expanding and developing this market, as first the U.S. airlines and later many large foreign carriers found themselves with surplus piston fleets. Airlines of all sorts and aircraft manufacturers became participants in this market. There are also a number of brokerage houses that act as dealers and assume the price risk of holding an inventory.

Used aircraft prices in this relatively perfect market respond quickly

[10] Perhaps half of the nations in the world have fuel taxes, either on fuel purchased or in throughput-charges. Most taxes are less than one cent a gallon, with some exceptions. Iceland charges a tax of 7 cents per gallon, Paraguay 5 cents, Peru 4.6 cents, and Denmark 7.7 cents. Argentina taxes jet fuel 13.75 cents per gallon, but aviation gasoline only 2.283 cents—an interesting protection for local piston carriers. Greece has a stiff fuel tax for the carriers of nations which have not signed bilateral agreements. See "World Guide to Airport Charges," *Aeroplane and Commercial Aviation News*, Vol. 109 (April 22, 1965), pp. 4–11.

TABLE IV-1. *Airport Landing Charge for Boeing 707 or Douglas DC-8, Selected Countries, December 1964*

(In U.S. dollars)

Airport	Landing Charge	Airport	Landing Charge
North America		Paraguay	116
Bahamas-Nassau	180	Trinidad	220
Bermuda	48	Uruguay	15
Canada-Montreal	445	Venezuela	165
Cuba	85		
Jamaica	80	*Europe*	
Mexico	124	Austria-Vienna	200
Puerto Rico	63	Belgium	185
		Cyprus	140
United States		Czechoslovakia	240
Boston	55	Denmark-Copenhagen	210
Chicago (O'Hare)	95	Finland-Helsinki	178
Honolulu	450	France	300
Houston	28	Germany (excluding Berlin)	279
New York (Kennedy)	88	Greece	195
San Francisco	48	Hungary	157
Seattle	60	Ireland	394
Washington, D.C. (Dulles)	52	Italy	
		Rome	190
Central and South America		Milan	160
Argentina-Ezeiza	150	Venice	74
Barbados	112	Luxembourg	50
Bolivia (flag)	290	Netherlands-Amsterdam	210
(foreign)	580	Norway-Oslo	200
Brazil	5	Poland-Warsaw	244
British Guiana	183	Spain	84
British Honduras	87	Sweden	203
Chile-Santiago	100	Switzerland	155
Colombia	290	Turkey	119
Costa Rica	28	United Kingdom	
Dominican Republic	111	(intercontinental)	570
Ecuador	227	U.S.S.R.-Moscow	50
El Salvador	40	Yugoslavia	350
French Guiana	300		
Guatemala	180	*Middle East*	
Haiti	385	Aden	518
Honduras	50	Bahrain	400
Nicaragua	150	Egypt	106
Panama	122	Iran	37

Source: "World Guide to Airport Charges," *Aeroplane and Commercial Aviation News*, Vol. 109 (April 22, 1965), pp. 4–11. (These figures were compiled by the International Air Transport Association.)

TABLE IV-1—*Continued*

Airport	Landing Charge	Airport	Landing Charge
Middle East (cont.)		Rwanda	256
Iraq	105	Senegal	291
Jordan	105	Sierra Leone	155
Kuwait	135	South Africa	290
Lebanon	160	Sudan	720
Saudi Arabia	158	Tanganyika	265
Syria	110	Tunisia	246
		Uganda	265
Africa		Zanzibar	265
Algeria	310		
Burundi	256	*Far East, Pacific*	
Central African Republic	290	Afghanistan	115
Chad	290	Australia	535
Congo: Brazzaville	290	Burma	160
Congo: Leopoldville	256	Cambodia	446
Ethiopia	375	Ceylon	158
Ghana	280	Hong Kong	385
Guinea	245	India	275
Kenya	376	Indonesia	350
Liberia	285	Japan	250
Malagasy	460	Malaysia (excluding Singapore)	222
Martinique	300	New Zealand	525
Morocco	210	Pakistan	158
Nigeria	280	South Vietnam	380
Reunion	300	Taiwan	200
Rhodesia	322	Thailand	240

to reductions in operating costs or marketing advantages of new technologies. Used aircraft prices tend to decline to the point where direct operating costs (including the depreciation costs implied by the aircraft sale price) of various plane types suitable for the same operation are essentially the same. The persisting differences in available seat-mile costs reflect principally marketing differences, which are revealed in differences in load factors and hence in revenue per seat-mile. In short, in the used aircraft market, the market valuation of capital equipment is responsive both to changes in technology and to the rate at which equipment wears out.

The introduction of the jets is the best and most dramatic example of this sort of market price adjustment. In the period prior to the late 1950s, used aircraft prices had been high—often as high as original prices. The larger U.S. carriers continually enjoyed capital gains as

TABLE IV-2. *Used Aircraft Prices, Selected Dates, 1957–62*

(In thousands of dollars)

Model of Aircraft	January 1957 (1)	January 1958 (2)	December 1958 (3)	June 1959, Bid-Asked (4)	July 1960, Asking Price Range (5)	1962 Sale Prices (6)
Douglas DC-3	165	115	75	65–75	35–70	50
Martin 202	. . .	270	270	. . .	. . .	. . .
Martin 404	. . .	400	400	. . .	. . .	120
Viking	98	84	62	. . .	. . .	. . .
Bristol 170/31	98	. . .	56	. . .	. . .	. . .
York	98	84	56	. . .	. . .	. . .
Convair 240	450	300	. . .	195–259	130–160	125
Convair 340	. . .	550	300	278–430	. . .	240
Convair 440	. . .	. . .	550	400–585	. . .	300
Curtiss C-46	140	125	125	. . .	42–200	40
Douglas DC-4, 4B	650	350	270	188–230	190–265	115
Douglas DC-6/6A	1,200	1,350	1,200	425–635	380–575[a]	375
Douglas DC-6B	. . .	1,430	900	608–738	450–470	400
Lockheed 049	1,000	800	460	200–364	150–185	700
Lockheed 749	1,250	900	500	250–400	250–400	200
Douglas DC-7	. . .	1,500	1,150	965–1,200	700–1,200	500

Sources: Col. 1, *Aviation Report Supplement* (London: Aviation Studies International, Ltd., February 1957), p. 3; Col. 2, *Aviation Report Supplement* (January 1958), p. 32; Col. 3, *Aviation Report Supplement* (January 1959), pp. 35–36; Col. 4, *Airlift* (July 1959), p. 27; Col. 5, *Airlift* (August 1960), p. 33; Col. 6, various aviation journals.

[a] The asking price for a DC-6 was between $380,000 and $575,000 and for a DC-6A, $725,000.

they sold depreciated piston aircraft to U.S. local carriers and to carriers abroad.[11] However, the introduction of jets produced a sharp reduction in operating costs, which made the piston planes expendable. The economic obsolescence of the DC-7C, Lockheed 1649, and Britannia were perhaps the most dramatic examples; these aircraft were placed at a huge cost disadvantage by the jets almost immediately after their introduction. The great supply of used piston planes subsequently offered for sale resulted in a sharp break in prices. In 1958 the used piston aircraft market was still strong. By mid-1959, prices had fallen by 50 percent or more; they fell another 25 percent by mid-1960. (See Table IV-2). Some piston aircraft were converted to cargo service. Air-

[11] *Reinvestment of Capital Gains on Sale of Airlines Flight Equipment*, Hearings before the Senate Committee on Interstate and Foreign Commerce, 84 Cong. 2 sess. (April 12, 1956), pp. 7–22; and *Reinvestment of Capital Gains by Air Carriers*, Hearings before the Senate Committee on Interstate and Foreign Commerce, 85 Cong. 1 sess. (August 16, 1957), pp. 76–95.

craft manufacturers accepted some piston planes as a means of offering a discount on jet purchases, and a few manufacturers even considered conversion of these planes by installing turbine engines. The used aircraft market has remained essentially in a depressed state since 1960, with piston planes available at very low prices.

The developing countries were the logical source of demand, as their high capital and low labor costs made depreciated piston aircraft the rational choice. Airlines in these countries have, in fact, been the major purchasers of used piston planes. As jet technology has been extended to shorter-haul designs, the replacement of piston aircraft in the developing countries has continued. Some displaced piston aircraft, however, have been cannibalized for spare parts or simply scrapped for lack of a market. As will be seen below, the latest jet technology of the DC-9 type may well alter this pattern somewhat. The DC-9 appears to be the optimal technological choice in the near future for all but those countries with very high capital costs and thin route densities.

Since the purchasers of surplus piston aircraft have generally been small carriers in the less developed countries, it can be questioned whether it is in the best interests of the major carriers to supply potential competitors. It is almost always beneficial for an individual carrier to sell its unwanted piston fleet since the buyer probably will not be in direct competition. This is also generally true for all carriers taken together. The purchasers generally have been conducting regional operations and hence provide a benefit in terms of traffic generation for the long-haul routes. There have, of course, been exceptions. Some of the piston planes have remained in important markets and siphoned off a share of business. Icelandic has profitably operated cast-off DC-6Bs in the North Atlantic, but this is a special case. In addition, some carriers that began with used piston fleets have gone on to provide jet service later. But generally the major carriers have been fortunate to find buyers, although the selling prices have been low.

Labor Market

Fuel, landing, and aircraft markets actually have a relatively insignificant effect on relative costs of firms in a given market. The labor and capital markets contain a much wider variation in relative factor prices. These variations, based on differences in factor availability among nations, have the most important implications for comparative

TABLE IV-3. *Average Annual Wage Levels, Selected International Air Carriers, 1964*

(In dollars)

Carrier	Average Annual Wage of Pilots	Average Annual Wage of All Other Labor
Pan American-Grace Airways	$23,630	$3,024
Braniff International	23,598	6,236
Pan American Airways (PAA)	21,637	6,685
Trans World Airlines (TWA)	20,914	6,952
Northwest Airlines	20,853	6,441
Royal Air Maroc	19,092	2,860
Air France	18,050	3,761
KLM Royal Dutch Airlines	15,215	3,712
Air Canada	14,657	5,796
Canadian Pacific Airlines	14,621	5,096
Caribbean-Atlantic Airlines	14,117	5,229
Sabena Belgian World Airlines	12,354	1,279
Iberia Airlines of Spain	11,593	2,120
Swissair	11,581	3,979
El Al Israel Airlines	11,496	2,816
Alitalia Airlines	11,145	4,420
British Overseas Airways Corporation (BOAC)	10,689	3,353
Scandinavian Airlines System (SAS)	10,572	3,879
Austrian Airlines	10,398	2,454
Lufthansa German Airlines	9,971	3,021
Finnair	9,775	3,352
East African Airways	9,661	1,456
Aerlinte Eireann	9,549	5,863
British European Airways (BEA)	9,441	3,088
Qantas Empire Airways	9,206	3,446
Aviacion y Comercio	9,170	2,731
Aerolineas Argentinas	9,000	2,000
Karhumaki, Veljeksef (Kar-Air)	8,571	2,857
Tasman Empire Airways	7,466	3,307
South African Airways	7,456	3,326
Aer Lingus	7,112	2,623
Japan Air Lines	6,514	1,973
Pakistan International Airlines	5,404	467
Philippine Air Lines	4,792	1,644
Sociedad Aeronautica Medellin	4,651	1,057
United Arab Airlines	3,550	1,319
Aerotransportes del Litoral Argentino	3,000	1,400

Source: International Civil Aviation Organization, *Digest of Statistics, Fleet and Personnel,* No. 116 (1964), pp. 33–134.

costs. Table IV-3 shows the price of labor for selected international carriers for 1964. Pilots, though a relatively homogeneous factor, receive widely different wages. In the United States, pilots' salaries are set by individual firm labor-management bargaining. In many foreign countries, the pilots must be trained extensively by the airlines themselves, and they are much less able to strive for wage increases. (There have been some occasions when pilots in Europe have been enticed by the much higher salaries paid in the United States.) Substantial differences exist in wages in the "all other labor" class as well. These can be partially explained by differences in productivity levels—but not entirely, since the productivity of stewardesses and much of the ground personnel is not markedly different across national boundaries. Adjustment for productivity differences has not been made, but there would appear to be substantial differences in the wages for unskilled labor.

Capital Market

The capital market also contains some significant inter-firm price variation, though less than the labor market. While there are some differences in capital costs across national boundaries, the principal reasons for variation in capital prices lie in the effects governments have on the perceived costs to their carriers and in the availability of foreign aid and certain special forms of outside financing.

Special financial arrangements have kept capital costs to many carriers close to zero. For example, some governments have provided their "chosen instruments" with capital and have financed all deficits. The less developed countries, in particular, have provided capital at a perceived cost to the firm far below its true opportunity cost. Private capital markets presumably would not finance these losing operations, either in the case of many of the less developed countries' carriers or in the case of many of the large, established carriers which continually lose money, such as Air France. The investments by private carriers in subsidiaries have been a source of low-cost capital to the recipient carriers. Equipment leasing or lending is often a low-cost capital grant. The BOAC subsidiary airlines which have regularly lost money are a specific example.

In addition to these low-cost sources, capital has also been acquired from the private capital markets. U.S. banks and insurance companies have been important sources for re-equipment financing in the form of notes, bonds, and convertible debentures. Rates have been competitive with those in the long-term capital market—between 4 and 5 percent in the 1950s and about 6 percent in recent years. Capital for jet aircraft has become quite readily available of late. The mobility and strong possibility of resale of jet aircraft, along with the profits which jet operations generally produce, make such equipment financing sound by conventional banking standards. Banks have been willing to make loans, even to some of the less developed countries, based on jet aircraft as collateral.

The effect on the industry of this capital market has been the obvious one of encouraging considerable expansion. The fact that the capital market has made funds available at low cost, in the form of foreign aid grants or whatever, should not, however, be construed as the sole causal factor. The willingness of states to bear a subsidy burden is the primary impetus to a capital market with very low costs to the airlines.

This survey of international airline factor markets suggests that the differences between factor prices and real opportunity costs are not too great in most countries, with the exception of capital. Markets for fuel, aircraft, and parts are relatively perfect. Wages for pilots and skilled labor in most developing countries probably understate the real cost. Capital is, of course, often provided far below its real cost, and airport facilities have been provided at less than their real cost. The operating cost comparisons to be made in the next chapter, which exclude capital costs, are therefore a reasonable approximation to real cost comparisons.

Factor Substitution: Plane Choice

The considerable differences in relative factor prices have resulted in firms altering their factor mix and have also affected comparative costs. Though there are certain fixed relationships between crew size, fuel, and a given output of seat-miles for any particular plane type, the production function for airline service is characterized by variable proportions. Plane choice is a principal means of factor substitution. For each seat-mile which can be produced with a DC-3 or a DC-9, the DC-9 is the more capital-intensive and labor-conserving choice.

Labor Costs

The opportunity for input substitution by an appropriate plane choice can be seen by examining direct operating and capital costs for various plane types. Direct operating costs (flight crew, fuel and oil, insurance, maintenance and overhead, and depreciation) comprise slightly more than one half of total air costs and are the components most sensitive to the choice of technology.[12] The opportunity for factor substitution arises because the proportion of costs attributable to particular inputs varies among plane types. The percentage breakdown of costs by plane type for the U.S. domestic trunklines is shown in Table IV-4. Differences in factor prices—labor and capital costs in particular—are often such that the optimal plane choice differs for carriers in different countries.

A second important area which permits substitution of labor for capital is ground operations—baggage handling, reservations, etc. Another important possibility is in the use of more or fewer stewardesses and labor-intensive services on the plane. Finally, an additional effort can be made to improve safety, navigational, and traffic-handling procedures so as to provide a high percentage of flights arriving and departing on schedule. U.S. carriers, for example, substitute capital for labor by using the latest jet equipment, by offering frequent flights which have good records on safety and punctuality, and by conserving labor in terminal operations and in the passenger service on board. This is in direct contrast to the labor-intensive operation which is conducted by many carriers.

Comparison of Factor Prices and Productivity for U.S. Carrier and Developing Country Carrier

Appendix A develops cost comparisons for the years 1962 and 1965 for different plane types as a function of factor prices and scheduling, at stage lengths of 250, 500, and 750 miles. The possible effects of different factor prices and productivity costs for various aircraft are numerous. Factor prices and productivity levels were compared for a U.S. carrier and a typical carrier in one of the developing countries, which

---

[12] Direct costs can in large part be explained by the nature of the route system, the choice of plane, the level of wages, and the quality of input scheduling. These determinants of direct costs will be developed at length in Chapter V.

TABLE IV-4. *Direct Operating Costs of Selected Aircraft Used by U.S. Domestic Airlines, 1965*

Cost Component	Boeing 727	Boeing 720/720B	Elec- tra	Doug- las DC-7/ 7B	Doug- las DC-6/ 6B	Convair 340/ 440	Doug- las DC-3[a]	Fair- child F-27[a]
I. Costs								
Direct operating costs (cents per seat-mile)	1.59	1.42	2.14	2.68	2.53	2.76	3.05	2.50
Stage length (miles)	481	678	241	225	191	129	87	126
Utilization (block time: revenue hours per day)	8.1	10.0	8.2	6.5	6.3	7.6	6.3	8.4
II. Percentage of Direct Operating Costs Borne by Various Components[b]								
Flight crew	22.5	17.0	22.7	24.1	28.6	32.9	40.5	26.5
Fuel and oil	24.0	26.2	15.9	22.4	22.6	19.0	19.6	17.1
Maintenance and overhead	27.4	32.5	37.6	43.2	44.2	43.7	37.1	39.5
Insurance	2.7	2.8	1.1	0.4	0.3	0.8	0.7	3.1
Depreciation	23.3	21.5	22.6	9.8	4.3	3.4	2.0	13.8
Total	100.0	100.0	100.0	100.0	100.0	100.0	100.0	100.0
III. Estimated Direct Operating Costs at Selected Stage Lengths (in cents per seat-mile)								
250 miles	2.25	2.75	2.10	2.60	2.37	2.52	2.80	2.40
500 miles	1.60	1.68	1.85	2.28	2.13	n.a.	n.a.	n.a.
750 miles	1.44	1.41	1.75	2.20	2.04	n.a.	n.a.	n.a.

Sources: Figures for Parts I and II are from Federal Aviation Agency, *Direct Operating Costs and Other Performance Characteristics of Transport Aircraft in Airline Service, Calendar Year 1965* (1966), pp. 18–22 and 28–32. Figures in Part III are based on cost curves derived in Chapter V, pp. 85–90.
n.a. Not available.
[a] Local service airlines.
[b] Figures are rounded and will not necessarily add to totals.

had lower labor costs relative to capital costs and lower input productivity levels. As noted earlier, a simple proportionate reduction in labor expenses for carriers facing lower wages generally far overstates the realizable savings in view of productivity and scheduling differences. The case in Appendix A assumes interest rates of 6 percent for the U.S. and 10 percent for the developing country, flight crew expenses for the developing country carrier at three-fourths those of the U.S. domestic airline, and fuel and maintenance and overhead costs equal to the U.S. experience.[13] (The implications of alternative assumptions about relative factor prices could be easily developed.)

[13] Mahlon Straszheim, "Air Cost Functions and the Choice of an Optimal Air

The rationale for these specific assumptions about labor productivity is developed in Appendix A. Although only illustrative, this example typifies the experience of many of the developing countries, especially the smaller ones serving markets of shorter stage lengths.

VARIATION IN OPPORTUNITY COST OF CAPITAL. The assumption of a different opportunity cost of capital has considerable significance in view of the large differences among aircraft in the amount of capital involved. In adjusting for interest rate differences, care must be taken to choose the appropriate investment outlay. In considering a firm's decisions as to plane choice, depreciation should approximate real capital consumption (that is, the difference in market valuation of capital assets at the year's beginning and end). The relatively perfect used aircraft market makes these data readily available. Table IV-5b, based on the data in Table IV-5a, compares accounting write-offs of U.S. domestic trunklines with an estimate of principal and interest on a straight line basis, using market prices for aircraft in 1965 (new prices for jets and used prices for piston planes). Utilization rates chosen were those which approximated the average for U.S. domestic carriers. It can be seen that the jets are being written off at near their real costs, while the piston aircraft are being charged for capital losses which, in fact, have already been sustained. Thus, airline accounting write-offs which use straight line depreciation of purchase prices do not provide a close approximation to actual capital consumption because of the sharp fall in piston aircraft prices. The low level of prices for piston planes in 1965 resulted in capital costs, in an opportunity cost sense, which were very low.

PLANE PRODUCTIVITY. The other major determinant of aircraft depreciation expense is plane productivity. Productivity is dependent on daily utilization rates, which for American carriers average nine to ten hours per day for jets and six hours per day for piston planes. As noted earlier, aircraft utilization is related both to route density and to the carrier's scheduling abilities. Utilization is important in the optimal plane choice. Since jets entail a larger capital outlay, utilization will ob-

Technology for the Developing Countries," Discussion Paper No. 28 (processed; Harvard Transport Project, October 1965). This paper develops the cost comparisons made in Appendix A in greater detail, with particular emphasis on decision rules for less developed countries. The effects of stage length and route density on plane choice are examined in detail.

TABLE IV-5a. *Productivity of Selected Aircraft, 1965*

Model of Aircraft	Average Speed (miles per block hour) Stage Length (miles)			Number of Seats per Plane	Daily Utiliza- tion (hours)	Millions of Available Seat-Miles per Year Stage Length (miles)		
	250	500	750			250	500	750
Douglas DC-9	375	425	—	115	9	141.7	160.6	—
Boeing 720B	—	390	410	148	9	—	189.6	199.3
Boeing 727	—	376	—	115	9	—	141.9	—
Electra L-188	253	290	315	90	8	66.5	76.2	82.8
Douglas DC-7B	213	233	248	90	7	49.5	53.6	57.0
Douglas DC-6B	198	216	228	90	7	45.5	49.7	52.4
Fairchild F-27	185	—	—	48	7	22.7	—	—
Convair 340/440	165	—	—	40	6	14.4	—	—
Douglas DC-3	135	—	—	27	6	8.0	—	—

Source: Data on average speed and number of seats are the author's estimates. Daily utilization data are averages for 1964 reported in International Civil Aviation Organization, *Digest of Statistics, Fleet and Personnel* No. 116 (1964), pp. 26–31.

viously have a greater impact on costs. The effect of differing utiliza- tion rates is discussed in Chapter V. The cost comparisons include as one alternative the case where utilization rates were 20 percent less than the levels used in the basic cost comparisons, permitting a sensi- tivity check on this important variable.

There are additional cost elements which should properly be in- cluded in examining input substitution implied in the plane choice. Ground equipment, historically about 10 percent of aircraft costs, is one such item. Also 8 percent of the sale price of the jets is added for crew training, to cover the incremental cost of training jet pilots (see Chapter V). There are some components of indirect airline costs, such as cabin personnel, which are also dependent on plane choice insofar as they relate to aircraft speed. Airport user charges, if they were to reflect appropriately the costs of handling different plane types, would also vary. Data are not available on the indirect cost elements by plane type. Fortunately, these elements are empirically small. The compari- sons made in Appendix A and summarized in Tables IV-6 and IV-7, for

TABLE IV-5b. *Capital Costs of Selected Aircraft, 1965*

Model of Aircraft	Reported Depreciation (cents per available seat-mile)	Aircraft Sale Price (thousands of dollars)	Plane Life Residual Value (percent of sale price)	Real Capital Costs (in cents per available seat-mile)					
				Stage Length (miles) (6% interest rate)			Stage Length (miles) (10% interest rate)		
				250	500	750	250	500	750
Douglas DC-9a	0.375	3,100	10–15	0.30	0.26	—	0.36	0.31	—
Boeing 720B	0.305	4,800	10–10	—	0.34	0.35	—	0.41	0.39
Boeing 727	0.370	4,500	10–15	—	0.43	—	—	0.51	—
Electra L-188	0.484	1,500	8–0	0.36	0.32	0.29	0.42	0.37	0.34
Douglas DC-7B	0.263	150	6–0	0.06	0.06	0.05	0.07	0.06	0.06
Douglas DC-6B	0.109	250	6–0	0.11	0.10	0.10	0.13	0.12	0.11
Fairchild F-27	0.345	1,000	8–0	0.71	—	—	0.83	—	—
Convair 340/440	0.093	100	6–0	0.14	—	—	0.16	—	—
Douglas DC-3	0.061	40	6–0	0.10	—	—	0.11	—	—

Sources: This table is illustrative of costs; data are based on author's estimates and on manufacturers' data, except for depreciation figures, which are derived from Federal Aviation Agency, *Direct Operating Costs and Other Performance Characteristics of Transport Aircraft in Airline Service, Calendar Year 1965*, pp. 18–32.
a DC-9 reported depreciation is for 1966. *Air Transport World*, Vol. 4, No. 1 (January 1967), pp. 34–35.

1962 and 1965, respectively, include direct operating costs and capital costs. The latter include aircraft and spare parts depreciation, ground equipment expense of 10 percent, and the marginal costs of jet crew training.

JET VS. PISTON. The choice between jet and piston is the most important dimension of the input substitution implied in plane choice. Jets save on maintenance and crew costs but involve much higher capital costs than piston aircraft, which are available at very low prices. For the major carriers in the medium- and long-haul markets, jet technology has such great passenger appeal that it is almost a competitive necessity. The cost comparisons in Table IV-7 show that for countries where factor prices resemble those in the United States or Western Europe, and where the opportunity cost of capital is considered to be approximately 6 percent, jets are much the cheaper plane to operate. Most carriers in these countries have been replacing piston with jet aircraft since the latter were introduced. As Table IV-7 indicates, jets in

TABLE IV-6. *Direct Operating and Capital Costs of Selected Aircraft, by Stage Length, 1962*

(In cents per available seat-mile)

Stage Length and Model of Aircraft	Costs		
	10% Interest Rate[a]	10% Interest Rate[a] (utilization 20% less)	20% Interest Rate[a]
Stage length 750 miles			
Boeing 707	1.742	1.901	2.011
Electra L-188	1.730	1.839	1.927
Douglas DC-7/7B	1.559	1.578	1.582
Douglas DC-6/6B	1.887	1.922	1.931
Stage length 500 miles			
Boeing 720	2.006	2.126	2.244
Electra L-188	1.769	1.888	1.983
Douglas DC-7/7B	1.607	1.626	1.630
Douglas DC-6/6B	1.899	1.937	1.946

Source: Appendix A, including Table A-10.
[a] Rate of interest refers to the opportunity cost of capital.

1965 were the preferred choice for countries with factor prices resembling those of the United States, even at 250-mile stage lengths. The DC-9 promises to have quite an impact on short-haul operations.

Carriers of the developing countries with higher capital costs have the most difficult problem with respect to equipment decisions. Table IV-6 shows comparative aircraft costs for jets and piston planes in 1962. Capital for jet aircraft in 1962 was somewhat scarcer than at present. The jets available at the time were designed primarily for long-haul, dense markets rather than for regional operations, and the cost differential with piston planes was only gradually widening as "learning experience" reduced jet costs. The costs in Table IV-6 show that at higher interest rates, used piston aircraft were cheaper to operate. On the other hand, their marketing disadvantage could not be neglected. Many carriers of the developing countries found themselves in the difficult position of having to use jet equipment to remain competitive in the major international markets since their better financed competition from North America and Europe was generally so equipped, despite the fact that this equipment was more costly to operate when the cost accounting included anything like the real opportunity cost of capital (that is, foreign exchange). Nevertheless, polit-

TABLE IV-7. *Direct Operating and Capital Costs of Selected Aircraft, by Stage Length, 1965*

(In cents per available seat-mile)

Stage Length and Model of Aircraft	U. S. Factor Prices and Productivity		"Low" Relative Factor Prices and Reduced Crew Productivity		
	6% Interest Rate[a]	6% Interest Rate[a] (utilization 20% less)	10% Interest Rate[a]	10% Interest Rate[a] (utilization 20% less)	20% Interest Rate[a]
Stage length 750 miles					
Boeing 720	1.584	1.694	1.579	1.713	1.825
Electra L-188	1.757	1.819	1.690	1.799	1.887
Douglas DC-7/7B	2.045	2.061	1.924	1.943	1.947
Douglas DC-6/6B	2.120	2.162	1.947	1.982	1.991
Stage length 500 miles					
Boeing 727	1.814	2.021	1.804	1.979	2.126
Electra L-188	1.840	1.995	1.800	1.919	2.014
Douglas DC-7/7B	2.128	2.147	1.992	2.011	2.015
Douglas DC-6/6B	2.166	2.198	2.034	2.072	2.081
Stage length 250 miles					
Douglas DC-9[b]	1.959	2.061	1.883	2.035	2.138
Electra L-188	2.085	2.201	2.044	2.179	2.287
Douglas DC-7/7B	2.419	2.438	2.262	2.284	2.289
Douglas DC-6/6B	2.407	2.442	2.264	2.306	2.316
Convair 340/440	2.610	2.655	2.412	2.463	2.475
Fairchild F-27	2.863	3.062	2.962	3.229	3.443

Sources: Appendix A, especially Tables A-7 through A-9.
[a] Rate of interest refers to opportunity cost of capital.
[b] DC-9 data are for the period October 1, 1965 to September 30, 1966.

ical pressures to participate with jets often pushed any consideration of the real costs of capital far in the background. There are a number of cases where carriers appear to have been too hasty in switching to jets. In many instances these nations sought to protect themselves from jet competition by imposing restrictions on their jet competitors, in the form of restrictions on schedule frequency or plane type. These policies, which were discussed in Chapter II, have their foundation in these comparative costs.

It does appear, however, that the worst is over for the developing countries, at least for a few years, until the jumbo jets and supersonic equipment appear. This same type of cost comparison using 1965 data (see Table IV-7) indicates that the recently developed three- and two-engine jets appear to yield such large cost savings in medium- and short-haul markets that they are competitive even at somewhat higher interest rates. Moreover, piston maintenance costs are increasing. The DC-9 appears to be the superior equipment choice even at interest rates up to 20 percent if route density is reasonably high and good scheduling is achieved. In view of the changes in capital availability, the future role of this short-haul jet technology appears very promising, even for some of the developing countries. With capital available (and jet financing was reasonably easy in 1965), the optimal plane choice depends essentially upon stage length, route density, and the ability of the carrier to schedule equipment.

This predicted role of jet technology has implications for the used aircraft market. Used piston aircraft may have an even more limited market in the next few years. On the other hand, Lockheed Electras may be in considerable demand by the less developed countries. As shown in Table IV-7, the Electra—somewhat discounted in price from $1.5 million—would have been cheaper for the developing countries to operate in 1965 than the jets. To acquire Electras, however, is another matter. There are only some 130 Electras presently in commercial service, and these are being used mostly by major carriers. The Electra is cheaper to operate than the DC-6 or other piston planes at 250-mile stage lengths. Only the DC-9 jet is able to meet its costs at this short range. Other jets have been more costly. The DC-9 may gradually make the Electra expendable in North American and European fleets. Its sale price, however, should not fall as sharply as did that of piston planes earlier. The Electra's operating cost disadvantage compared with jets is not so great as that of piston aircraft; Electras reduced in price by one-half from the price of $1.5 million used in Table IV-5b will be competitive with the DC-9s in developing countries with higher capital costs. The demand for used Electras by the developing countries with capital costs which are too high for the DC-9 may well keep the sale price of used Electras on the order of $500,000 each in the next few years as airlines of the United States and other developed countries sell this aircraft.

These comparisons also illustrate the rapidity of change in technology in the aircraft industry, which makes it difficult to choose the appropriate equipment. While the quantitative nature of input substitution implied by this evolving technology is changing rapidly, its qualitative nature remains basically constant. Those carriers with higher capital costs will always find themselves in the position of having a technology which is "a generation old" because it is available at low prices on the used aircraft market.

Capital costs are the fundamental determinant upon which a carrier's optimal aircraft choice turns. While used aircraft prices respond to changing technology, the differences in factor prices among airlines mean that total operating costs of various plane types are still only approximately equal. Different relative factor prices among nations will still create different optimal plane choices for different carriers, and the cost of capital is the most important of these. Capital market differences largely explain why the less developed nations have generally been the buyers of piston planes, and capital availability has been, and will continue to be, a major explanation of which carriers can economically sustain jet operations.

Capital-Labor Trade-offs

The capital-labor substitution in the form of aircraft choice described here can be observed in cross-section data describing capital, labor, and output. Appendix A examines this factor substitution in the context of a general production function and summarizes the effects of scheduling on input requirements and unit costs. In this model the firm substitutes capital (in the form of aircraft) for labor, in response to relative factor prices. Aircraft as a measure of capital is a proxy for all capital that is variable and is a good approximation since aircraft make up most of a firm's capital and since much of the remainder (hangars, ground equipment, etc.) is relatively fixed.

The model indicates that higher-wage firms have chosen equipment (jets) which conserves pilot requirements, as evidenced by an inverse correlation of flight crew requirements with pilots' wages. It was noted earlier that high-wage firms are better schedulers of their crews. Despite this superior scheduling and the substitution of capital outlay for larger flight crews, high-wage firms still incur higher pilot costs per seat-mile. In short, firms paying high wages have reduced but not eliminated an inherent cost disadvantage by both better scheduling and the substitution of capital for pilots.

A trade-off of capital with all other labor has also occurred. Labor's wage has been an important determinant of the amount of labor employed, with substitution occurring in ground and support operations.

Despite this substitution there is a negative correlation of labor cost per seat-mile with labor's wage. Capital per seat-mile is also slightly correlated with the wage, suggesting that firms with high relative capital costs—that is, the developed countries' carriers—use less capital. Moreover, observed capital per seat-mile is influenced by scheduling abilities, implying that firms with high relative capital costs have been comparatively poor jet schedulers. If adjustment is made for these scheduling differences, the correlation of capital per seat-mile with labor's wage is more evident. Subsidy commitments have apparently not completely negated the effects of differences in real opportunity costs of capital in equipment choices of firms.

Summary

The production function of the various international carriers is reasonably homogeneous, with one important exception—considerable differences exist in input scheduling ability. There are also substantial differences in relative factor prices. Such differences, customarily important determinants of comparative advantage in an international industry, are fairly unimportant to airlines. The production function is characterized by variable proportions and allows considerable input substitution. Different wage levels can be nearly offset by an appropriate factor mix, with high-wage firms choosing all jets and offering a utilitarian service. Potentially the most significant factor price in determining comparative costs is the price of capital, which greatly influences the choice of aircraft and entry policies for the carriers of the less developed countries. However, the commitment of governments to subsidize the major international flag carriers has resulted in a uniformly low perceived capital cost to the firm and hence has done much to negate the importance of capital costs in industry decisions.

CHAPTER V

Costs

THE CAPITAL AND OPERATING COSTS reported by the various airlines differ greatly. Some of this variation reflects comparative efficiency; some reflects such factors as stage lengths, passenger volume, weather, fuel prices, or landing charges. The structural model of airline costs developed in this chapter separates the variables that pertain to type of operation from the variables peculiar to a given firm (for example, factor prices paid, choice of factors, and scheduling of equipment and personnel). In addition to indicating the relative efficiency of the producers, this model will be useful in suggesting an optimal pricing structure for the airline industry and in determining explicitly the cost of inappropriate entry and inefficient scheduling.

Operating Costs by Plane Type: U.S. Domestic Experience

The major determinants of direct operating costs (roughly one-half of total costs) for any airline are the choice of planes and the route systems on which they perform. Direct operating costs include direct flying expenses (flight crew salaries and related expenses such as lodging, fuel and oil, insurance, and rental of flight equipment), maintenance and overhead, and depreciation. These costs differ widely among various types of aircraft, depending upon the efficiency of scheduling and the nature of the route system.

83

Operating Efficiencies of Various Types of Planes

A number of excellent discussions exist on the operating efficiencies of different plane types.[1] Over the last two decades, seat-mile costs have steadily declined as plane size and speed have increased. The bigger, faster planes have lower fuel and labor costs, and the ratio of payload to aircraft weight has increased as plane size has increased.

The evolution of piston aircraft through a succession of increases in size and speed resulted in decreases in operating costs until the last class that was produced just before the introduction of jets—the Douglas DC-7C, Lockheed 1649, and Boeing 377. The fuel and capital costs of this group, which represented the final extension of range and speed of the piston planes, proved to be higher than the fuel and capital costs of their piston forerunners. The next-introduced turboprop planes (propeller aircraft driven by turbine engines) caused costs to turn downward again because of speed increases. The Viscount, introduced in the mid-1950s, and the subsequent Electra, Britannia, and Vanguard have higher speeds and lower costs than equivalent piston planes.

Jet technology, largely because of the turbine engine, has produced a sharp discontinuity in the gradual reduction of aircraft operating costs. The turbine engine produces greater thrust, greater speeds, and hence much lower costs for fuel, maintenance, and labor per ton-mile of payload. Efficiency in converting fuel to thrust and the ability to perform for much longer periods between maintenance work or overhauls have been important. The jets typically fly 6,000 hours between engine overhauls, at least twice as long as the piston engines of ten years ago. Failures between overhauls have become much less frequent. Daily utilization rates for aircraft are largely a function of such factors as the number of hours between inspections and overhauls. As a result, jets have been able to achieve utilization rates on the order of ten hours a day as contrasted with a figure of about seven hours per day for piston aircraft. Similarly, crew costs have been sharply reduced because the bigger, faster planes use crews of the same size.

[1] See, for example, R. Dixon Speas, *Technical Aspects of Air Transport Management* (McGraw-Hill, 1955), or Civil Aeronautics Board, "General Characteristics of Turbine-Powered Aircraft," Staff Research Report No. 2 (CAB Office of Carrier Accounts and Statistics, February 1960).

Route Systems and Direct Operating Costs

The route systems over which aircraft fly have important effects on costs, and stage length is the most important consideration. Different planes are designed for different stage lengths. When average cost of any type of aircraft is plotted against stage length, a U-shaped curve is produced. The relatively fixed cost of take-off and climb to cruising altitude is the principal reason for the decreasing cost phenomenon. Fuel consumed in take-off is a disproportionately large share of total fuel consumed on a trip, and fuel reserves must be disproportionately large for short stage lengths. Similarly, crew time and aircraft time in the take-off and landing processes are a "fixed cost" which can be spread over more miles as stage length increases.

Stage length also has an indirect effect on costs through its effect on utilization of aircraft and other factors. Short hops and frequent stops make scheduling of aircraft and other personnel difficult. Lower block speeds reduce input productivity. There is also a tendency for short-haul passengers to be reluctant to begin flights in off hours in the middle of the night, whereas passengers making longer trips are more willing to sleep through a night flight or to tolerate a take-off at an odd hour. Thus scheduling is easier for long flights, and this promotes higher utilization rates.

The rising cost portion of the curve as stage length increases occurs because at some point payload must be reduced in order to carry extra fuel. In practice few airlines have operated at these excessive stage lengths.

Route density is also an important factor influencing direct operating costs in that it is an important determinant of unit costs. A low route density poses difficulties in maintaining high utilization rates of aircraft and also of maintenance personnel and flight crews. Airlines have solved these difficulties with varying degrees of success.

The specific effects of stage length and route density on direct operating costs for each plane type must be inferred from U.S. domestic data since very little international data on plane costs exists. The data on aircraft costs appear in Appendix B; the relevant cost curves for 1965 are summarized in Figure V-1.[2] Costs as related to stage length

[2] Figure V-1 also includes 1966 data for the new DC-9 for purposes of comparison, as noted below.

FIGURE V-1. *Direct Operating Cost Estimates for Selected Aircraft, U.S. Domestic Experience, 1965*

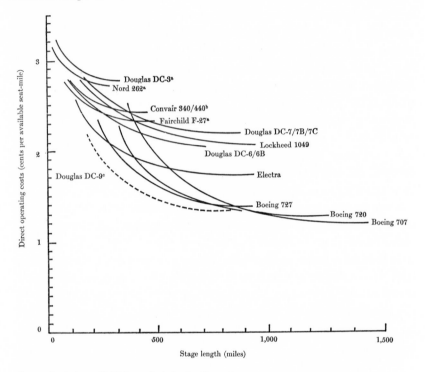

Source: See text, pp. 85–87, for method of estimating costs.
a U.S. local service airlines' costs.
b Average of trunkline and local service airlines' costs.
c This curve uses 1966 data.

were determined by using the Air Transport Association (ATA) formula for calculating direct operating costs. This formula, which has served as a standard method in the airline industry, is a complicated expression involving fuel, engine prices, aircraft weight, and similar variables. The formula yields cost curves which appear to be reasonably good approximations to industry experience with regard to shape, but less reliable with regard to the level of costs.[3] The estimates in Figure V-1 were based on cost curves produced by the ATA formula, adjusted for scale to fit the 1965 U.S. experience. Although cost curves for

---

[3] "Standard Method of Estimating Comparative Direct Operating Costs of Transport Aircraft" (processed; Air Transport Association, 1960).

other years are not presented here, both the shapes of the curves and the relationships between plane types appear quite stable.

ESTIMATES FOR PISTON AIRCRAFT. In estimating costs for piston aircraft, the adjustment for each plane type was based on an average cost of all carriers using the equipment. Insufficient data on the many factors affecting aircraft operating costs were available to allow inferences at the firm level of disaggregation. An example of information that would be desirable is whether a carrier used the plane on a standby basis (for peak loads and emergency situations) rather than on regularly scheduled flights.

The cheapest piston aircraft is the DC-6; its costs have generally been fairly close to those of the Electra. The later piston models—the DC-7C, L-1049G, and L-1649—have experienced higher operating costs because of higher design speeds. The piston operating cost disadvantage as compared with jets lies in higher fuel, crew, and maintenance costs; this gap has widened as jet costs have declined and will probably continue to do so as maintenance requirements for the piston aircraft grow and the sizable depreciation charges which jets now carry are reduced.

TURBOPROP COSTS. The turboprops (Electra, Viscount, Britannia, and Vanguard) stand on a middle ground between piston aircraft and jets. The Viscount and Electra have been the most efficient. The later turboprops—the Britannia 100s and 300s and the Vanguard 950—have not fared well, as shown by the cost experience of British European Airways (BEA). The Electra still appears to be the best in this class. BEA, in particular, has not achieved costs levels with its Viscounts or Vanguards that are comparable to the Electra costs in 1965 of 2.1 cents per seat-mile over stage lengths averaging 240 miles. The Fairchild F-27 is a two-engine turboprop being operated by U.S. local service carriers over stage lengths of approximately 125 miles. However, after several years of operations, its costs are only slightly lower than those of the Convair 340/440, its piston competitor for short hauls.

JET COSTS. Cost data for jets are available at the firm level and were used to verify the shape of the cost curves, as well as to adjust their scale. The historical jet cost data for individual firms are consistent with ATA cost curves as related to distance. A considerable decline has occurred in jet costs in absolute terms since 1959, partly because of such improvements as the turbofan engine,[4] but mostly because of a general increase in knowledge and experience as the jets were phased in. Longer intervals between overhauls has been one such cost-reducing factor. Increases in utilization rates, on the order of 25 percent in the initial three years of use of a new aircraft, typified the experience of the airlines in phasing in the jets. Data showing this increase in utilization rates appear in Appendix B.

The correlation of aircraft utilization rates with longer stage length (as noted earlier, scheduling is much easier for longer flights) makes it difficult to separate the individual effects of these two factors on costs. The relationship between jet costs and utilization rates is shown in Appendix B. Reduced utilization has less impact on costs for turboprops and piston planes since capital, insurance, and other fixed costs are proportionately less than for jets.

The most striking feature of the cost curves for jet and piston aircraft in Figure V-1 is the huge cost savings of the jets. The Boeing 707 and the DC-8 have long dominated the longer range jet market. Only the curve for the 707 is shown here; the DC-8 cost curve is nearly identical. Cost curves for the other long-range jets have not been presented.

A simple comparison of operating costs of the American-built Convair 880 and 990, France's Caravelle, and the British Comet 4B and 4C —based upon the experience of U.S. carriers with the French and American models and the experience of British Overseas Airways Corporation (BOAC) with the British planes (see Appendix B, Table B-5)— indicates that these planes have been more expensive to operate than the long-range American jets. The experience of BEA and BOAC with the Comets may be somewhat misleading due to various inefficiencies— excess labor, poor scheduling, etc.—and may therefore provide an overly pessimistic view of the costs of the Comet and the British turboprops as discussed above. Nevertheless, it seems safe to conclude that these planes have intrinsically higher operating costs than the Boeing 707 and DC-8.

The Boeing 720, introduced in 1961, and the 727, a three-engine jet initiated in 1964, have extended jet economies to shorter stage lengths.

[4] The turbofan engine uses a fan to increase the flow of air and hence raise propulsive efficiency. The turbofan engines reduced total direct operating costs of the jets by about 5 percent in 1964, through an increase in average utilization rates and a small reduction in fuel costs.

The 727 reduced costs in 1965 very sharply for medium stage lengths (about 1.6 cents per seat-mile at 500-mile stages). The 720 and 727 costs have been far enough below piston plane costs that U.S. carriers have begun using them for stage lengths as low as 300 miles. The DC-6, DC-7, and L-1049—piston planes designed for long-haul service —have, therefore, been switched to stage lengths in the 200 to 300 mile range, where they are as cheap to operate as the jets.

The DC-9, a short-range, two-engine jet, which first became available in 1966, promises to extend the jet economies to even shorter stage lengths. The relationship of DC-9 costs to those of other planes is not yet fully known, though the comparison shown in Figure V-1 is indicative of the potential economies of the DC-9 at short stage lengths. A slight decline in other jet costs from those shown in Figure V-1 occurred in 1966. It can be expected that DC-9 costs may fall in the next year or two as a result of increases in utilization rates above those achieved in its first year of operation. Thus, the DC-9 promises to have a major impact on even very short stage lengths.

"PLANE-STRETCHING." Another important change occurring in jet technology is the phenomenon known as "stretching" planes—essentially, lengthening the fuselage to include space for more seats. The payload of most models is limited in terms of space rather than weight (hence the switch in baggage limitations from pounds to number of bags). Most models also have sufficient power to allow an expansion in seating capacity, thereby reducing unit costs. Expanded versions of the DC-8 and the 727 are being produced and promise to reduce costs by at least 10 percent. The extra space gained by adding 30 feet to a DC-8, for example, will allow about sixty additional seats in a tourist configuration.

THE "JUMBO JET." Promised for the future are two new aircraft types, widely different in character, with the potential of producing major changes in air travel. The 747, referred to as the "jumbo jet," will seat 390 passengers in a very modest seating configuration of 90 percent tourist seats and can hold 490 seats in a conventional high-density tourist configuration. This aircraft is essentially a larger-scale version of existing jets, and will be capable of reducing unit costs by about 25 percent, it is expected. This innovation will extend considerably the economies accompanying higher route densities. Fares on routes dense enough to warrant use of jumbo jets could be 25 percent lower; this possible reduction could have considerable influence on modal choice.[5] There will be some new problems created, of course, such as the necessity for efficient ground operations to support the enplaning or deplaning of 500 passengers at one time. The delays and difficulties associated with present airports—their location, parking facilities, and procedures for handling tickets and baggage—are familiar. The 747 technology will require some new solutions to these problems. On the other hand, the reduction in number of plane departures at peak hours, implicit in use of aircraft of this size, may be important in meeting some of the problems of airspace and runway congestion which currently plague larger airports.

SUPERSONIC AIRCRAFT. The supersonic transport is a technology of an entirely different order, with its own special problems. Despite the arguments as to whether the plane should be developed and how it should be financed, it now appears that such a plane will be available by 1975. Much uncertainty exists at present as to its technological and economic attributes. The United States will probably produce a plane capable of flying the North Atlantic at a top cruising speed of almost three times the speed of sound and carrying about 280 passengers; on the basis of an estimated sale price of $30–40 million, its cost levels will probably be only a few percent above the subsonic jets with which it will compete. These cost estimates are based on predictions of utilization rates for the supersonic transport (SST) of about nine hours a day (somewhat lower than those for existing jets).

International Airline Costs

A cross-section comparison of international airline costs indicates a high variation among firms. Table V-1 shows average operating costs per available tonne-kilometer for the year 1962 for a sample of 56 firms reporting to the International Civil Aviation Organization (ICAO). Subdividing the sample into five groups by size (as measured in millions of seat-miles) reveals some considerable differences; the most noteworthy is a decrease in costs as size increases. Breaking total costs into

[5] Mahlon Straszheim, "Intermodal Cost Structure for Future Passenger Travel in Less Developed Countries," Discussion Paper No. 42 (processed; Harvard Transportation and Economic Development Seminar, May 1966).

TABLE V-1. *Average Operating Costs of Sample of Carriers, by Seat-Miles Flown and by Cost Component, 1962*
(In cents per average available tonne-kilometer)

Cost Component	Millions of Seat-Miles Flown				
	0–50	50–100	100–200	200–500	500 and Over
Direct flying expenses	10.04	7.34	8.60	5.52	5.28
Crew expenses	2.17	1.67	1.99	1.42	1.66
Fuel and oil	3.67	3.35	3.91	2.87	2.45
Other (insurance, etc.)	4.20	2.32	2.70	1.23	1.17
Maintenance and overhead	6.26	4.81	4.30	3.39	3.44
Depreciation	2.53	3.05	2.34	2.62	2.69
Station costs	3.01	3.24	2.20	2.77	3.16
Passenger services	1.34	2.27	1.84	1.50	1.55
Ticketing, sales, and promotion	2.91	4.38	3.36	3.52	4.45
General and administration	1.91	1.70	1.34	1.07	1.02
Total	28.00	26.79	23.98	20.39	21.59
Number of carriers in sample	21	10	7	10	8

Source: International Civil Aviation Organization, *Digest of Statistics, Financial Data* (1962).

components and categorizing by firm size indicates some of the sources of the variation among groups. Direct flying expenses decline sharply with size. Economies of scale are one possible explanation; this cost decline, however, may have its explanation in plane type and route structure. Maintenance and overhead show sharply declining costs; again, explanations other than scale might be correct. The large carriers are those flying many jet-hours, and jets have proven quite economical in this respect.[6] Costs for passenger services, ticketing, sales, and promotion are quite low for the group of smallest carriers. These small carriers as a group are serving smaller markets—in size and geographical area. Many do only the minimum in the way of ticket selling and promotion, and their passenger service is not comparable to that of larger carriers competing in the long-haul international markets.

When costs at the individual firm level are examined (Appendix B,

[6] Figures in the maintenance and overhead category provide an interesting contrast to Caves's results (Richard E. Caves, *Air Transport and Its Regulators* [Harvard University Press, 1962], pp. 59–60) for the U.S. domestic airlines for 1958, which showed no real scale effects except for local service carriers. His were essentially pre-turbine data. The large carriers at that time were flying DC-7s and L-1049s on long-range flights, and these aircraft proved to be very costly in every respect.

Table B-6), even greater variation exists. This variation is the result of considerable differences in wage levels, scheduling abilities, route densities, stage lengths, and firm size. To extend the analysis of these costs beyond the simple descriptive stage, the causal relationships or structure of costs must be ascertained. In general, the larger carriers are using jet equipment over dense long-haul markets; this source of lower costs must be segregated before significant statements can be made concerning scale effects or inferences can be drawn as to the relative efficiency of various producers of airline service.

A Cross-Section Model of Costs

There are three kinds of variables which have important effects on costs: input prices, scheduling abilities, and route system variables. The most important of the input prices is the level of wages. The second class of variables, scheduling abilities, was described in Chapter IV, and measures were derived for pilot, labor, and aircraft scheduling. Of these, aircraft scheduling probably has the most important impact. Route system variables include all those influences which are a function of the particular route system operated by a firm and the area in which it flies; these variables would be the same for any firm serving the same route system. The latter condition is the important defining characteristic of this class of variables. Three of the most important route system variables—stage length, route density, and passenger trip length—are considered explicitly in the model below. The literature on airline costs has been concerned primarily with route system variables.

The previous discussion of direct operating costs for each aircraft type indicated some of the relationships of route system variables to costs. The effect of stage length was made explicit. The effects of route density on costs are twofold: first, it is an important factor in determining the choice of plane size; second, it affects utilization rates. (Thin route densities, for example, require use of smaller planes and result in lower utilization rates.) Both these effects tend to raise costs.

Average indirect or nonoperating costs (as well as operating costs) also decline as stage length, passenger trip length, and route densities increase. A number of authors have given good descriptions of the factors which produce this cost decline.[7] A portion of indirect expenses

[7] Harold D. Koontz, "Economic and Managerial Factors Underlying Subsidy Needs of Domestic Trunk Line Carriers," *Journal of Air Law and Commerce,*

is relatively fixed and can be regarded as an overhead charge incurred when a station exists regardless of its use. Longer stage lengths reduce indirect unit costs because of two general factors. A number of costs which are incurred for each aircraft flight regardless of trip length can be spread; for example, landing charges and the costs of station personnel engaged in the landing process. Also, as speed increases with longer distances, the result is increased productivity of labor and other inputs; for example, the costs of meals and of other in-flight services are lower on a plane-mile basis as trip lengths rise and speed increases. Similarly, wages and work requirements for crews and cabin staff are directly related to ramp-to-ramp time, which increases less than proportionally with distance.

Excellent a priori reasoning has supported these explanations of airline costs. Statistical costing is not far advanced in the airline industry, however; evaluating the exact extent of particular variables, including separation of the various interdependencies, is a problem on which little progress has been made. Most explanations have settled for relating costs to a single variable—usually some measure of firm size. The cost model developed in Appendix B and summarized here is a multi-variate one which attempts to separate the effects of the several variables discussed above. Cross-section data for 1962 describing a sample of ICAO firms were used. All cost data were converted to U.S. dollars at exchange rates used by IATA. The data and sources appear in Appendix B.

ADJUSTMENTS FOR FIRM EFFECTS. The use of cross-section observations on costs and output to provide information on the nature of firms' cost functions assumes that the firms in an industry have a common production function and are purchasing inputs in perfect markets. The differences in factor prices and production functions among the international airlines noted earlier obviously pose some conceptual problems. Such differences imply that all firms' cost functions are different. If a single cross-section sample is to yield meaningful estimates of the structure of airline costs, the data must be adjusted for these differences among firms (generally called "firm effects") so that the observations approxi-

Vol. 18 (Spring 1951), pp. 127–56; Stephen Wheatcroft, *The Economics of European Air Transport* (Harvard University Press, 1956), pp. 23–58; Paul W. Cherington, *Airline Price Policy: A Study of Domestic Airline Passenger Fares* (Harvard University, Graduate School of Business Administration, Division of Research, 1958), pp. 42–66; and Caves, *op. cit.*, pp. 303–87.

mate a common cost structure or a "representative" cost function. Varying efficiency in scheduling is the most important difference in the production function which must be taken into account when airline costs are considered; and the price of labor is the one significant difference among factor prices.

The cost model developed in Appendix B includes adjustments for these differences. An equation was estimated for each component of airline costs, with average seat-mile costs the dependent variable in each case. Costs were related to the route system, input prices, aircraft choice, and scheduling ability.

SUMMARY OF MODEL. While the model is developed fully in Appendix B, a brief description and summary of the results are given here. The variables used in the model are:

n/SM = number of stations per seat-mile (route density)
h = average passenger hop (miles)
d = average flight stage length (miles)
d/h = average flight stage length per average passenger hop (miles)
$AC(d)$ = expected average direct operating cost per seat-mile, as a function of plane choice and flight stage length
S_l = nonflight crew scheduling
S_c = flight crew scheduling
S_a = aircraft scheduling
C/SM = flight crew (in man-years) per seat-mile
K/SM = capital expenses (cents) per seat-mile
L/SM = all other labor (man-years) per seat-mile
W_P = pilot wage (dollars per year)
W_L = wage of all other labor (dollars per year)

A summation of the equations by components gives the model for total costs:

$$\frac{L}{SM} = -0.7885 + 1{,}700{,}000\frac{n}{SM} + 0.5640\,AC(d) - 91.8\frac{1}{d} + 50.10\,W_L$$

$$\frac{C}{SM} = -0.3228 + 0.3094\,AC(d) - 21.8\frac{1}{d} + 1{,}300{,}000\frac{n}{SM}$$

$$AC\frac{\cancel{c}}{SM} = 0.2398 + 68.694\,W_P\frac{C}{SM}\,S_c + 0.1889\,S_c + 0.9310\,AC(d) - 249.5\frac{1}{d}$$

$$+\ 3{,}800{,}000\frac{n}{SM} + 0.1599\frac{K}{SM} + 25.9W_L\frac{L}{SM} + \frac{W_L}{10{,}000}$$

$$\cdot\left[0.2633 + 876{,}400\frac{L}{SM} + 4{,}800{,}000\frac{n}{SM} - 0.00034h + 0.00024d\right.$$

$$\left.+\ 3.4376\,S_c - 0.3513\frac{d}{h}\right]$$

The most important omissions from the model appear to be fuel and landing prices, which vary considerably by region; however, no system-atic bias is evident from an examination of the residuals (estimation errors) of the equations. Although the residuals do not reveal any omissions or faulty specifications in terms of factor prices, production technique, or the nature of operations, there is a definite pattern among firms. Certain firms are always below the cost function, while others are always above it. This indicates systematic differences among firms not included in the equations; in Chapter IX these systematic firm residuals or differences will be used in determining the relative ef-ficiencies of various producers of airline service.

Important Structural Determinants of Costs

EFFECTS OF FIRM SIZE ON COSTS. A number of studies have made con-vincing arguments regarding the existence of scale economies as firm size increases. These studies usually relate costs to some measure of firm size as the one explanatory variable, and have generally used the same evidence (U.S. cross-section data) and drawn the same con-clusions—that the U.S. local service carriers are so small that they suffer serious diseconomies of scale.[8] Such cross-section comparisons are not, however, proper evidence to resolve scale economy ques-tions. There are many important differences between the local service carriers and the trunklines other than firm size, such as plane type or route structure. These other factors can be considerably more impor-tant than firm size and hence must be considered explicitly. This cost analysis provides new evidence on the issue, since many of these in-terdependent operating characteristics have been taken into account more adequately here than in the earlier studies. Although still more observations on small firms would be desirable, the issue of scale economies can be considered on the basis of the newly added evidence.

[8] Jesse W. Proctor and Julius S. Duncan, "A Regression Analysis of Airline Costs," *Journal of Air Law and Commerce,* Vol. 21 (Summer 1954), pp. 282–92; Wheatcroft, *The Economics of European Air Transport,* pp. 59–63; Stephen Wheatcroft, "Airline Competition in Canada: A Study of the Desirability and Eco-nomic Consequences of Competition in Canadian Transcontinental Air Services," prepared for the Ministry of Transport, George Hess (Ottawa, Canada, 1958), pp. 40–41; Stanford Research Institute, *Air Transport Development and Coordination in Latin America: A Study of Economic Factors* (SRI for the Organization of Ameri-can States, 1961), pp. 58–61.

The sharp decline in direct costs generally observed as firm size increases appears to have its major explanation in terms of plane choice, stage length, and route density. Since the cost equations developed here take account of these variables, any systematic effect of size on costs would appear in the residuals of the fitted equations. The residuals of these equations for direct costs show no relationship to scale. Plane choice and input utilization prove to be the important cost determinants. Small firms report higher costs mainly because they fly thin routes or are forced to choose planes less economical to operate than the big jets and fly them over short stage lengths. Size thus affects costs in an indirect way that is different from what economists generally mean when they discuss scale economies, since firm size per se is not the important variable.[9]

No scale effects are evident in the indirect costs. This is clear from the residuals of the cost functions and the function for labor requirements. The decline frequently observed in the "general and administrative expenses" category as a simple function of firm size has its explanation in large part in route density.

EFFECT OF WAGE RATES ON COSTS. Conclusions can also be drawn from the cost model about the effect of different wage rates. If all other things are equal, lower wage rates should mean lower costs. All other things are not equal, however: firms can substitute capital for labor and vice versa, depending on relative prices. The data used in estimating the cost model reflect this input substitution. For a firm with route density, stage length, and trip length equal to the industry average, and a pilot's wage also equal to the industry average (estimated as $10,919 in 1962), an annual wage to all other labor of $2,000 would produce an average cost per available seat-mile of 5.408 cents; an annual wage in the industry of $3,000 would produce an average cost of 5.898 cents; and an annual wage of $4,000 would produce an average cost of 6.660 cents. These cost estimates also assume average scheduling ability. The conclusion is that the opportunity to substitute capital for labor has converted a large difference in wage rates into a fairly small difference in costs. In point of fact, even this cost difference has not appeared among the international carriers since the superior scheduling

[9] This confirms the suggestion made by Cherington, in his analysis of U.S. trunklines' costs, that length of haul and route density are the principal determinants of cost levels rather than scale per se. Caves also suggested this sort of explanation for apparent scale economies. Cherington, *op. cit.*, pp. 42–66; Caves, *op. cit.*, pp. 58–62.

ability of the firms which pay higher wages has done much to offset their wage handicap.

EFFECT OF ROUTE SYSTEMS ON COSTS. The cost model also allows important conclusions to be drawn as to the effects of important route system variables. The effect is different for different wage levels. Figure V-2 shows costs for different levels of stage length at varying wage levels, and Figure V-3 shows costs for different levels of route density at varying wage levels. The costs represent the variation attributable to each of these independent variables taken singly, with everything else held constant. In the cost model, average values for the industry are assumed for the other variables, including passenger trip length, pilot wages, aircraft choice, and scheduling ability. The cost curves in Figures V-2 and V-3 indicate that less than average route density and less than average stage length have a serious impact on costs. The figures also show the effects of reducing each of these important variables by 50 percent. The percentage cost effects are greater in the case of thin route density, a fact which is especially evident for firms paying above average labor costs. In short, the cost disadvantage of shorter stage lengths can be overcome in large measure by proper plane choice and good scheduling, but it is more difficult to reduce the cost impact of fixed charges of underutilized stations.

On the other hand, passenger trip length does not appear to be an important cost determinant. Once flight stage length is included in the cost estimates, whether passengers fly one stage only or remain on the plane for several stages appears to have only marginal effects on costs.

The cost model, it should be noted, only approximates the specific relationship of costs to stage length and route density. The model is based on data aggregated at the firm level and hence conceals a wide range of cost variation in particular city-pair markets. Any number of factors may affect costs in a particular link (for example, landing or fuel charges, terrain, weather, altitude); none of these is included in the cost model. The problem of allocating common costs at this level of disaggregation is difficult to solve. Finally, the specific form used for the cost model is limited to a linear model for which parameter estimation was simple.

The cost estimates generated by the model are of course approximations; airline accountants should be able to refine these estimates considerably for application to particular cases or routes. There is little indication, however, that the international carriers actually make calcula-

FIGURE V-2. *Air Carrier Costs as a Function of Wages and Stage Length*

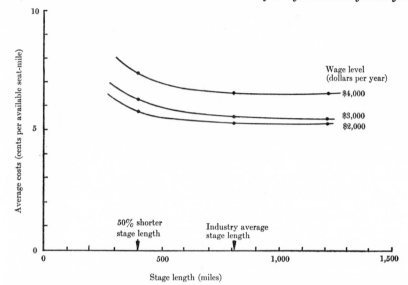

FIGURE V-3. *Air Carrier Costs as a Function of Wages and Route Density*

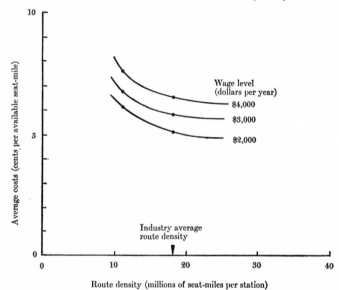

Source: For Figures V-2 and V-3, see text, pp. 97–99.

tions of the marginal costs of serving a particular route. Rational decision-making by any individual firm would seem to require careful calculation of cost information at this level of disaggregation in order to
make capacity and pricing decisions. As will be seen in Chapter VII,

prices on particular routes show little taper with respect to stage lengths or route density. The following estimates may, therefore, be of some interest.

Assuming wages and scheduling equal to the industry average,[10] costs decline as stage length increases as shown in Figure V-4. The shape of these curves is closely related to the curves of direct operating costs by plane type; there is less curvature, however, since indirect costs do not fall as sharply with longer stage length as do direct costs.

Changes in route density can be considered in a similar fashion. The model provides an estimate of the marginal cost of an additional station: $1/100$ $(3,800,000 + 89.622W_P + 6294W_L)$, where W_P and W_L are the annual wages of pilots and all other labor, respectively. This assumes values for scheduling and other route system characteristics (such as stage length) equal to the industry averages. The marginal cost of a station is estimated at $239,825 for the firm paying average wage rates. (This is the fixed operating cost per year for a station of average size and is not to be confused with the capital investment.) This cost must be spread over all seat-miles flown in and out of a station. Stations located on thin routes obviously create a higher fixed station cost per seat-mile.[11] For firms with a route density equal to the industry mean, fixed station costs amount to 1.338 cents per seat-mile, or 22 percent of the total costs. This is clearly a substantial fixed expense and shows why costs in the model are far more sensitive to route density than to stage length. The earlier observation on the importance of route density as a cost determinant is re-emphasized.

In addition to this estimate of fixed costs per station, the model yields an estimate of costs as a function of route density in a particular link. Figure V-5 shows average costs per seat-mile at different route densities, assuming average values for wages and scheduling. In this model of costs, each additional station bears a constant fixed charge plus variable costs which are a function of output.

[10] The cost model (see pp. 92–95) can be simplified to show the effects of the nature of the route system by assuming values equal to the industry average for wages and scheduling. Substituting $W_L = \$3,000$, $W_P = \$10,919$, $S_c = 1$, $S_a = 1$, and $S_l = 1$ into the model yields the cost equation:

$$AC(\text{¢}/SM) = -0.6946 + 2.6751\,AC(d) - 502\frac{1}{d} - 0.00072(d)$$

$$+ 23,975,100(n/SM) + 0.1599\frac{K}{SM} - 0.000102(h) - 0.108\frac{d}{h}$$

[11] If n is the number of stations and SM is available seat-miles, the seat-mile cost of fixed station expense can be represented by $\$239,825(n/SM)$.

FIGURE V-4. *Air Carrier Costs as a Function of Aircraft Choice and Stage Length*

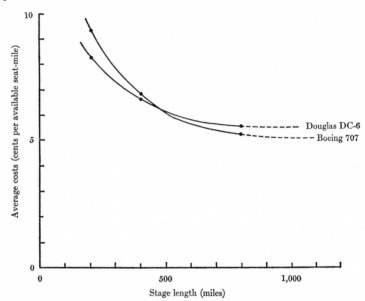

FIGURE V-5. *Air Carrier Costs as a Function of Route Density and Stage Length*

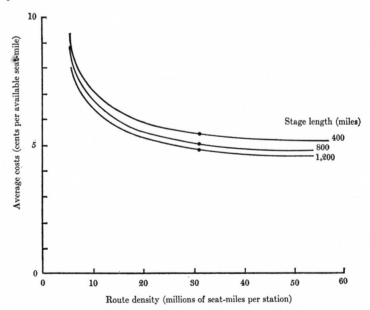

Source: For Figures V-4 and V-5, see text, pp. 99–101.

The cost model is of the general form: $TC = \alpha_0 + \alpha_1 n$, where n is stations, α_1 is the marginal cost of a station, and α_0 is a linear function of a number of variables. The model was fitted using average costs, which are linearly related to route density, n/SM. Costs when plotted against SM/n thus produce the downward sloping curves shown in Figure V-5. The resulting cost curve looks much like past estimates and preconceptions.

Costs of First Class Service versus Coach Service

The difference in costs between first class service and coach service is determined largely by differences in seating density; most other airline cost factors are associated with the number of plane departures and flight hours rather than the number of passengers on board. The ratio of first-class seats to coach seats depends upon plane choice. For a DC-3 the ratio of highest density coach to first class seating is 1.30; for the DC-6 and DC-7, 1.43; and for the big jets, 1.50.[12] The bigger planes obviously have more flexibility for crowding in coach seats. On the big jets first class seats are four abreast; coach service seats six abreast. One European carrier has a model which quickly converts from two- to three-abreast seating.

Calculation of the cost ratio of first class to coach service appears in Table V-2, assuming a 1.5 to 1.0 trade-off in seats. A cost ratio of 1.40 is the estimate for the big jets; similar computations on the basis of the seat ratio between first class and coach service give a cost ratio of about 1.37 for the turboprops and four-engine piston planes and 1.28 for two-engine aircraft.

The Level of Capital Requirements

The transition to jets has sharply raised the capital requirements in the industry. Firms with a high percentage of jet equipment have capital-output ratios of about 1.0. This is in contrast to a figure of about 0.60 for the industry in 1950. The industry represents a mid-point, for example, between the capital-intensive steel industry and the less capital-intensive large retailing firms.

[12] Based on historical seating configurations listed in International Civil Aviation Organization, *Digest of Statistics, Fleet and Personnel,* No. 102 (1962).

TABLE V-2. *Coach Service Costs Distributed by Plane Hours and Seating Density, and Ratios of First Class to Coach Service Costs*[a]

(In percent)

Cost Component	Direct Flying	Station	Passenger Services	Ticket Sales and Promotion	General and Administrative	Total
Coach service costs dependent on						
Number of plane hours	52.0	10.2	10.0	5.3	2.5	80.0
Number of seats	0.0	6.8	0.0	10.7	2.5	20.0
Total	52.0	17.0	10.0	16.0	5.0	100.0
Cost ratio of first class to coach service[b]	78.0	22.1	15.0[c]	18.6	6.2	139.9

[a] A seat trade-off of 1.5 to 1 for coach to first class service is assumed. All costs which are independent of the number of seats on board are given a weight of 1.5 for first class seating, versus a weight of one for coach seating. Costs dependent upon the number of seats are a simple addition in each case. The assumptions concerning the amount of costs dependent upon the number of seats were as follows: all direct flying costs were assumed independent of the number or type of seats on board. Approximately 60 percent of station costs were assumed a result of aircraft handling (e.g., landing charges) and are therefore independent of the number of passengers on board. Baggage handling accounts for the rest. Passenger service is better on first class, but by reducing the number of seats by one-third when switching from coach to first class, there is "more service" to be distributed per passenger. Fifty percent more service per first class passenger was assumed a fair estimate of the differential. Two-thirds of ticketing, sales, and promotion expenses were assumed determined by the number of passengers, while the remainder were assumed independent and determined by the number of aircraft flights. Finally, general and administrative expenses were estimated as one-half a function of the number of flights and one-half a function of the number of passengers. These assumptions as to the costs dependent upon the number of seats yielded the above cost differential, which is reasonably insensitive to the assignment of indirect costs to passenger seats or to aircraft flights.

[b] Based on a ratio of 100 for coach service.

[c] Allocated to one-third fewer seats for first class and raised by 50 percent, assuming same cabin costs as on coach flight.

Capital investment is made up of three basic components: aircraft (approximately 80 percent), terminal and ground equipment (10 percent), and operating capital (10 percent). It is noteworthy that airports, which are publicly provided, are not included as a component of capital investment. Both U.S. and foreign carriers lease from airports, municipalities, or other carriers a good portion of the hangars, workshops, and terminals needed for jets and therefore do not tie up capital in these facilities. These leased facilities include line-haul terminal buildings, hangars, and sometimes even major overhaul and maintenance bases. If a jet fleet is operated, this type of base requires an investment of several million dollars at a minimum.[13] Leases generally run from 20 to 30 years on facilities built to the carriers' specifications. The rent includes depreciation, and thus the base essentially is an in-

[13] "Big Jet Investment Analysis of Operating Costs," *Aviation Report Supplement*, No. 113 (London: Aviation Studies International, Ltd., April 1962).

TABLE V-3. *Aircraft and Related Equipment Investment, Selected Models, 1962*

Model of Aircraft	Quantity	Investment (thousands of dollars)			
		Planes (first cost)[a]	Spares[a]	Ancillary Equipment[a]	Total Unit Investment
Boeing 707/707B	212	5,900	1,180	590	7,670
Boeing 720/720B	119	5,000	1,000	500	6,500
Convair 880/880M	63	4,500	900	450	5,850
Convair 990	37	5,000	1,000	500	6,500
Douglas DC-8	177	5,900	1,180	590	7,670
Viscount 10	52	6,100	1,300	675	8,075
Average		5,400	1,093	551	7,044

Source: "Big Jet Investment Analysis of Operating Costs," *Aviation Report Supplement*, No. 113 (London: Aviation Studies International, Ltd., April 1962), p. 4.
[a] Figures reflect average cost for each type of aircraft.

vestment paid for by the airlines collectively but on loans granted to national or local governments. The rental charge is a fixed annual cost, in addition to any interest charges the carrier has on facilities it may own.

Table V-3 shows the average investment as of 1962 in planes, spares, and additional equipment. Investment other than aircraft raises the total investment by 30.5 percent. While the level of investment in spare parts has been quite stable over time (18 to 20 percent of the value of the aircraft for both piston and jet planes), investment requirements in ground equipment are increasing as terminals grow in size and become more crowded. The trend is clear in the aggregate investment of U.S. airlines in recent years. Investment in flight equipment has grown from $593 million in 1960 to $644.5 million in 1964. Ground equipment investment in the same period has grown much faster from $45.7 million to $80.6 million.[14]

When jets are purchased, additional capital must be invested in crew training. The bigger jets require a four-man crew—three pilots and one navigator—and each needs a minimum of three crews to keep the plane running (because of the constraint on a pilot's flying time and because of the need to use planes 8 to 10 hours a day). The basic training procedure requires between 15 and 20 hours per man on an electronic flight simulator and an equal amount of time in live flying.

[14] *American Aviation*, Vol. 28 (May 1965), pp. 17–18.

Firms generally buy, but can lease, flight simulators. The total training costs for pilots to staff a jet has amounted to between $250,000 and $400,000—fully 6 to 8 percent of the plane's cost.[15]

There are several implications in this level of capital requirements. The investment per seat-mile now for Boeing 707s is only slightly higher than it was for Douglas DC-7s ten years ago. The absolute magnitude of investment in a jet operation, however, is large. Several jets are a minimum fleet for efficient operations, and this minimum depends upon participation in spares pools and negotiation of reasonable subcontracting arrangements for overhaul and maintenance work. The level of capital requirements thus represents a certain entry barrier to jet operations. Though a 707 has roughly four times the productivity of a DC-7, the capital investments differ by a magnitude of 25 to 1 at current used piston plane prices. Entry into piston operations is therefore far less expensive. However, the political stimulus to jet entry appears so far to have overridden the deterrent caused by this increase in capital costs of jet operations.

Summary

The existence of a homogeneous production function and reasonable homogeneity among factors makes direct international comparison of airline costs possible. Industry costs are characterized by a very high variation among carriers, which is explained by differences in factor markets, in the nature of operations, and in relative efficiency. The introduction of jet aircraft has also been a source of considerable variation, depending upon the firms' plane choice and route structure; the jets have raised capital requirements in the industry and given rise to a number of cost-saving pooling arrangements.

A large part of the variation in costs can be explained by plane choice, route density, and input scheduling variables. Firm size in itself was shown to be a less important factor in costs than has previously been supposed: the nature of small firms' operations—short stage lengths, small aircraft, poor station and labor utilization—are the important explanations of their higher costs rather than firm scale per se.

[15] See "The Cost of Introducing the Jets in Terms of Additional Airline Investment," *ITA Research Paper No. 333* (Paris: Institut du Transport Aérien, May 1960), pp. 7–58.

CHAPTER VI

Demand

THE DEMAND FOR INTERNATIONAL AIRLINE SERVICE has grown spectacularly since World War II as a result of increases in real income, reductions in air fares relative to fares on alternative modes, and improvements in the quality of air service. Service changes—basically the consequence of jet technology—have included more frequent schedules, reduced travel times, and more comfortable flights. Major innovations which have led to greater comfort are the pressurized cabin and the reduction in cabin noise and vibration on jets.

Price, schedule frequency, and passenger service are the basic determinants of demand at the discretion of the airlines. In terms of explaining the tremendous growth rate, the first two are decidedly the most important. The considerable service competition in the industry—the expected strategy in a market where prices are fixed—far overstates the role of service quality as an explanation of total demand. There is little evidence that efforts to compete on the basis of service have had much effect on total demand. The significance of service competition lies in its effects on market shares.

Product Differentiation

The nature of service competition as a differentiation attempt is worth examination. In the period immediately after World War II, such efforts were extreme. Free gifts were distributed, including handbags, cigarettes, theater tickets, toilet articles, perfume, and wine and

105

champagne. The value of these gifts really made them a form of fare discounting. It was not until the early 1950s that International Air Transport Association (IATA) resolutions were passed ending this practice. The differentiation efforts, however, have continued, along with disputes concerning what forms of differentiation are proper and what form of regulation should exist. The introduction of tourist service in 1952 posed problems of class definition. Seating density and type of passenger service became the two important criteria which distinguished the different classes. Passenger service, however, is not easily controlled; IATA regulations limiting the food service on certain classes to a sandwich produced considerable dispute as to what constituted a sandwich.

The inflight movie is the latest product-improvement issue. Trans World Airlines (TWA), Pakistan International Airlines, and Philippine Airlines were the first carriers equipped for showing films, and TWA increased its market share in the North Atlantic considerably as a result. IATA and the other carriers have reacted by pressuring TWA to cease showing movies. The arguments on both sides are old hat. A TWA vice president has argued, "Anything that attracts more persons to air travel, that eases the tension of first-time riders and relieves the long flight boredom of experienced travelers, has great therapeutic value for customers of the airline industry."[1] The reply is that inflight movies are a costly product improvement which will not significantly raise airline demand once adopted by all carriers; movies are therefore a differentiating gimmick which will raise costs for all carriers and result in higher fares. The inflight entertainment question will be considered in Chapter VII. The opportunities for, and efforts at, product differentiation seem as important now as they were fifteen years ago.

These efforts notwithstanding, the airline industry has a fairly limited scope for product differentiation. Caves found that product differentiation is very difficult in the U.S. domestic industry, with two important exceptions—improved flight schedules and the use of faster, newer, more comfortable aircraft.[2]

The international airline industry can be similarly characterized, though it has some important additional dimensions for differentiation. One is the opportunity of a traveler to choose in-flight surroundings

[1] "What's New in Air Fares?" *New York Times*, November 29, 1964, Section XX, p. 23.
[2] Richard E. Caves, *Air Transport and Its Regulators* (Harvard University Press, 1962), pp. 48–54, 331–35.

(food, drink, and cabin service by stewardesses) of his own nationality or of a different country. It is difficult to estimate the traveling public's underlying preferences, but many American tourists contemplating a trip to the Orient or to Europe appear to be influenced by the prospect of, for example, a Japanese or French or Italian setting en route. This aspect of traveling is exploited to its fullest and receives considerable attention in each carrier's advertising. Another important dimension concerns the preference by certain travelers for their own flag carrier. In this regard, American travelers appear much less wedded to U.S. carriers than are other nations' travelers to their own, as evidenced by the percentages of travelers choosing their own flag carriers.

The international airline industry also has more plane types available and in use. In general, the introduction of new equipment is a step which no carrier can afford to neglect if it is to retain its share in competitive markets. As newer and better equipment is introduced on more competitive routes, existing equipment is relegated to monopoly situations or less competitive routes. The North Atlantic, in particular, has been a market in which new equipment has been almost essential for a firm to remain competitive. As noted in Chapter III, the effect of new equipment is so important that provisions regulating its use have occasionally been included in bilateral negotiations. Finally, and most importantly, the variation in relative factor prices creates relative advantages for particular carriers in different service levels. High-density seating on frequent jet service, however, seems to be the type of product predominantly in demand.

While product differentiation efforts have been considerable, it is generally not necessary for a carrier to introduce something new and different in order to enter a market. A new carrier can enter successfully if it uses equipment comparable to that of existing carriers, offers reasonably frequent and reliable flights, and meets minimum safety standards. These requirements are largely unrelated to the subtleties of product competition described above.

Characteristics of Airline Demand

Policy decisions in the industry reflect considerable differences of opinion as to the nature of demand. For example, the Civil Aeronautics Board has generally argued that price elasticity is greater than 1.0 when it asks for fare cuts. The international carriers have disagreed; IATA generally has been reluctant to reduce fares on the presumption that the price elasticity is small. Similarly, the reluctance of IATA to permit new classes of service which are less luxury-travel oriented is based on the judgment that new classes would not create new markets, but would rather divert traffic from existing classes and hence lower the average revenue per seat.

Previous research has produced less than conclusive results. Much of the work has concerned the U.S. domestic experience, for which data are available. Many of the important questions, however, remain unanswered. Plausible a priori arguments can be made supporting the importance of all of the variables mentioned earlier and others besides as an explanation of demand, and scattered evidence exists to support each. However, determining the relative importance of all the variables affecting demand is a very large task. The use of customary procedures for estimating demand parameters entails both empirical and methodological difficulties, arising in large part from the quality and availability of data. In this chapter a number of these techniques will be used—survey methods, case studies, cross section models, and time series models. The difficulties of each approach will be evident. A synthesis of information from all these approaches incorporated in a time series model, however, appears to provide reliable parameter estimates of price and income elasticities.

The Growth of Markets

Perhaps the most dramatic feature of airline demand is its amazing growth—roughly 15 percent each year since World War II. Few industries have grown so rapidly. This advance has been even more rapid than that of international passenger travel, with air transport having made inroads on the markets of competing surface modes. In the North Atlantic, 76 percent of all passenger traffic went by air in 1962, whereas travel by ship was predominant at the end of World War II. Other markets have experienced this same change as evidenced by these air travel percentages: North Pacific, 90 percent; South Pacific, 70 percent; South America-to-United States, 94 percent; Central America-to-Europe, 70 percent; South America-to-Europe, 48 percent.[3]

[3] R. Arnoult and G. Besse, "Principal Air Passenger Traffic Flows," *ITA Documents 65/11-E* (Paris: Institut du Transport Aérien, 1965), pp. 31–32.

TABLE VI-1. *Growth in International Air Service, by Region, 1947–61*

Year	All Carriers[a] (billions of passenger kilometers)	North Atlantic (thousands of passengers)	Markets (billions of revenue passenger-miles)							
			U.S. Domestic	Canada	Europe	Latin America	Asia	Pacific	North America to and from Latin America	Other
1947	18.9									
1948	20.9	240								
1949	23.0	267								
1950	27.3	311		0.5						
1951	34.7	330	11	0.6						1.3
1952	40.0	432	14	0.7	1.7		1.2		1.3	2.0
1953	46.5	507	16	0.8	2.3	2.1	1.3		1.3	2.8
1954	52.5	550	17	0.9	3.6	2.3	1.5		1.4	2.8
1955	62.0	652	21	0.9	4.2	2.4	1.6		1.6	3.2
1956	71.0	782	24	1.2	5.3	2.9	1.8		1.9	3.6
1957	81.0	968	28	1.4	5.9	3.5	2.0	1.0	2.0	4.1
1958	85.0	1,195	28	1.5	6.2	3.6	2.1	1.2	2.1	4.1
1959	97.1	1,367	32	1.7	6.8	3.7	2.5	1.4	2.5	4.5
1960	108.8	1,761	33	1.9	8.4	4.0	2.8	1.7	2.7	5.3
1961	116.7	1,919	34	2.3	9.5	4.2	3.1	2.0	3.0	6.0
Percentage increase, 1952–61	192	344	143	254	459	100[b]	158	100[c]	131	200

Sources: ICAO, *Digest of Statistics*; IATA, *World Air Transport Statistics;* Stanford Research Institute, *An Economic Analysis of Supersonic Transport*, Project No. ISU-4266 (under contract to Federal Aviation Agency), 1963.

[a] All carriers reporting to the International Civil Aviation Organization.
[b] 1953–61.
[c] 1957–61.

The regional pattern of market size and development clearly indicates the important role of income and economic activity in general. Air travel developed first in the United States, Canada, and Europe; this was followed by a considerable growth in Latin America during World War II, while European travel fell off, and a subsequent revival in Europe after the war. This growth record is shown in Table VI-1. The North Atlantic has been both the largest and the most rapidly growing major market.

Regional Distribution of Markets in Terms of Density

The regional distribution of markets is important also because it determines the sort of market opportunities available to particular flag carriers. Passenger densities of the major air routes are given in Table VI-2. It will be shown subsequently that the long stage lengths of the

TABLE VI-2. *Passenger Densities of Major Air Routes, 1962*

Number of Passengers by Route or Region	Number of Routes	Approximate Stage Length (kilometers)
More than 2,000,000	1	
North America to Europe		6,000
Between 1,000,000 and 2,000,000	4	
Los Angeles to San Francisco		560
Boston to New York		300
New York to Washington		330
Chicago to New York		1,140
Between 500,000 and 1,000,000	7	
Osaka to Tokyo		400
Miami to New York		1,760
New York to Puerto Rico		2,580
London to Paris		350
Rio de Janeiro to São Paulo		360
Melbourne to Sydney		700
U.S. West Coast to Hawaii		4,000
Between 200,000 and 500,000		
U.S. Domestic	30	...
Europe–Mediterranean	15	...
U.S.–Canada	2	...
Japan	1	...
South America	3	...
Australia	2	...
Others	6	...

Source: R. Arnoult and G. Besse, "Principal Air Passenger Traffic Flows," *ITA Documents 65/11-E* (Paris: Institut du Transport Aérien, 1965).

North Atlantic market, plus pricing policies which have kept fares up, have made this market a key source of profits. U.S. carriers are therefore well situated, especially since they have some inherent marketing advantages in attracting U.S. passengers.

Of the intra-continental routes, half of those which carried between 200,000 and 500,000 passengers in 1962 were U.S. domestic routes, one-fourth were in the Europe–Mediterranean region, and one-fourth in various other parts of the world.

Since fares do not usually taper as the length of journey increases and are not related to route density, the densest routes are the most profitable—and the longer they are, the greater the increase in profits.

Survey Studies of Air Transport Demand

Much of what is known about airline demand has come from survey studies of U.S. passenger demand. Surveys generally concentrate on data giving various socio-economic characteristics of airline passenger travelers. An attempt is then made to infer from the data causal factors or explanations of demand. The variable most often discussed in these survey studies is income.[4] Surveys of domestic air travel demand show that most air travelers are in the upper income brackets, their number is small, and most of them fly fairly often. They also indicate that as personal income rises people are more likely to travel, to travel longer distances, and to choose to travel by air.[5]

The role of income in international air markets is even more important, but differs in several respects from its role in the U.S. domestic market. Income levels of international travelers are lower than income levels of U.S. domestic travelers, and distances are relatively greater. (The average distance flown by ICAO scheduled passengers is about 1,000 kilometers, or $50–$60 at European fare levels,[6] which is a substantial amount in terms of many nations' income levels.) Thus an even greater percentage of passengers in the international air market is drawn from the upper income brackets than is true for the U.S. domestic market. A greater share of the international market is made up of business or government travel. International air travel generally has evolved from use predominantly by government and administrative personnel, to increasing use by business people supervising new investment, and finally to the development of more personal and tourist use. This evolution has occurred as investment and income levels have risen. At the early stages of this process the growth rate of income is most important since it generally indicates an increased rate of economic acitivity and an accompanying rise in outside investment and trade which can be supervised and facilitated by air travel. The subsequent development of personal travel depends upon incomes reaching a level at which people can afford air travel.

[4] See John B. Lansing and others, *The Travel Market* (University of Michigan, Institute for Social Research, Survey Research Center, 1963); Wharton School of Finance and Commerce, *Study of Consumer Expenditures, Incomes and Savings* (University of Pennsylvania, 1957).

[5] Caves, *op. cit.*, pp. 40–44.

[6] G. Desmas, "Air Transport Passenger Fares," *ITA Studies 62/63* (Paris: Institut du Transport Aérien, 1962), pp. 41–42.

This role of income is shown in an extensive survey conducted by the Port of New York Authority.[7] A large sample was taken of all air travelers passing through New York City in the years 1956 and 1963. The passengers were classified into four groups, depending on their destination, or (if they were returning to New York) where they had come from: North Atlantic, Caribbean, Bermuda, and Latin America. A summary of some of the highlights of the survey appears in Table VI-3. It is clear that air travel is more important to the higher income classes. However, the median income of air travelers has increased proportionately less over the seven years than the national median income. While there is a high proportion of professional and government personnel who travel, this percentage has fallen as more students and housewives have entered the market. The average age of travelers has fallen. Pleasure travel has increased faster than business travel with the percentage of pleasure travel increasing from 73 percent in 1956 to 76 percent in 1963. While those at the upper income levels travel more, there is a growing market among middle and lower income groups. Fare reductions may have been the major cause of this change.

While business travel has not grown as fast as pleasure travel, it has nevertheless increased considerably. Business demand is less sensitive to price reductions but was probably stimulated by the reduction in travel time made possible by jets. In 1956, 2,500 business trips were made to Europe by American residents for every billion dollars worth of direct foreign investment as reported by the U.S. Department of Commerce. By 1963, the number had increased to 3,700. In this same year 25 percent of the business trips were one week or less in duration as compared with 7 percent in 1956.[8]

This survey information suggests relationships of income levels and growth rates to airline demand, as well as hypotheses about other variables. The importance of income implies that price may be an important variable and may have different effects on different classes of travelers. Price elasticities cannot easily be determined, however, from the above survey studies. Comparisons of survey results over time face the difficulty of distinguishing between the effect of price changes and the effects of a host of other variables which have also changed.

The importance of the reduction in travel time as a result of the in-

---

[7] Port of New York Authority, Aviation Economics Division, *New York's Overseas Air Passenger Market, 1963* (1965).

[8] *Ibid.*

TABLE VI-3. *Travel Patterns and Characteristics of Air Passengers Originating in New York, 1956 and 1963*

(In percent)

Travel Pattern and Characteristic	Respondents by Residence					
	American Residents		Foreign Residents		Total	
	1956	1963	1956	1963	1956	1963
Purpose of trip						
Business	23	21	39	30	27	24
Touring or visiting a resort	43	40	10	11	33	31
Visiting friends and relatives	21	26	16	26	20	26
Other pleasure	5	5	18	19	9	9
Personal affairs	8	8	17	14	11	10
Total	100	100	100	100	100	100
Age of passengers (years)						
12–24	13	18	14	18		
25–44	43	39	49	46	n.a.	
45–64	38	36	34	32		
65 and over	6	7	3	4		
Total	100	100	100	100		
Family income[a]						
Under $6,000	24	17				
$6,000–$9,999	21	18				
$10,000–$14,999	18	23	n.a.		n.a.	
$15,000–$19,999	9	11				
$20,000 and over	28	31				
Total	100	100				
Duration of trip (weeks)						
One	17	20	8	12		
Two	19	15	12	13		
Three	11	15	12	17		
Four	12	13	15	13	n.a.	
Five to seven	16	13	18	11		
Eight or more	25	24	35	34		
Total	100	100	100	100		

Source: Port of New York Authority, Aviation Economics Division, *New York's Overseas Air Passenger Market, 1963* (1965), pp. 16–40.

n.a. Not available.

[a] Data obtained for American resident travelers only. The median income of these travelers in 1957 was $11,400 and in 1963 was $13,300. The median income of the U. S. adult population in 1957 was $4,950 and in 1963 was $6,190.

creased speed of new equipment exemplifies the difficulty in interpreting survey study data. The policy question is whether the public has been willing, in fact, or would have been willing to pay for such product improvements. The proposed supersonic transport raises this problem in particularly acute form. There is really no answer concerning the effect of speed increases that is obvious from the surveys of historical data.

Demand has grown fairly steadily year after year regardless of product improvements. The introduction of jets in place of piston aircraft did not result in any great immediate demand increase in most markets. (This generalization is for the market as a whole and is not to be confused with the advantage an individual carrier gains when introducing new equipment that is not matched by its competitors.) The jets have had their biggest impact in creating new, very long-haul markets, with stage lengths in excess of 4,000 miles. Flights from North America or Europe to South America, flights across the Pacific, and polar routes over the Arctic Circle are prime examples of markets which have received such an added impetus.

Cross-Section Model

The inherent difficulties of survey studies in determining the effects of variables which are changing simultaneously suggest that cross-section models might be useful. One advantage is that changes over time are eliminated, such as changes in tastes or technology. Another big advantage is the large variation in passenger income levels appearing in international data, which might yield an estimate of the income elasticity of demand.

Cross-section demand studies have explained differences in city-pair traffic flows by examining certain characteristics of each city, including income, population, and attractiveness to tourists. The most common approach has been some form of a gravity model, where traffic is positively related to the populations, incomes, or alternative measures of "traffic creating or attracting" quality of the two cities, and inversely proportional to distance.[9] Distance acts both as a proxy for the price

[9] The simple gravity model is of the form: $x_{ij} = f(P_i P_j)/d_{ij}$, where x is travel between cities i and j, P is population, and d_{ij} is distance. For a discussion of gravity models, see Walter Isard, *Methods of Regional Analysis* (The Technology Press of MIT, and John Wiley, 1960), Chap. 11.

and as a measure of remoteness (related to the likelihood that there will exist a reason for intercity business or tourist travel).

A number of these kinds of models have been constructed for the domestic industry;[10] they are equally applicable to international air transport demand, though the process of estimation is somewhat more difficult. For international travel more attention must be placed upon getting the proper estimate of a city's traffic-generating ability; per capita income varies considerably among cities, hence city population is not a useful measure by itself. Population must be weighted by income levels.

Origin-Destination Data Needed

The unavailability of origin-destination data because of the political interests in what constitutes fifth freedom traffic poses perhaps the biggest problem for cross-section models. The available traffic flow data are considerably affected by a city's position in the overall route structure. Much of the traffic between cities a and b may be "system traffic," arising because b is a stopping-off spot on the way to c, for example. The presence of system traffic in the flows may obscure the importance of measures of traffic generation, such as city income or population. This problem effectively makes cross-section models in any detail very complex.

The extent to which system traffic may distort cross-section models can be seen by examining Besse's survey[11] of traffic in 800 of the world's largest airports. He defined "terminal traffic" as all passengers commencing or terminating their journey at a particular airport plus "connecting passengers"—that is, those continuing on a different flight and generally a different aircraft. (A connecting passenger was therefore counted as an arrival and a departure.) "Passengers in through transit" were defined as those making a temporary stop and continuing

[10] For example, George K. Zipf, "The P_1P_2/D Hypothesis on the Intercity Movement of Persons," *American Sociological Review,* Vol. 11 (October 1946); F. C. Ikle, "Sociological Relationship of Traffic to Population and Distance," *Traffic Quarterly,* Vol. 8 (April 1954); Carl Hammer and F. C. Ikle, "Intercity Telephone and Airline Traffic Related to Distance and the 'Propensity to Interact,'" *Sociometry,* Vol. 20 (December 1956); John B. Lansing, Jung-Chao Liu, and Daniel B. Suits, "An Analysis of Interurban Air Travel," *Quarterly Journal of Economics,* Vol. 75 (February 1961), pp. 87–95.

[11] G. Besse, "World Airport Passenger Traffic: A Tentative Analytic Survey," *ITA Studies 63/16-E* (1963), pp. 8–18.

their journey in the same aircraft. The percentage of "passengers in through transit" of total traffic is a good approximation to the percentage of system traffic. The extent of the problem can be seen in Table VI-4, which lists the airports where there were over 100,000 passengers in through transit in 1962. The system-traffic problem is greatest at airports located strategically on certain long-haul routes, such as the Europe-to-South America or Europe-to-Asia routes. Shannon, Ireland, is a fueling stop in the North Atlantic; Kano and Khartoum are stopping points between Europe and South Africa; Curaçao and Bridgetown are islands just north of South America and are conveniently reached from North America.

Cross-Section Gravity Model Based on Paris Data

A simple cross-section gravity model was developed, using traffic flow data to and from Paris in September 1962,[12] plus explanatory variables—population, distance, income, and price. Traffic flows were adjusted to remove system traffic; observed demand between city i and Paris was reduced by the percentage of through traffic passing through airport i each year according to the Besse data. This adjustment seems to be a reasonable means of eliminating system traffic between city i and Paris. The remaining traffic from Paris to city i was expressed as a linear combination of the effects of income, population, distance, and whether or not the city was a national capital.

The variables were:

x_i = adjusted traffic flow, city i to and from Paris, for September 1962
P_i = population, city i
d_i = distance, city i to Paris
y_i = per capita income, city i.

The estimating equation, for forty-nine cities, was:

For non-capitals:
$$\log x_i = 2.5845 - 0.3405 \log d_i + 0.6991 \log P_i + 0.3716 \log y_i.$$
$$(0.2086) \qquad (0.1765) \qquad (0.2991)$$

For national capitals:
$$\log x_i = 3.5896 - 0.3405 \log d_i + 0.6991 \log P_i + 0.3716 \log y_i.$$
$$(R^2 = 0.3989)$$

[12] ICAO provides only March and September traffic data for its sample each year.

TABLE VI-4. *System Traffic, by Airport, 1962*

| Airport | Through-Transit Passengers (counted once) | |
	Number	Percentage of Terminal Traffic
San Francisco	591,341	10.9
Rome	472,596	20.4
Chicago	380,697	2.8
Frankfurt	317,752	11.8
Athens	276,170	27.1
Shannon	250,008	205.8
Honolulu	227,139	13.5
Burbank	218,486	37.6
Memphis	215,484	22.2
Toronto (1961)[a]	201,200	10.4
Montreal (1961)[a]	187,300	9.6
Paris	181,557	4.2
Cairo	178,569	32.5
Zurich	178,215	11.4
Beirut	174,015	26.4
Kano (1958–59)	171,531	334.0
Dakar	165,388	108.8
Bangkok	164,731	45.9
São Paulo	160,457	11.6
Prestwick	154,804	79.6
Oakland	153,322	49.0
Istanbul	152,754	39.7
Salvador	152,598	56.6
Marseilles	149,998	15.8
Nice	149,872	19.3
London	145,448	1.8
Dusseldorf	142,213	15.1
Milan	141,047	12.8
Khartoum (1958–59)	137,032	291.8
Rio de Janeiro	130,058	7.4
Recife	128,497	47.4
Kansas City	125,053	7.6
Munich	121,873	13.7
Geneva	116,416	12.4
Tokyo (1961)	115,328	6.5
Copenhagen	115,274	5.6

Source: G. Besse, "World Airport Passenger Traffic: A Tentative Analytic Survey," *ITA Studies 63/16-E* (Paris: Institut du Transport Aérien, 1963), p. 18.
[a] Estimated.

Use of a dummy variable for nations' capitals yielded an estimate of the difference in intercepts, equal to 1.0051, with standard deviation of 0.4656, significant at the 5 percent level.

This model was only moderately successful. City population had a significant positive effect on demand, and longer distances had a negative effect, as expected. The basic hypothesis of the gravity model is thus supported by the empirical results. However, this model will not provide an estimate for total income elasticity, and the demand elasticity of income in the cities connected with Paris was estimated as 0.372, which is suspiciously low. Inclusion of fares was unsuccessful, perhaps because fare differences are small (the result of various IATA agreements), but probably because the distance variable includes much of the "fare effect."

This relatively simple gravity model could be extended in a number of directions. Distance and price might be included in a nonlinear fashion since there is probably some discontinuity in the significance of travel time and the nature of surface competition on trips longer than a couple of hundred miles. Perhaps a dummy variable reflecting tourist attractiveness would be useful. However, it seems unlikely that much improvement could be made in the way "system traffic" is estimated. Estimating price, scheduling, or travel time coefficients with even more elaborate cross-section models seems unlikely to yield results significantly better than those above, because of the difficulties of representing cross-sectionally the overall traffic potential between cities and because there is no substantial price variation.

Case Studies

A case-by-case analysis of particular markets can be a useful source of information. If attention is confined to the two or three years of a price or service change on a particular route, many extraneous changes are eliminated. Many substantial changes in price, scheduling, and service have been made. A large number of case studies could provide reasonably good estimates of important parameters.[13]

[13] Cherington has essentially followed this procedure in his study of the U.S. domestic airlines. See Paul W. Cherington, *Airline Price Policy: A Study of Domestic Airline Passenger Fares* (Harvard University, Graduate School of Business Administration, Division of Research, 1958).

FIGURE VI-1. *North Atlantic Demand for Air Transportation, by Class of Service, 1948–64*

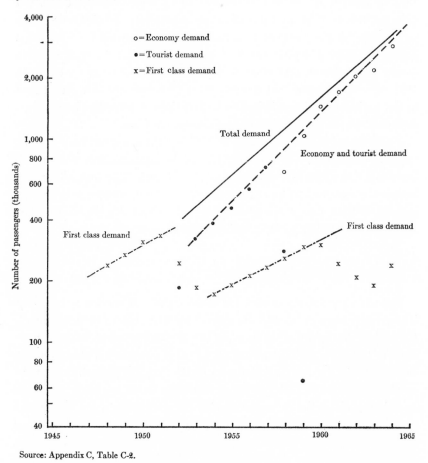

Source: Appendix C, Table C-2.

The North Atlantic case is considered here. Data used in the case study appear in Appendix C, Tables C-2 and C-3, and in Figure VI-1. Two questions of interest concern the price elasticity within each class of service and the consumer response to new classes of service.

Tourist fares were initiated on the North Atlantic on May 1, 1952. This fare cut produced a switch from first class to tourist as evidenced by the discontinuities in demand for first class; it also created a new class of travelers in view of the distinct rise in the growth rate of total demand. After 1954, switching of first class traffic to tourist class no longer appears. The extent of the switch can be estimated by using the 1954–60 growth rate of first class travel of 11.05 percent in a backward extrapolation to 1951. By this technique an estimate of 121,000 first class passengers, or 36.6 percent of actual traffic, is obtained for 1951. This could be labeled legitimate first class traffic—that is, traffic which would have chosen first class if both services had been available in 1951. It would appear that roughly 60 to 65 percent of first class travel in the period 1952–54 switched to tourist class as travellers became accustomed to the availability of the alternative class.

A second major fare reduction of 12.7 percent came on April 1, 1958, with the introduction of economy fares. The consequences were much less than those emanating from the 1952 change. The only difference between economy and tourist service was a slight difference in seating density. Within two years passengers had indicated a decided preference for the cheaper service, and the tourist class was dropped.

Price Elasticity in First Class Service

Estimating price elasticities for these classes of service is not easy. The airlines have presumed the market for first class to be price inelastic, and survey information showing the predominance of business travelers in this class would lend support to this assumption. However, the experience in the North Atlantic suggests that this inelasticity can be overstated. Since the alternative to first class travel is always air travel in a lower class, the fare and service differences between the classes may be an important determinant of first class demand. This has in fact been the case. After the shift from first class to tourist ended in 1954, first class traffic grew despite a slight, unfavorable increase in the fare difference. In 1961, however, the differential was sharply increased when first class fares from New York to London were raised from $462 to $500. Over the next three years passengers again switched from first-class to economy service. In April 1964, the fare difference was substantially reduced (from a ratio of 1.85 to a ratio of 1.61), and first class travel again expanded sharply. A fare differential of 1.6:1 seems, therefore, to be the approximate limit which will sustain the present first class market in the North Atlantic. At the existing load factors (slightly lower in first class than in economy), the average revenue ratio in the two classes is consistent with the cost ratio estimated in Chapter V of approximately 1.4 to 1.

The experience with "deluxe first class" service in the North Atlantic is further evidence that the business class will not pay infinitely higher prices for a higher level of service. A deluxe first class service, offering a lower seating density at a premium fare 12 percent above the regular first class fare, was tried in the North Atlantic from 1958 through 1960. After three unsuccessful years, the service was dropped.

The absolute increase in first class patronage in 1964 in the North Atlantic was the first encouraging evidence in years to the airlines of a renewed interest in first class service. First class demand has fallen relative to economy travel in every market as the market has developed. The North Atlantic experience suggests, however, that long-haul first class service may still be able to pay for itself. Only 10 percent of all passenger trips made in the North Atlantic and in Europe are first class trips, as pleasure travel predominates in this market; in markets where business travel is more important the amount of first class demand would be higher. It would be of interest to see how particular airline markets would separate by classes if the airlines were to set prices more rationally; present prices often subsidize first class service since the higher fare in first class is usually not sufficient to offset the much lower load factors.

Price Elasticity in Economy Services

The elasticity of demand for the economy services (grouping economy and tourist together) is more difficult to estimate. The fare cut in 1958 produced no noticeable demand increase. In April 1960, economy fares were raised 7.2 percent; yet traffic increased by 35 percent from 1959 to 1960. Without attempting any sophisticated measure of income or trend effects on demand, this suggests that the price elasticity was not large.

The record since 1961 is of interest. The 1961, 1962, and 1963 growth rates in economy traffic must be adjusted downward because of the rise in first class rates in 1961. Using the 11.05 percent growth rate in first class travel to estimate the approximate "normal" level of first class demand and hence the extent of the shift, the growth rates of economy traffic become somewhat lower—10.0 percent in 1961, 23.2 percent in 1962, and 6.6 per cent in 1963. The 4.5 percent economy class fare increase in 1963 probably helped produce the very low demand increase for that year. The fare cut of April 1964, in which first class fares (one way from New York to London) were cut from $475 to $375, economy fares were reduced by 3 percent in-season and 20 percent off-season, and excursion fares were lowered from $350 to $300 round-trip, reversed the unfavorable trend in demand growth rates. In the first quarter of 1964, passenger demand was up by 4.9 percent for economy service and by 1.2 percent for first class. These very modest increases were the result of the prevailing fare levels combined with anticipation of the new, lower rates previously announced. The huge demand increases in the last three quarters were so great that for 1964 as a whole, first class travel was up 22 percent and economy traffic increased 28 percent. The 1964 experience seems to indicate a substantial price elasticity.

Price Elasticity in Europe in 1953

A study of the traffic response in Europe in 1953 when tourist fares were introduced was conducted by the Air Research Bureau. The study examined the demand response in a number of city-pairs in Europe to the change in price. The city-pairs were selected to exclude routes involving much through traffic and also those which had been recently involved in substantial route changes. Quarterly and annual estimates were made of traffic growth for 1952 and 1953 on each of the routes, independent of any price changes. Price elasticities were estimated, based on demand increases above those which had been anticipated. Two potentially important sources of demand change were absent— that is, income and schedule frequency. Income in Europe, outside of West Germany, grew only slightly in the period from 1951 to 1953. Schedule frequencies were not raised, as traffic growth was accommodated by bigger planes and higher load factors.

This study found a substantial price elasticity (1.8 for 1953 as a whole, 1.9 for the summer, and 1.4 for the fourth quarter). The elasticity was reflected in a 27 percent traffic increase in 1953; the traffic increase in 1952 was 9 percent. The higher elasticity in the summer was the result of a predominance of tourist travel. The volume of business travel was also significant, as reflected in the fact that the Scandinavian routes, which normally carry a greater proportion of business travel than other European routes, exhibited a lower elasticity.[14]

After presenting this evidence of a substantial price elasticity, the Air Research Bureau (ARB) paper came to a questionable conclusion. Additional demand may, of course, produce higher load factors, or it may be met by adding capacity—by installing more seats per plane or by offering greater schedule frequencies. The ARB paper noted that tourist seating configurations used in Europe permitted no more seats per plane. It was implicitly assumed that if fares were to be cut, capacity would have to be increased by raising schedule frequencies; if load factors were therefore to be maintained as before at 50 percent, and direct costs assumed to be 50 percent of total costs, an elasticity of −2.0 would be required to pay for the added frequency supplied. The conclusion was that only London and the Mediterranean routes could justify fare cuts.[15] The possibility of not raising capacity and accepting higher load factors from the increased demand was overlooked. In general, the price elasticity for intra-Europe appears to be about −2.0. Further fare cuts therefore probably would have been beneficial.

These two cases could be supplemented by others to yield good estimates as to price and flight frequency or schedule elasticities. The difficulty with such a compilation of cases is that analysis of results depends on the accuracy with which basic trends can be predicted, independent of the price or service changes in question. The results thus have a subjective element. The final approach using time series models is slightly less flexible but provides an opportunity to make more precise estimates.

Time Series Model

The substantial changes in price, income, and type of service that have occurred in the airline industry over many years provide an opportunity to estimate elasticities with time series data. The failure of survey methods and case studies to focus on more than one variable at a time is a serious drawback; statistical time series models can more effectively consider the simultaneous effects of a number of variables. Such a model is developed in Appendix C and will be summarized

[14] *Intra-European Air Passenger Traffic, 1952–54,* No. 103 (Brussels: Air Research Bureau, 1955).

[15] *Ibid.,* pp. 48–49.

here. The model uses annual data from the North Atlantic, a market chosen because the data are reliable and because considerable variations in price and class of service have occurred. The estimation in Appendix C specifies a demand function for total air service and also one for tourist service. The latter equation is intended to reflect tourist demand in the presence of first class service. The estimates are based on post-1954 data, adjusted to exclude "first class travelers" who switch in and out of tourist service in response to the relative prices of the two classes. First class travel in the North Atlantic has unfortunately been affected by too much switching in and out to be useful in a statistical analysis.

Airline demand was formulated as a linear function of price, income, and a time trend. The time trend was assumed to represent the sum of all those effects except price and income which have raised airline demand over time (for example, reduction of fear, rise in sea fares, and reduction in air travel time). The air fare from New York to London was used as the price variable, deflated by the Consumer Price Index of the U.S. Department of Labor. (For total demand, the fare was the weighted sum of first class and economy class fares.) The income variable was based on U.S. figures, also deflated by the Consumer Price Index.[16] Data problems precluded a more sophisticated form for the demand function.

The outstanding difficulty in estimating this sort of time series model is that historical data often show the cumulative effects of many variables. Moreover, the variables that are of interest sometimes show little independent variation over time, and therefore assessment of their effects can be difficult. When equations are estimated using data of this sort, the parameters may reflect very well the joint effect of several variables. However, the individual parameter estimates will be highly dependent upon the particular interrelationships between variables which prevailed during the sample period. The estimates will not be valid "structurally"—that is, for example, as a specification of the relationship of demand to price, with other things constant. Rather, such data will produce estimates based on observed price changes

[16] Because American travelers make up only a portion of the North Atlantic market the equation should properly include such variables as European income and price levels. Weighted averages of European and U.S. incomes and prices were computed, but their inclusion did not make an appreciable difference in the results, and hence the model is presented here in terms of U.S. income and prices.

which have been accompanied by a particular set of influences. These relationships may or may not prevail in the future. It is therefore dangerous to use the price elasticity, for example, estimated in the above manner to assess the effect of price changes, since the "milieu" of such changes may not closely resemble that of the historical changes.[17]

This problem is inherent in airline demand data. A rapid growth rate, noted earlier, has its explanation in a number of factors—the rise in real incomes, the reduction in real air fares (both absolutely and relative to sea fares), the reduction in travel time, the increased comfort of the jets, the increased convenience of better flight schedules, and a shift in preferences for air travel because of reduced fear of flying, improved safety records, etc. All of these factors have occurred simultaneously over the last fifteen years, making assessment of their individual effects difficult.[18]

Results of a Simple Time Series Model

The reasonably simple model postulated here, which includes only a few variables because of lack of data, involves a difficult estimation problem—of the multicollinearity of independent variables type—since both price reductions and income increases have been highly correlated with time.

The independent variables had simple correlations approximating 0.90 (see Appendix C). Letting x equal yearly passenger demand, t equal time, p equal price in real terms, and y equal real income, the estimated equations were as follows, where time was the only independent variable:

(1) all demand (1948–64)
$$\log x = 5.2316 + 0.1647 \ (t) \qquad\qquad (R^2 = 0.9956)$$
$$(0.0028)$$
(2) adjusted tourist demand (1954–64)
$$\log x = 6.2077 + 0.1616 \ (t) \qquad\qquad (R^2 = 0.9841)$$
$$(0.0068)$$

[17] This is the problem which economists have labeled "multicollinearity of independent variables." Time series data often exhibit this characteristic; independent variables are often highly correlated with time and hence with each other, with the result that historical data may contain insufficient information to determine the separate effects of each variable. This problem is discussed somewhat more rigorously in Appendix C.

[18] Caves refers to the same difficulty in his discussion of time series models for U.S. domestic airline demand. See Caves, op. cit., pp. 33–36.

The high R^2, the coefficient of multiple determination, indicates that "time" provides an explanation for almost all of the variation in demand.

The inclusion of price and income in the equations does not markedly increase the quality of the fit, nor does it provide estimates of the price and income elasticities which make sense as structural estimates. The coefficients of the variables in these logarithmic equations are the elasticities:

(1) all demand $\qquad (R^2 = 0.9971)$

$$\log x = 6.5496 - 0.3157 \log p - 0.7613 \log y + 0.1825t$$
$$\qquad (0.2565) \qquad\quad (0.4950) \qquad\quad (0.0229)$$

(2) adjusted demand $\qquad (R^2 = 0.9861)$

$$\log x = 11.6310 - 0.9074 \log p - 0.0026 \log y + 0.1933t$$
$$\qquad (0.9177) \qquad\quad (0.28885) \qquad\quad (0.0372)$$

In this case (an extreme one), the historical data were insufficient to estimate reliable elasticities for these three variables in an equation. The time trend alone was sufficient to explain most of the variation in demand. Price and income variables were of little added help, nor could reliable estimates of their effects be made. This is not to say that they are unimportant, but only that their importance is concealed in the large time trend coefficient.

The only solution to this problem is additional information about the relationships among parameters or their approximate values, which can be combined with the time series data in the estimation process. This sort of combination of data, based on information from the cross-section model and from the case studies combined with the North Atlantic time series data is developed formally in Appendix C. It produced seemingly reliable structural estimates of the price, income, and time trend elasticities.

The additional information included with the time series data necessarily plays a large role in the estimation process. The substantial dependencies in the sample data are such that estimation must weight the "outside information" heavily. The role of this "subjective" information (as it relates to the sample data) in the estimation process can best be seen by examining the estimation process sequentially, beginning with the "less subjective" approaches which weighted the sample data most heavily.

"Constrained Regression" Model

A minimal weighting of the "outside information" relative to the sample data was employed in the first approach, in which the estimates were constrained to fall within certain bounds. This is the so-called "constrained regression" model, developed by Meyer and Glauber.[19] The constraints on the parameter estimates are a representation of one's prior knowledge. In a model such as this there is a certain sensitivity of estimates to the values of the constraints; hence a number of constraints were employed to test this sensitivity. Tests for sensitivity were also advisable because the constraints themselves were estimates subject to error. The income elasticity was constrained to be below 2.0 and greater than 0.35 and 0.85 in successive trials. The price elasticities were constrained to be above -4.0 and below 0.0, -1.0, and -1.5 in various estimation attempts. These bounds are suggested by prior knowledge and by both the cross-section model and the case studies. The time trend was constrained to be greater than zero.

The results were not encouraging. In the constrained regression model at least one parameter must lie at a constraint if the constraints are to be effective. In this case, both the income and price elasticity estimates fell at a constraint: income elasticity at the lower level and price elasticity at the upper level of 0.0, -1.0, or -1.5. The time trend assumed some positive value less than its value when previously used as the single variable to explain demand. The resultant estimates were therefore highly dependent upon the specific values of the constraints. With various constraints on the parameters, a number of estimates were produced, including what would appear to be good structural parameters. Moreover, the resulting equations all were excellent fits for the historical data, as evidenced by the high values for R^2. Unfortu-

[19] John R. Meyer and Robert R. Glauber, *Investment Decisions, Economic Forecasting, and Public Policy* (Harvard University, Graduate School of Business Administration, Division of Research, 1964), pp. 181–85. The model is to choose estimates, b, of β, so as to minimize the sum of squared errors subject to linear constraints on b:

$$Y = \beta + \varepsilon$$

choose b to min $e'e$

subject to $b_l \leq b \leq b_u$

where $e = Y - Xb$

and b_l and b_u are lower and upper bounds on the regression coefficients.

nately, the high quality of the fits is not evidence in support of any one set of estimates, since a variety of constrained estimates had this property.

The proper conclusion is that the historical data are consistent with a variety of estimates, including both "reasonable" structural values and other values. Use of additional information in the way of constraints therefore has not solved the basic problem of estimation created by historical data that do not reflect sufficient independent variation in the relevant variables. This outcome, less than fully satisfactory, demonstrates both the severity of the data problem and the rather rigid way in which this model incorporates prior information into the estimation. Constraints in the form of absolute bounds are perhaps not the best reflection of outside information about the unknown parameters.

The "Bayesian" Model

Some of these difficulties were avoided in the second model used, the "Bayesian" model developed by Raiffa and Schlaifer.[20] This provides a more flexible format for incorporating prior knowledge and sample data into an estimation procedure. The model begins with all prior information about the parameters in the form of a probability distribution. The sample data are then used to modify the distribution and hence yield new parameter estimates. In this case the cross-section model, survey data, and case studies are used to formulate the prior probability distribution. The time series data are then incorporated as additional evidence, and revised probability distributions for the parameters are formed. These revised distributions of the estimates will reflect the information in the time series data. This sort of model is quite flexible and allows any weighting of prior knowledge with sample data. The results, of course, are only as reliable as the inputs.

In the model estimated in Appendix C, the prior information on the parameters was in the form of a multivariate Normal distribution. The prior distribution on the price elasticity was assumed to have a mean of -2.0 and a standard deviation of 1.0. This prior information therefore assigns little probability to the price elasticity falling beyond the

[20] Howard Raiffa and Robert Schlaifer, *Applied Statistical Decision Theory* (Harvard University, Graduate School of Business Administration, Division of Research, 1961).

TABLE VI-5. *Bayesian Estimates of Demand Function for North Atlantic Air Market, 1948–65*

Type of Demand and Elasticity, and Time Trend	Elasticities of Variables and Time Trends			
	Prior Distribution Assumed for Elasticities		Posterior Distribution	
	Mean	Standard Deviation	Mean	Standard Deviation
Total demand, 1948–65				
Income elasticity	1.75	0.585	2.0440	0.517
Price elasticity	−2.00	1.000	−1.5041	0.894
Time trend				
(annual growth rate)	0.10	0.050	0.0557	0.043
Adjusted tourist demand, 1954–65				
Income elasticity	1.75	0.585	1.8192	0.522
Price elasticity	−2.00	1.000	−1.4223	0.818
Time trend				
(annual growth rate)	0.10	0.050	0.0620	0.046

Source: See Appendix Table C-5.

limits 0 and −4.0. The distribution of the estimate of the income elasticity was assumed to have a mean of 1.75 and a standard deviation of 0.585.

This prior information employed and the resultant estimates, which are also normally distributed, are summarized in Table VI-5. The price elasticity determined for total demand was −1.50, which may reflect price effects within a class or shifts in demand with the creation of the tourist class. The price elasticity estimated for the adjusted tourist demand equation, which avoids the shifting between classes, was −1.42. The estimate for the income elasticity for total demand was slightly over 2.0, which is consistent with the fact that air travel has been growing faster than income. Annual growth, independent of price and income effects, was 5.6 percent. This implies that about one-third of the growth rate has its explanation in factors other than price and income, a fairly unlikely result; this suggests that the income elasticity may even be understated.

It is this use of additional information in the form of a prior distribution which essentially solves the collinearity problem of the historical time series data. The Bayesian model is more flexible than the constrained regression model in handling prior information. These two procedures are systematically compared in Appendix C. The success of the former when severe multicollinearity exists is due primarily to the fact that more prior information was included. The kind of time series sample encountered here necessitates subjective estimation procedures of this sort, with the results dependent on the credibility of the prior or outside information employed.

Conclusion

Combining data from the cross-section model, surveys, and case studies with time series data can provide reliable estimates of price and income elasticities. Given sufficient data, the approach used in this chapter could be used to estimate elasticities in other markets. Tourist or pleasure travel in the North Atlantic in economy class appears to have a price elasticity near −1.5, which is probably higher now than it was ten years ago. The fall in air fares and the rise in income levels are such that air travel is being chosen by people farther down the income distribution, who are more conscious of price. Even the business traveler in first class is not altogether insensitive to price; for this traveler the alternative is economy service, and he has demonstrated a willingness to choose this if price differences between the two classes become large. An important implication of this price elasticity (since it exceeds unity) is that a fare reduction could raise load factors enough to increase total revenue.

The price elasticity in other markets will depend both on the level of fares and service and on the mix of business and tourist travel. Price elasticity will be highest in those markets in which tourist travel predominates. This is borne out in the analysis of selected Caribbean city-pair markets in Appendix C. In other markets—in the Pacific, the Middle East, and Latin America—fares tend to be higher than in the North Atlantic, and the percentage of business travelers is higher. Although the latter implies price inelasticity, large fare reductions in the form of charter or other special services might well create a very much larger tourist market, especially in those areas where incomes are rising rapidly. If fare reductions reached this expanding market, total demand might well have a high elasticity with respect to price.

CHAPTER VII

Pricing and the International
Air Transport Association

A TRADE ORGANIZATION of more than one hundred firms, the International Air Transport Association (IATA) is responsible for setting all international air fares. In addition, IATA runs for its members a clearinghouse, through which it coordinates common ticketing, safety, operating, and navigating procedures.

Development of the Fare-Setting Role of IATA

IATA derives its fare-regulating function from the attempt to settle a pricing dispute that developed in the industry at the end of World War II. European companies stood as adamantly opposed to free pricing as they did to free entry. This position became apparent in the European response to a Pan American Airways (PAA) request to institute high-density service from New York to London at a one-way fare of $275, as opposed to the prewar price of $375. European carriers were not ready to meet this price nor able to supply enough capacity for high-density operations; hence the United Kingdom threatened to limit PAA flight frequencies to two per week. This threat was sufficient to rule the day, and the prewar fares were maintained during an interim period of more than a year until resolution of the dispute at Bermuda. In the Bermuda Agreement, the United States and the United Kingdom

131

accepted IATA as a means of setting fares, subject to government approval. This agreement was subsequently widely accepted as the industry model for fare determination.

The solution of the fare-setting dispute by a conference agreement was conditioned by a number of factors, including the existence of IATA as an on-going industry "trade organization" with a history of participation in setting fares. IATA was formed in 1919 by a group of European airlines and was then called the International Air Traffic Association. It acted as an industry cartel in the beginning and later became an organization which facilitated airline cooperation and provided opportunity for informal discussion and agreement on rates.[1] In 1944, IATA membership became worldwide when it took in a new rival organization, the Conference of International Air Transport Operators; this inclusion altered somewhat the former "club" atmosphere. By January 1945, when the Bermuda Conference took place, IATA had grown sufficiently in stature that the United States and the United Kingdom were willing to entrust responsibility to it. The belief by the British government, which insisted on price controls, that an effective means of controlling rate determination already existed was important in reaching the Bermuda Agreement.[2] At the same time, the United States and the Civil Aeronautics Board (CAB) felt that rate-setting by conference was probably the most feasible procedure at the time. The veto power which the United States held over fare agreements was thought to be a sufficient guarantee that unreasonable fares would not be imposed. Furthermore, since operations in 1945 were unprofitable and would therefore need considerable government subsidy, the advantages of competitive pricing did not appear overwhelming. When the United States conceded competitive pricing, it seemed a proper step and a reasonable means of compromise.

The rate-setting machinery within IATA consists of three Traffic Conferences, corresponding to geographical areas of the world. All carriers within a conference area may participate, and regardless of size,

[1] Ralph S. Cohen, *IATA: The First Three Decades* (Montreal: Head Office of the IATA, 1949); see also Stephen Wheatcroft, *The Economics of European Air Transport* (Harvard University Press, 1956), p. 123.

[2] Anthony Satterthwaite, lecture before the Aircraft Recognition Society, in Great Britain (October 20, 1948), as reproduced in Walter H. Wager, "Some Selected Readings on International Air Transportation" (processed, undated), pp. 59-66. See also "Air Services Agreement, signed at Bermuda, February 11, 1946," *Treaties and Other International Acts Series,* No. 1507 (1946).

each has a single vote. Fare agreements require unanimous approval, which ostensibly assures that no carrier or government will have an unacceptable fare forced upon it. Fare agreements resulting from each Traffic Conference meeting are subject to approval by each carrier's government. The CAB acts as the approving body for the United States. The Bermuda Agreement reads as follows:

(b) The Civil Aeronautics Board of the United States having announced its intention to approve the rate conference machinery of the International Air Transport Association (hereinafter called IATA), as submitted, for a period of one year beginning in February, 1946, any rate agreements concluded through this machinery during this period and involving United States air carriers will be subject to approval by the Board. (Annex II, par. (b).)

Rate-Making in Practice: Recurrent Crises

IATA Traffic Conferences meet each year to establish fares (which are generally effective for only one year) and to determine stopover privileges, mileage limits, or multi-stop trips and service characteristics for each class of travel. With the exception of the intervention by the CAB, discussed below, IATA behavior appears consistent with that of an industry price cartel. The secrecy attending the proceedings of these meetings is such that details of the bargaining are not public information. What evidence is available permits a rationale to be developed which appears to provide a good explanation of IATA price negotiations and the fares which result.

IATA's history has been one of recurrent crises, each seemingly worse than the last; yet a compromise is always reached eventually. Many disagreements have been settled only at the last minute, after carrier bargaining has threatened to break down the entire rate-setting procedure. It is in time of crisis that IATA receives most of its publicity and criticism, even though the organization has managed over the years to produce compromises among widely divergent views. Only occasionally has lack of agreement left an open-fare situation.

The fundamental problem which IATA faces is that of reconciling very different positions. Carriers presumably bargain for a profit-maximizing price based on their own demand and cost curves, which often differ considerably. In the early postwar years these differences were quite pronounced, with U.S. carriers holding a considerable edge.

Their advantage, however, appears to have been exaggerated by the European airlines and governments. The desire of PAA to reduce fares and raise seating densities was in direct opposition to the interests of European carriers. PAA continually pushed its advantage; the airline equipped itself with a large fleet of DC-6Bs and eventually was able to reap the benefits when tourist service was introduced in the North Atlantic in 1952.

DIFFERENCES BETWEEN ESTABLISHED CARRIERS AND NEW ENTRANTS. The difference in viewpoints between American and European carriers has diminished as the latter have expanded and somewhat rationalized their operations. However, the entry of carriers from the less developed countries in recent years has introduced a set of interests not unlike those of the European carriers in the immediate postwar period. This range of interests can be illustrated by the bargaining pertaining to service in the North Atlantic. The American and Canadian carriers were the first to become efficient operators and have led the campaign for fare reductions. PAA and Air Canada in particular have championed lower priced, higher-density service. These carriers have a competitive advantage for such a product since capital is readily available and their customers are probably very price conscious. On the other hand, labor costs are relatively high, which means that these carriers are at a disadvantage in service competition. The other end of the spectrum, initially occupied by the European carriers, has now been taken by such market entrants as Air-India and Pakistan International Airlines. These carriers tend to serve a more captive market which is probably less price-elastic. Their profit-maximizing fare will thus be higher. Also, they face capital constraints and could not as readily expand capacity if the market were to switch to more competition on the basis of increased schedule frequencies and high-density seating. The large European airlines now represent a middle ground. These carriers, however, have been slow to change their position to favor fare cuts, even though the evolving pattern of entry and changes in competitive costs would suggest that their competitive advantage may lie in this direction. British Overseas Airways Corporation (BOAC), for example, does not face a capital constraint and would probably be better off competing on the basis of lower fares and more frequent flights using the latest equipment. Probably fear of the uncertainties of a fare cut explains to some extent why BOAC and some European carriers have continued to support higher fares.

MAJOR POST-WAR PRICING DISPUTES. Two major IATA "crises" have occurred since World War II. Both times it was doubtful for a while that
a compromise could be achieved. In both cases the important divergent
view was that of the CAB, which was looking after the "public welfare." The first incident of crisis magnitude occurred in 1956. The question which precipitated the crisis concerned a proposed luxury surcharge and also a surcharge on berths, which many carriers felt certain
passengers would be willing to pay. The surcharges were discussed at
the IATA meeting in Miami in the fall of 1955. Unable to agree on a
luxury surcharge, the carriers decided instead to institute a 10 percent
increase in first class rates, to be effective October 1, 1956.[3] In March
the CAB, acting for the U.S. government, refused to accept the proposed fares. (This was the first time a government had opposed an
IATA decision.) The CAB also felt that a reduction in tourist fares was
in order. Accordingly, an emergency conference was convened at
Cannes in May 1956, and a number of subsequent sessions were held.
These sessions were marked by considerable drama and uncertainty for
the airlines, the governments, and the traveling public. Eventually a
compromise was reached, which provided that the fares agreed upon
at Miami be accepted until March 31, 1958, at which time a reduction
in tourist fares would take place. The reduction agreed on was to be 20
percent, with the understanding that the one-way fare not be below
$232 and that higher-density seating would be introduced.[4] This compromise did in fact serve as the basis for the introduction of economy
class service two years later.[5]

The second major incident was the "Chandler crisis,"[6] named for the
resolutions passed at Chandler, Arizona, in the fall of 1962, which precipitated fare disputes the following year. The IATA Traffic Conference agreed at Chandler to a reduction in the round-trip discount on
North Atlantic routes from 10 percent to 5 percent; American carriers
opposed this fare increase but felt that they had struck the best possible bargain. The CAB had told U.S. carriers prior to the meetings that

[3] "Report on the 1955 Traffic Conferences at Miami," IATA Bulletin, No. 22
(December 1955), pp. 100–02.
[4] "Report for the Cannes Traffic Conferences," IATA Bulletin, No. 24 (December 1956), pp. 99–100.
[5] "Reports by the Chairmen of the Traffic Conferences, Miami-Paris, 1957,"
IATA Bulletin, No. 26 (December 1958), pp. 95–97.
[6] International Air Transportation Rates, Hearings before the Senate Committee
on Commerce, 88 Cong. 1 sess. (1963).

it would not approve a fare increase, and on March 18 the Board issued a disapproval of the proposed IATA rates. Canada followed a policy similar to that of the CAB. When the European carriers continued to support the Chandler fares, the issue was joined.

The effective date of the Chandler fares was first postponed until April 29 and then until May 12, pending further discussion—which did not resolve the dispute. The Board then ordered U.S. carriers to continue to provide service at the old rates,[7] while Britain, Italy, France, West Germany, Spain, and the Scandinavian countries all insisted that U.S. carriers charge Chandler rates.[8] Operations by U.S. carriers at the old fares after May 12 led to threats by the United Kingdom and other European governments that landing rights would be denied, penalties imposed, and the U.S. carriers' equipment impounded if they continued operating at the illegal rate. Exchanges were made at the foreign ministry level, with the U.S. State Department deciding against backing the CAB. The Board consequently ordered U.S. carriers to charge the higher rate, and the 5 percent round-trip discount went into effect.[9] A provisional compromise was subsequently reached in intergovernmental negotiations which maintained the Chandler fares until July 15 (thus covering one-half the peak season); thereafter the one-way economy fare was to be cut from $270 to $263 between New York and London. The overall increase after July 15 on a round trip was therefore $13.70, rather than $27, which the Chandler rate increase entailed. This provisional solution was to apply until March 31, 1964, and conferences were scheduled at Salzburg in October 1963 to produce a permanent agreement. Thus a worldwide open-rate situation was avoided —but only barely.

PAA announced that it favored a $320 round-trip fare from New York to London—36 percent below the existing economy fare of $499.70. There was to be no cabin service, and 707s or DC-8s with 190 seats were to be used. Air Canada's proposal was a one-way economy fare of $145 during the off-season and $180 during the peak season. Prior to the Salzburg meetings, European carriers in conjunction with their governments worked out a compromise plan among themselves at meetings held in Bonn and in Stockholm in August. The basis for this cooperation was to oppose the more extensive fare reductions proposed by PAA and Air Canada.

[7] *Aviation Daily,* Vol. 146 (May 3, 1963), p. 17.
[8] *Aviation Daily,* Vol. 146 (May 9, 1963), p. 53.
[9] *Aviation Daily,* Vol. 146 (May 15, 1963), pp. 89–90.

When the conference at Salzburg convened, the PAA and Air Canada cuts were immediately opposed as too extreme, on grounds that they discriminated against small carriers that were not so well equipped. Nor did European carriers want to do away with cabin service. The Salzburg meetings adjourned, reconvened, and again adjourned without settlement, though all carriers did agree to some fare cut (as yet undetermined).[10] The U.S. carriers (and the CAB) indicated a willingness to accept a $230 economy fare (down from $263) and a $300 excursion fare—fares roughly in line with the European carriers' proposals. Air Canada, however, stuck by its more extreme proposal. Also, El Al Israel and Aerlinte wanted the retention of certain special group fares, opposed by other carriers because they implied a more liberal definition of a group fare than was customary industry practice. El Al had been offering a "group flight" from New York to Tel Aviv at a round trip fare of $535, well below standard rates, which gave passengers considerably more leeway than normal group flights. Additional stopping-off privileges in London, Rome, and other cities were allowed, and no common affinity among travelers (the customary definitive requirement of a group flight) was required. This flight had been very profitable for El Al because of its high density and long stage length. Other carriers wanted the flight cancelled or wanted the right to compete on equal grounds. Such an unrestricted flight essentially amounted to a license to make a fare reduction considerably below basic IATA rates.

A series of meetings followed, and a "near compromise" was reached at Nassau in December. First class fares were to be reduced 21 percent and economy fares reduced 3 percent in-season and 20 percent off-season.[11] This agreement was accepted by all carriers except Air Canada, El Al Israel Airlines, and Aerlinte.[12] While this lack of unanimity would ordinarily have meant continued IATA bargaining for a solution, IATA was bypassed in this instance. The agreeing carriers filed the new fares with their respective governments, presenting the three dissenting carriers and their governments with the alternatives of either agreeing or negotiating separately with each government.[13] The three

[10] *ITA Bulletin,* No. 43 (Paris: Institut du Transport Aérien, November 25, 1963), pp. 1172–73.

[11] *Aeroplane and Commercial Aviation News,* Vol. 106 (October 31, 1964), p. 11.

[12] *ITA Bulletin,* No. 3 (January 20, 1964), pp. 57–59.

[13] *Aviation Daily,* Vol. 150 (January 6, 1964), p. 18.

eventually gave ground. In April 1964, all governments unanimously accepted the fare structure in a mail vote, and IATA had a single agreement to enforce.[14]

The final solution was thus reached in this important, different way, with the unanimity rule effectively bypassed by a near-unanimous government consensus. IATA was originally created to handle the fare problem at the carrier level, and concern has continually been voiced about the amount of state intervention and the presence of CAB observers. Open-rate situations have been predicted as the consequence of governments' participation in the bargaining. In this instance, however, IATA bargaining among carriers served to narrow and define the issues so that governments could effectively reach a solution.

OTHER IATA NEGOTIATIONS. Other IATA bargaining and rate agreement meetings have been less spectacular, and only scattered evidence is available on the proceedings. Groups of member carriers have occasionally agreed on a particular position outside the formal IATA framework. European carriers reached a consensus prior to the formal IATA discussion of tourist fares in 1952 and again prior to the Salzburg meetings in 1963. The African states organized themselves prior to the Rome meetings in October 1963, at which they made a political effort against South African Airways and Transportes Aéreos Portugueses.[15] Such prior agreements have probably facilitated the bargaining in that they help to define issues and positions quickly.

IATA proceedings on the whole are time-consuming, expensive, and ineffectual. The expense has kept some small carriers away and has often resulted in carriers leaving the meetings early. The Rome meeting in 1963 was largely wasted by the African effort to unseat South African Airways delegates from certain committees.[16] At Athens the following year, 300 delegates spent six weeks and about $750,000 in expenses to accomplish almost nothing. The in-flight movie controversy was debated and then shelved, nor was agreement reached on the question of baggage allowances. The CAB request for a 15 percent across-the-board fare cut in the Pacific was discussed, but no agreement resulted. Provisional fares have been in effect since 1962,[17] with

[14] Sir William P. Hildred, "1964 Annual Report of the Director General," *IATA Bulletin*, No. 32 (September 1964), pp. 68–70.
[15] Frank M. McGuire, "Inside Story of African Walkout and IATA Crisis," *American Aviation*, Vol. 27 (December 1963), pp. 54–60.
[16] *Ibid.*
[17] "What's New in Air Fares?" *New York Times*, November 29, 1964, Sec. XX, p. 1.

a fare agreement on Pacific traffic not reached by IATA until 1967.

The apparent trend for IATA proceedings to become more complicated and overburdened with a mass of detailed proposals is discouraging. However, most industry observers point beyond the formal proceedings to informal meetings of the top officials of a few airlines as the real fare-setting mechanism in IATA. There is surely no single or simple cure-all for IATA bargaining difficulties, in view of its task of resolving very diverse interests. A trade organization making pricing decisions in an industry of more than 100 firms with different cost and demand functions has at best a formidable task. In such a context, bargaining will always be a precarious affair.

The CAB and IATA Rate-Making

The Civil Aeronautics Board has long been one of IATA's harshest critics. The Board has labeled IATA an ineffective rate-making body at best, and a dangerous cartel harmful to the public welfare at worst. The IATA meeting at Athens in 1964 was disappointing to the CAB, since no Pacific rate reduction was obtained, and evoked comments not unlike those of the previous decade on the same subject. Alan S. Boyd, then CAB chairman, said:

From what we have learned so far, the Athens conference was a model of ineffectiveness.

It is of considerable concern to the CAB that so much high-priced talent has been tied up so long with virtually no results.

The onus rests no less on the United States than on the foreign flag carriers. The CAB is seriously concerned also with the U.S. carriers' apparent disregard of the Board's stated position and their failure to push this position by hard negotiations.[18]

In a speech to the International Aviation Club in Washington, Boyd said:

IATA is a very fine organization. It includes the best airlines in the world, and the worst. It has a fine staff of competent people. The only thing I have found they lack is persuasive power.

IATA and the Board have had a number of communications over the recent years, and we have said with honest sincerity that we do not want to see the demise of IATA. . . .

[18] *Ibid.*

We have been told from time to time that IATA is an absolutely essential organization, that there would be chaos without it, and at times IATA will not be able to reach agreement but that we should be patient because these things can be worked out. This is our hope and belief. . . .

IATA . . . should not live in a fool's paradise that the U.S. government or other governments of the world are going to sit on their hands while the membership of IATA spend their time in in-fighting without reaching any conclusions.

If they cannot do the work for which they were established, I think that the sovereign governments in the world can do it for them. Now we don't want to do it, and I'm sure I speak for most governments when I say this.

The U.S. government doesn't want to do it, but we are not going to have, for the burgeoning industry of international air travel, a situation where a group of some self-centered, selfish, short-sighted and narrow-minded air carrier representatives are unable to reach agreement on either basic or unimportant items.[19]

This criticism by the CAB is perhaps a little harsh. As noted earlier, the diversity of interests represented in IATA makes reconciliation a difficult job. More fundamentally, it is inconsistent to criticize IATA for operating as a private cartel, when in fact governments have not acted to supervise its rate-making.

On the other hand, the role that the CAB has played in IATA crisis periods has generated considerable criticism of the Board around the world. IATA officials accuse the CAB of excessive meddling or intervention in the orderly process of rate determination by the airlines themselves. Europe in general has looked upon IATA rate control as a great boon toward preserving order in the industry. A typical European editorial following the Chandler crisis charged the CAB with using "dangerously unilateral authority" over rates:

This particularly serious crisis came as a justification, in retrospect, for the stand taken by the U.K. in Bermuda in 1946. Although unable to organize Order in the Air in every respect, as defined in the U.K. thesis at Chicago, the U.K. at least secured, through the only contractual arrangements henceforth acceptable to States—under bilateralism—some measure of regulation in air transport competition . . .

. . . We have been obliged, then, to wait this long to appreciate fully the positive contribution made by the U.K. in the Bermuda compromise.[20]

[19] "CAB Chairman Takes a Firm Stand on IATA," *New York Times,* February 7, 1965, Section XX, p. 15.
[20] "Bilateralism in the Light of Recent International Air Transport Developments," *ITA Bulletin,* No. 35 (October 5, 1964), pp. 911–12.

This is an unfair criticism of the CAB and an unrealistic picture of IATA's role. The charge of government meddling is somewhat incongruous in view of the facts that IATA derives its rate-setting power through government acceptance, and approval of agreements lies with governments. The CAB rejection of IATA fares was no more a unilateral action than was the threat by European governments to seize aircraft unless IATA rates were followed.

The CAB has been labeled a "meddler" because its function of protecting the interests of the traveling public really does not exist in other nations' international aviation policies. The aeronautical authorities of other nations apparently have not defined the public interest in any larger sense than the interests of their own flag carriers. In addition, since most major flag carriers are chosen instruments, a close liaison is created between carrier and government. U.S. carriers are private firms, and therefore a conflict of interests can easily arise between the CAB and the carriers. The CAB as representative of the U.S. government is by no means bound to give rubber stamp approval to IATA fares. Nor is any other government so bound.

The Effectiveness of IATA Fare Controls

IATA fares have not been accepted by all of its members all of the time; some carriers on occasion have refused to abide by IATA rates in some areas. Also, IATA faces competition from a number of nonmember carriers, the best example being Icelandic in the North Atlantic. In Latin America, non-IATA carriers, which often charge one-third less for service on older equipment, account for perhaps a quarter of the market. IATA carriers have been known to discount as well, and hence a near open fare situation has often prevailed in Latin America.[21] The Middle East is another region where discounting has been prevalent; the problem has been especially serious since 1960, when a huge increase in capacity resulted from the replacement of Comet 4s by Boeing 707s.[22] Middle East Airlines has entered into a number of pools

[21] *International Air Transportation Rates,* Hearings before the Senate Committee on Commerce, 88 Cong. 1 sess. (1963), pp. 58–60.
[22] Eric Bramley, "Drive Is On To Wipe Out Rate Cuts," *Airlift,* Vol. 26 (October 1962), pp. 17–18.

with the express purpose of avoiding fare discounting brought on by excess capacity.[23]

Illegal Fare Discounts

The explanation for discounting or fare cutting is obvious. In marketing a commodity which cannot be stored and in a market in which everyone is supposedly maintaining a set price, the fare cutter is always rewarded. In addition, discounting is frequently difficult to trace or detect. One discounting device is to grant excess mileage or additional stopovers or to allow excess baggage. Another method is to use private ticket agents who later receive a rebate. Finally, in many parts of the world bargaining over a selling price is a natural procedure, unlike Western practice. Hence, IATA fare enforcement is difficult.

IATA has made an effort to curb these practices and has an annual enforcement budget of over $1 million. Conviction of discounting results in a fine, which may be as high as $15,000, but convictions have been only occasional. Judging from the complaints of carriers about unjust fines and about the manner in which IATA enforcement officials operate, the IATA price enforcement must be judged neither popular nor terribly successful. Sabena received a $15,000 fine in 1961 when an agent was found rebating tickets at the expense of his own commission. There have been many such complaints.[24]

In the period 1960-61, the excess capacity brought about by the switch to jets resulted in discounting almost everywhere. The subject was debated by IATA, and all carriers pledged to discontinue discounting—with little result. By 1963, the problem had largely vanished (except for Latin America and the Middle East), not as a result of the IATA effort but because of the growth in demand. Generally speaking, the international airline market is sufficiently dominated by IATA members that the IATA price can be maintained; the IATA carriers themselves have abided by the fare agreements reasonably well (except during the 1960–61 period).

[23] "Airline Profile: Middle East Airlines," *Flight International*, Vol. 85 (April 16, 1964), pp. 607–11.

[24] Robert Burkhardt, "Major Issues Threaten IATA Unity," *Airlift*, Vol. 25 (October 1961), pp. 16–17.

Problems Stemming from Product Definition

A consideration related to price control is product definition. IATA has made efforts to achieve agreement among carriers on a common definition of product, but with only limited success. The organization has been able to produce an enforceable agreement on the seating densities which define each class of service, but the subtler types of product change have been more elusive. Control by IATA agreement of such items as the expensive gifts of the early 1950s and lavish food service has required considerable discussion and debate.

The issue of in-flight movies has been equally difficult to resolve. The in-flight movies initiated by TWA in the North Atlantic have proved so popular that all carriers must offer them if a single one does. At the IATA meetings in October 1964, the in-flight movie question was debated but unresolved, since TWA was unwilling to discontinue movies. An accord was subsequently reached at a meeting of airline presidents in Paris; in-flight entertainment was banned, effective April 27, 1965, and payment of $600,000 was to be made by PAA and fifteen non-U.S. carriers to TWA for removal of its equipment.[25]

The issue remained settled only until the CAB reviewed the inflight entertainment resolution. One advisor to the CAB was the U.S. Justice Department, which pointed out that the ban was discriminating against the U.S. motion picture industry. That industry produced data showing that IATA had greatly overstated the extent of the cost increase due to the movies, hence had overstated the pressure to raise fares. In-flight Motion Pictures, Inc., provided its movies to TWA at a total cost of $1.06 per seat for the North Atlantic trip. Another company offered PAA a system of closed circuit television, radio, and stereo at $1.70 per seat. This is small in comparison to PAA costs on a North Atlantic flight for passenger food and other amenities.[26] After hearing complaints from the entertainment industry and evidence as to the costs involved, the CAB decided on June 1, 1965, to disallow the ban as

[25] *ITA Bulletin*, No. 22 (May 31, 1965), pp. 599–600.

[26] *Interavia Air Letter*, No. 5752 (May 20, 1965), p. 1, gives these figures:

Item	Per Atlantic Flight	Per Atlantic Passenger
Passenger commissions	$936	$12.50
Food and beverage	427	5.70
Advertising	683	9.10
Other costs	406	5.40

an agreement contrary to U.S. antitrust principles.[27] With the Paris agreement nullified, TWA has continued to show movies, and other carriers have prepared to add the necessary equipment.

The debate was renewed in October 1965 at Bermuda, again with no agreement. The airlines appear to have accepted the CAB disapproval of a ban on films, and the recent debate has centered on the appropriate surcharge (proposals from $2 to $10 per passenger), whether the surcharge should be paid only by those renting headsets, etc.

This dispute points again to the role of governments in the international airline market. The reasoning behind the CAB decision that the ban discriminates against the motion picture industry and is therefore contrary to U.S. antitrust principles should not be of major importance in resolving the issue. There have been other decisions made in the industry which are similarly discriminatory; for example, limiting food and beverage service discriminated against both U.S. and foreign food industries. The prohibiting of gifts such as toiletries, theater tickets, and luggage could also be regarded as discriminatory. The United States in this instance is acting under pressure from the motion picture industry and in the belief that the U.S. carriers will probably have a comparative advantage in this form of product competition. In addition, the additional cost seems small for what appears to many to be a considerable product improvement. The outcome of the dispute depends upon how firm a stand the respective governments and airlines are willing to take, just as resolution of other fare disputes has come to this.

The Structure of Fares

The IATA rate-setting process has produced a fare structure which deviates in a number of ways from marginal cost pricing. The fare structure constitutes a value-of-service pricing system with a considerable degree of cross-subsidization. Generally, economy-class travelers on the high-density long-haul routes in the off-season are paying excessive prices. Pricing decisions have been somewhat attentive to the elasticity of demand and the availability of surface competition. The more elastic the demand, presumably in cases where substitutes are available and tourist travel is important, the lower should be the expected fare.

[27] "CAB Rejects IATA Entertainment Ban," *Interavia Air Letter,* No. 5760 (June 2, 1965), p. 1.

Fare Levels for Various Classes of Service

The cost ratio of first class to economy service has been shown to be about 1.40 to 1 (see page 101 and Table V-2), the comparative values determined in large part by the differences in seating density. Demand at present for the two classes indicates that in many markets first class service is being subsidized by economy service. Though price differences between the two classes are often large, and generally larger than the ratio of costs, load factors in many instances have been so low in first class that average revenue for this service does not cover costs.

The airlines have several choices—and unfortunately have often made the wrong one. Increasing the fare differential to increase first class revenues has been one tack,[28] on the assumption of inelastic demand for first class service. This has generally produced a switch to the economy class, as for example in the North Atlantic. Reducing the fare difference appears a more reasonable procedure. Another possibility when first class average seat revenues fall short of costs is to lower first class capacity. The difficulty here is that altering seating configurations in existing equipment often presents a problem. Consequently, first class service must be reduced by offering it on selected flights, perhaps every other flight. This may so reduce the scheduling convenience that demand is discouraged and switching to economy service is induced.

In many markets even small price differences (ratios of 1.2/1 or 1.3/1) will not yield first class revenues which cover costs. This has been true for many short hops where first class service has been abandoned (or should have been). African carriers have quite properly gone to economy service only on many of the short hauls. On the other hand, European carriers continue to maintain mixed service on even the shortest trips, with very low load factors on many first class flights.

Improvements could be made that would rationalize the classes of service offered and their prices. Experiments with varying service levels and prices should be encouraged. The airlines have gradually raised their seating densities with no adverse effect on demand. To the extent that seating density is the fundamental determinant of cost levels, the

[28] G. Desmas, "Air Transport Passenger Fares," *ITA Studies 62/63* (Paris: Institut du Transport Aérien, 1962), pp. 57–62.

important question airlines need to ask is what price various classes of travelers will pay for different seating densities. In the past, consumers have shown a preference for lower-priced, higher-density seating. The use of 190 seats on the big jets is a service which warrants trial, particularly on important tourist routes. Parenthetically, price differences between classes should closely approximate service differences. Often in the past, excessively high-priced services have lost their market. The switch from first class to economy is one case in point. Another is the failure of tourist service in the North Atlantic after the economy class was introduced.

The major barrier to improvement in the variety of service offered is the competitive advantage which some carriers have in service competition. The high labor costs of first class service are a disadvantage to the United States and Canada and to a lesser extent to some European carriers with relatively high labor costs. The many carriers with a competitive advantage in service competition, however, prevent the introduction of new classes of service at lower prices. Similarly, other steps at rationalizing fares with respect to stage length or route density, for example, tend to founder on a conflict with some nation's interest in the status quo.

Relationship of Fares to Stage Length

A second consideration of fare structure is the relationship of fares to stage lengths. Rational pricing requires a reduction in price as stage length increases, consistent with the reduction in costs. In many areas, international airline fares are nearly constant irrespective of distance. Value-of-service considerations often explain this pricing; only where other competition is important, have air fares come down. Generally the long-haul routes face little competition from surface travel and are traveled by people able to pay high prices; hence fares exceed costs.

An examination was made of a sample of fares as related to distance, in major city-pair markets as of April 1, 1964. The general failure to conform with costs was striking.[29] Intra-African fares appeared most closely to approximate the cost changes with stage length. Intra-European fares showed some tendency toward lower per-mile rates as stage length increased. The fares through the Middle East and Asia, and in

[29] Mahlon R. Straszheim, "Efficiency in the International Airline Industry" (Ph.D. thesis, Harvard University, 1965).

the Far East and Pacific, showed little, if any, reduction. Latin American fares are quite heterogeneous. Since there is little evidence of a correlation of load factors with stage length, the consequence of this fare structure is a subsidy from long-haul to short-haul travelers.

The level and structure of fares in particular regions is also of interest. The North Atlantic is the most important international air market and has enjoyed the most competition and marketing innovation. Fares of about six cents per seat-mile are considerably below the long-haul fares in the Pacific and throughout the Middle East and Far East. Excursion and charter fares were first introduced in the North Atlantic and represent a larger percentage reduction from standard fares in this market than in any other important market. Still, fares remain above those of transcontinental flights in the United States. North Atlantic fares also exhibit a rising per-mile rate as stage length increases; for example, the New York to Rome fare is higher on a per mile basis than the New York to London fare. The most important explanation of this lies in the stopover privileges in Europe which are allowed on tickets from departures in North America to interior points in Europe. Since ticket prices generally have not differentiated between non-stop and stopping travelers (within broad agreed limits as to route circuitry), and since these stopover privileges sharply increase costs, a rising per-mile price is quite rational. The fare increases on a per-mile basis are not, however, sufficient to offset the cost increases of these stopover privileges, and hence this portion of the trip is subsidized. European governments apparently have implicitly agreed to spread the tourist travel around Europe by this subsidization scheme. Presumably the interior nations have represented the strongest lobby in favor of this scheme, especially in the past when direct service to interim points was less economically feasible, given the demands and the available equipment.

The most interesting feature of the fare structure in Europe is the much higher level of fares from Scandinavia to Europe and to the Middle East, relative to fares on the continent. The lack of good surface substitutes on routes departing from Scandinavia and the preponderance of business travelers have kept Scandinavian fares high. Much Scandinavian traffic is now using the inclusive tour charters. Such price discrimination because of the absence of surface competition is to be expected. European fares are generally quite high—considerably above those of U.S. domestic flights of comparable length. The explanation probably lies in the pool arrangements and in the overall absence of marketing innovation. Because of surface competition by rail, European carriers have argued that raising short-haul air fares in Europe would result in loss of traffic to the rails. The air network for very short hops in Europe may well be overextended; on the other hand, considerable reduction in fares on the medium- and longer-haul routes would be in order. Fares in Europe and in the Middle East are above those of Africa and Latin America.

Fares in the Pacific are quite high. The airlines have presumably kept fares high because profits are high and demand is less price elastic because of the high income of long-distance travelers. Also, with the exception of PAA, the other major carriers in the Pacific (Northwest, Qantas, and Japan Air Lines) might not be able to raise capacity easily if fare cuts sharply increased demand.

Fare Structure and Route Density

A final feature of the fare structure concerns route density. Traffic density data by city-pairs are not readily available. The cross-section sample used in the demand estimation is one source; this sample of passenger travel in fifty city-pairs to and from Paris during September 1962, classified by both stage length and number of passengers, showed no relationship between fares and route density. The sample suggests that the IATA fare structure is irrational, since prices do not reflect the lower costs accompanying increased density.

This fare structure has produced considerable geographical cross-subsidization. The North Atlantic has historically been the industry's most profitable route, but it has now been far surpassed by the Pacific. Those carriers fortunate enough to be in this market are earning returns of about 25 percent (see Chapter IX). Most airlines have been in favor of this cross-subsidization via fare structure, because the profits from dense long-haul routes can be used to finance losing operations which have political motivations. Such an internal subsidization through price discrimination has existed in other modes of transportation. The internal subsidization through the IATA pricing structure has also produced a considerable income transfer among nations. The United States and U.S. travelers have paid a substantial subsidy in this form for some time, especially in the Atlantic and more recently in the Pacific.

Summary

The IATA fare structure does not conform to rational pricing, but rather is a complicated value-of-service scheme, resulting from the political process by which fares are established. This is part of the price being paid for an industry structure in which political processes are substituted for competitive ones. Neither IATA as a rate-making body nor its administrative procedures should be held primarily accountable. The most important economic failing—the level of fares—would probably not be much better under any alternative political fare-setting arrangement. As long as countries with an interest in irrational pricing retain their influence, and as long as governments are content to permit IATA (or any alternative conference procedure) to set prices in cartel fashion, the structure of prices as described above must be considered a likely outcome. The long-run achievement of more rational pricing must lie in altering the motives of IATA participants and in including more competitive influences.

CHAPTER VIII

Economic Efficiency

THIS CHAPTER FORMALLY DEVELOPS the concept of economic efficiency. The specification of an economically efficient or rational industry configuration includes both a description of an efficient pattern of entry and criteria for rational capacity and pricing decisions in any city-pair market. In the following chapter, industry performance is evaluated on this basis.

Static Economic Efficiency in an International Trade Model

Efficiency in an international industry cannot be defined without recourse to an international trade model and the Law of Comparative Advantage. Static economic efficiency in such a model is defined in terms of a pattern of production in all sectors which follows comparative advantage, derived from differences in relative opportunity costs or internal marginal rates of transformation. "Efficiency" of a particular industry in such a general trade model context can be defined as that entry pattern which is optimal in view of production and trade in all other sectors. Since an efficient industry configuration depends on the opportunity cost of each nation's resources—that is, the alternative goods sacrificed—its determination is a complex general equilibrium problem.

By making some specific assumptions about the nature of world trade and world markets, this general trade model context can be simplified so that statements can be more easily made about efficiency in one sector. The first assumption is that money costs reflect real alternative costs in each country. If factor markets are perfect and all factors completely mobile, the price of a factor equals the value of its marginal product in each of its uses, and goods of least cost (in monetary terms) are therefore those which use the least amount of real resources. Second, the price of each product must equal its marginal costs in each country. Third, nations must produce those goods in which they have a lower money cost. The third assumption implies that consumers buy the good from the cheapest source (neglecting transport costs), that all product markets are perfect, and that foreign exchange is available to firms and households at the same rates.

These assumptions simplify the determination of comparative advantage since they imply that production of any good by the least-cost nation will produce an efficient result. If money costs in each nation reflect real opportunity costs and also determine the pattern of production, monetary cost comparisons indicate which nation should produce any particular good. No good of greater comparative advantage can be passed by in favor of one with less. Inferences as to industry efficiency can be made from intra-industry cross-section cost comparisons.

These assumptions—for example, that of no trade or exchange restrictions—are of course only approximated in the real world. Varying sorts of market imperfections in both product and factor markets are rather widespread throughout most economies. Price may be near to or far from long-run marginal costs. Optimization in any one sector should take account of these market imperfections. The problem of optimization in view of one or more constraints arising from market imperfections belongs to the general class aptly labeled "second best" problems. Finding an optimal solution in these circumstances is considerably more complicated and requires much more information. Empirical descriptions of market imperfections are usually difficult; specification of production and utility functions is also necessary in this sort of analysis.[1] "Second best" solutions require inclusion of all market imperfections as constraints in the objective function. Solution also requires

[1] See R. K. Lancaster and R. G. Lipsey, "The General Theory of Second Best," *Review of Economic Studies,* Vol. 24 (December 1956), pp. 11–32; and M. McManus, "Comments on the General Theory of Second Best," *Review of Economic Studies,* Vol. 26 (June 1959), pp. 209–23.

knowledge of the cross partials of all production and utility functions.[2] Recourse here to a static model of economic efficiency based on perfect market assumptions is a simplification dictated largely by the difficulties of introducing market imperfections in a manner which is meaningful and can be empirically specified.

The degree to which the necessary assumptions are violated and the resulting implications for the model deserve attention. The first assumption required, if cost comparisons are to indicate comparative advantage, is that foreign exchange be freely traded and available at the exchange rate used. In actuality, foreign exchange availability is restricted, and multiple exchange rates (such as differences between market and official rates) sometimes exist. These pose conceptual problems in choosing the relevant rate for cost comparisons. Since the market rate is the one which most directly affects the distribution of production and trade, it is probably the most relevant.

The exchange rate used in the empirical analysis of international airline costs was that used by the International Air Transport Association (IATA), which serves as an important clearinghouse among the airlines. Carrier participation in the clearinghouse requires that its government fulfill certain guarantees of exchange rate stability. The rate that IATA uses is that one at which foreign exchange is available for foreign transactions, either on the free market or through the exchange authorities.[3] The IATA rate is the official rate only if the official rate is the same as the market rate. In cases of multiple exchange rates, IATA generally uses the rate at which most import and export transactions take place.[4] Given the importance of IATA clearinghouse transactions,

---

[2] Aside from the difficulty of assembling meaningful data, the problem becomes complicated very quickly. For an example of a "second best" model in a transport setting, see the discussion by Robert Mnookin in a manuscript in preparation by John R. Meyer and others on the economics of transport pricing and project evaluation. Mnookin considers a two-input, three-sector model, which includes a transport sector. The effects on welfare of imperfections in the markets are discussed, as well as policies which could be undertaken. Extending this simple model becomes cumbersome fairly quickly.

[3] In 1962 most nations maintained an official rate at which foreign exchange transactions took place. There were some exceptions. In Colombia, for example, the official rate was 9 pesos to the dollar, while the free market rate averaged 11.094 pesos to the dollar; the latter was used by IATA. In cases where devaluation occurred or where the exchange rate was allowed to change—Argentina, Brazil, Chile, Syria, and Colombia—IATA used the market rate or an average of rates before and after devaluation.

[4] For example, Brazil maintained especially high rates for petroleum imports

all carriers and governments have keen interest in seeing that IATA rates resemble the real cost of foreign exchange, and hence the IATA rate is a useful empirical approximation.[5]

A second question concerns trade restrictions. In addition to the multiple exchange practices mentioned above, there are import duties, licensing restrictions, and export subsidies. Trade is not conducted in accordance with money cost differences. The relevant question for present purposes is how this affects the determination of comparative advantage in producing airline service. Trade distortions may be such that selected nations should produce airline service even at an absolute cost disadvantage so that production will conform more closely to comparative advantage. The determination of which countries should produce airline service depends, of course, upon the source of the resources used.[6] Empirical determination of comparative advantage in these circumstances is very difficult. If all resources are earning domestically the same return at the margin, it is meaningless to speculate on the alternative which would be sacrificed if resources were switched into producing airline service. Students of international trade have made little progress in empirically assessing the effects of trade restrictions on resource allocation. Disentangling the effects of trade restrictions on the patterns of world production and trade is well beyond the scope of the present study; short of such an effort, money-cost comparisons are probably the best means of selecting efficient producers.

The assumption that factor prices reflect real costs was necessary so that money costs could represent real marginal opportunity costs. If, for example, capital inputs or certain skilled labor such as pilots are paid a factor income less than their opportunity cost, the real cost of producing airline service by that nation will be understated. Factor markets in the international airline industry were shown to be reason-

---

and low ones for cocoa bean and paste exports. IATA used the market rate at which other transactions occurred. In Venezuela, "essential" imports and exports occurred at official rates, while market rates were used for other transactions. IATA rates coincided with the latter.

[5] International Monetary Fund, *Fourteenth Annual Report on Exchange Restrictions, 1963.* The report describes exchange rates and trade restrictions. IATA rates appear in International Civil Aviation Organization, *Digest of Statistics,* various years.

[6] Resources must be drawn from an inefficient sector if a carrier which is at a cost disadvantage is to be selected to remain on the basis of comparative advantage.

ably competitive for the most part. Fuel, aircraft, and spare parts are purchased in competitive markets; thus input prices for these factors reflect real costs. Skilled labor may be paid less than its real cost in many less developed countries. Capital is the input with the greatest divergence between real and money cost, but since the operating cost comparisons do not include capital costs, they are probably satisfactory approximations to comparisons of real opportunity costs.

Ascertaining deviations in costs of other goods from their real costs is largely speculative given the present state of the art, especially with regard to many of the less developed countries. Skilled labor in the developing countries probably is paid less than its real costs in most other sectors as well as in the airline sector. No effort was made to assess these various imperfections. Rather, it was assumed that rationalizing the international airline industry in terms of specifying those carriers with lowest money cost and extending output to the point where price equals marginal cost would approximate an efficient outcome.

Optimal Entry, Pricing, and Capacity Decisions

The above discussion of efficiency can be interpreted explicitly for the international airlines industry in terms of three questions: Who should produce? How much capacity should be provided? How should it be priced?

Entry and the Role of Subsidy

The question of "who" should produce—the entry question—can be answered in terms of the Law of Comparative Advantage: the lowest-cost producers should provide the service. If choosing the lowest-cost producers assures an economically efficient pattern of entry, this immediately raises a question as to the proper role of subsidies. The lowest-cost criterion means that the common industry practice of subsidizing higher-cost carriers leads to an inefficient outcome.

One possible justification offered for subsidies is that subsidies are payments for external effects. The existence of these external benefits implies that output might properly be expanded beyond the point where price equals marginal cost, with the subsidy payment for losses regarded as an appropriate compensation because the market price does not reflect all of the marginal social benefits. However, the discussion of external effects of the industry in Chapter II indicated that industry participants seem to have greatly exaggerated the importance of these effects. The industry has, in fact, received a considerable subsidy in the form of public provision of much of the overhead capital and improvements in technology. Other industries of course could also produce a list of social or external benefits emanating from their product or service, most of which are unrewarded. Rewarding external effects in one industry and not in another is a questionable practice. It appears that expansion of this industry into nonprofitable operations cannot be justified on the basis of external effects alone.

Another customary rationale for subsidy is the "infant industry" argument. In its early developmental stage the entire industry needed operating subsidies, but this need has long since passed. This argument persists, however, in the claims that new carriers still require subsidy support.

Any assessment of this argument is somewhat complicated, and a number of questions are raised immediately: What amount of subsidy is reasonable to establish an additional firm in the industry? How close should a potential entrant's cost be to existing industry levels, and how quickly should they converge? Who should bear the subsidy costs of the new firms? If demand growth is less rapid than new entries, what are the costs of excess capacity versus the contraction of existing firms' capacity? Protagonists of subsidies for "infant carriers" have generally not offered answers to these questions.

The nature of the industry structure is such that strong practical arguments can be made against subsidies for "infant carriers." It is always politically difficult to remove subsidy commitments once they are initiated. Moreover, since the industry behaves as a cartel behind political barriers, the subsidized entry of new carriers would add to the difficulty of rationalizing the industry and would raise the total subsidy burden in the interim. Indeed, the fundamental premise that having more competitors is preferable to having fewer can be questioned, especially when the entrants are subsidized flag carriers generally supporting restrictionist policies. There is even considerable doubt whether new carriers really need subsidy support. A number of charter operators and smaller regional carriers have been initiated by private capital. Entrants with efficient managements can be profitable from the very beginning. Entry would be even easier if price controls were not so tight and more opportunity were given to serve charter markets. In short, there are neither strong conceptual nor strong practical arguments in support of subsidies as part of an efficient industry. The "who" decision should be answered by cost comparisons.

Interdependence of Pricing and Capacity

The airline market is a sum of many city-pair markets, and hence pricing and capacity criteria must be developed on a disaggregated basis. Airline demand is related to the capacity offered, with consumers willing to pay for the higher schedule frequencies associated with greater seating capacity. The relation of capacity to demand is complicated by the fact that airline demand exhibits random fluctuations and has significant seasonal and hourly peaks, especially in markets where business travel comprises a significant portion of the total. Consumers' valuations of the marginal benefits of additional capacity are affected by how that capacity will be scheduled, how the service is priced, and the load factor on previous capacity. High load factors mean that the probability of not being served on any given flight is increased; many travelers appear willing to pay substantial amounts to avoid this problem.

This interdependence of demand and supply functions is very important in making optimal pricing and capacity decisions. It exists in varying degrees in other industries as well. This interdependence implies that market clearing prices do not reflect all of the marginal social benefits of added capacity. If demand and supply functions are interdependent, solutions based on the concept that price equals marginal cost will not, in general, be optimal. The question of specifying the optimal capacity level is one of determining from market information the level of demand at each price, the relevant marginal social benefits, and the marginal cost of added capacity. In particular, the question is raised as to how consumers value the "convenience" and "service reliability" of empty seats.[7]

Figure VIII-1 illustrates the number of seats which will be de-

[7] The problem of ascertaining consumer preferences for more or less airline capacity versus more or less of all other goods can be straightforwardly solved in a utility maximization format which includes airline capacity as one of the arguments. The difficulty arises in attempting to infer marginal benefits from market information only, which is far less than the information needed to make an estimate of the marginal social benefit of added capacity. The latter will require some form of consumers' surplus measure of net benefits.

FIGURE VIII-1. *Airline Demand Related to Capacity Available, Average Revenue Curves Dependent on Pricing Policy*[a]

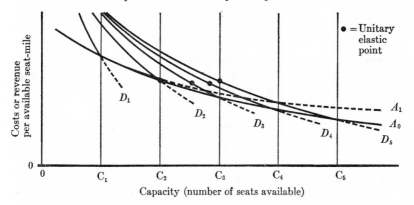

FIGURE VIII-2. *Long-Run Marginal Cost of Airline Capacity*

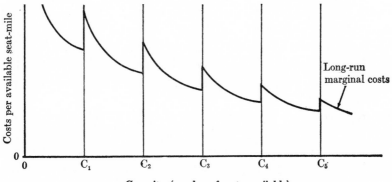

FIGURE VIII-3. *Long-Run Capacity Costs, Revenue Curves, and the Choice of a Capacity Level*[a]

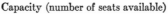
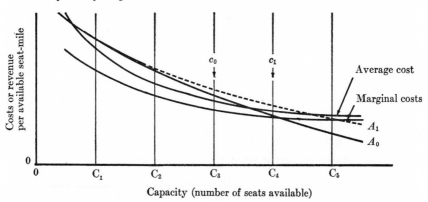

[a] Curve A_0 = average revenue per seat priced for full seat capacity; curve A_1 = average revenue per seat priced to maximize revenue; curves D_i = demand related to capacity available.

manded at various fares for a given level of capacity in any given city-pair market: $C_1, \ldots, C_5$ show increasing levels of capacity in the route (with C measured in available seats). The dotted portion in each demand curve represents fares at which all seats are occupied. A series of curves appears rather than one, reflecting the increased demand due to better schedules as capacity increases. As schedule frequencies increase, the demand shifts become much smaller.

Two pricing policies are also illustrated in Figure VIII-1. One is the set of prices which maximize use, represented by curve A_0, the average revenue per seat. The second, curve A_1, is that set of fares which maximize revenue for each level of capacity. Airline demand functions are such that pricing to achieve 100 percent load factors generally does not maximize average revenue per seat since the point of maximum use lies in the inelastic portion of each demand curve. By an appropriate price increase it is possible to raise average revenue and thus finance a greater level of capacity. The maximum revenue per seat for each level of capacity is given by pricing at the unitary elastic point on each demand curve. These points are denoted by dots in Figure VIII-1. The curve A_1 (fare $\times$ load factor) represents the maximum average revenue per seat.

Capacity costs are illustrated in Figure VIII-2. The marginal cost curve will be discontinuous, with the discontinuities occurring when another plane must be added to the schedule. The empirical cost analysis in Chapter V indicated that route density has important effects on costs, and, in particular, that marginal costs will decline as capacity increases. Marginal costs will therefore lie below average costs. The analysis below employs average costs in making pricing and capacity decisions. This is a deviation from customary welfare criteria, which are generally defined in terms of marginal cost pricing. Customarily, marginal cost pricing is recommended and "price neutral" lump sum transfers are then used so that revenues will cover costs. This solution is only formally correct. "Price neutral" transfers are not easily devised, and they are by no means costless. Moreover, most airlines, private or public, will be motivated by average cost considerations. In view of the conceptual and practical difficulties in strict marginal cost pricing, the criterion to be used here requires that revenues cover costs, and therefore average cost pricing is used.[8]

---

[8] The choice of an appropriate pricing standard is by no means clear-cut in many circumstances. For a discussion of alternative pricing procedures of trans-

PRICING TO ACHIEVE LOAD FACTORS OF 100 PERCENT. Two pricing decision rules and capacity levels are of particular importance. One employs the fare (after netting out passenger-carrying costs) that yields 100 percent load factors. The capacity level is chosen so that the receipts of another flight will not cover its marginal cost. This alternative is illustrated in Figure VIII-3, where c_0 denotes capacity level. Figure VIII-3 includes only a schematic representation of the discontinuous cost curves shown in Figure VIII-2. At point c_0 a few people would pay for added seats at the prevailing fare, but not enough to finance another flight.

This simple model was abstracted from stochastic or peaking demand. The stochastic element in demand is actually such that 100 percent load factors are not feasible. There are upper limits on realizable load factors, determined partly by the particular peaking or seasonal characteristics of the market and partly by the utilization of aircraft. With respect to the latter, load factors are inversely related to equipment utilization rates. As aircraft utilization rates are pushed higher, flight departures become increasingly less convenient, and hence load factors decline. Hourly peaking and seasonality characteristics of demand vary with the market. Short-haul markets with many business commuters, such as the Northeast Corridor shuttles in the United States, face an acute hourly peaking problem. In other markets seasonal and directional imbalances may have important effects on the level of load factors which can be achieved. Flights in the North Atlantic and Northern Europe to the Mediterranean exhibit considerable seasonal peaking. A very high load factor for scheduled service is 60 to 65 percent; beyond these levels, increasing numbers of travelers in peak hours or seasons are disappointed. (In the North Atlantic market, Icelandic Airlines maintains load factors of about 76 percent over the entire year, but this is achieved by turning away many people in the peak summer months.) While the present description of this model has defined the "maximum use" alternative as 100 percent load factors, this is an abstraction which should be interpreted as a "high" load factor—"high" defined in terms of the stochastic and peaking characteristics of the particular market.

---

port facilities and the implications for welfare, see the manuscript in preparation by John R. Meyer and others on the economics of transport pricing and project evaluation.

A PRICING POLICY MAXIMIZING AVERAGE REVENUE PER SEAT. The second important pricing alternative is one in which prices maximize average revenue per seat. As noted, airline demand functions are such that the revenue-maximizing price (the unitary elastic point on each particular demand curve) is higher than that at which consumers demand all of the capacity offered. Specifying a revenue-maximizing fare will therefore result in less than 100 percent load factors, with some travelers being rationed out of the market. Pricing to maximize revenue permits a larger level of capacity to be financed than pricing to maximize use. This is denoted in Figure VIII-3 by the point c_1. As long as the unitary elastic points on the demand curves are at a point where demand is such that load factors are less than 100 percent, it will be possible to finance more capacity by using revenue-maximizing pricing. There will thus exist a range of capacity levels where a single-price policy will cover costs.

The optimal capacity level depends on consumer preferences as to fares and schedule frequencies. The best choice between a price that maximizes use on a smaller capacity and a revenue-maximizing price which finances a larger capacity is not evident on a priori grounds. In particular, 50 percent load factors are not necessarily nonoptimal, although they are a frequent target of ridicule by skeptics of industry performance. In city-pairs where capacity is low, the additional welfare of improved schedules is probably large. In city-pair markets in which there are only a few flights a day (this includes most international routes) the added welfare of increased frequency probably warrants pricing at the unitary point in order to finance the largest capacity possible. From a dynamic viewpoint such pricing, which leads to improved schedules, may help create future demand. By contrast, in the markets with many departures per day (for example, some of the North Atlantic markets) the increase in welfare of additional capacity is probably small. Prices in these markets should probably be lowered below the unitary elastic point, increasing use but reducing average seat revenue and hence financing less capacity.

The above discussion has been developed on the basis of a single price. A price discrimination scheme, especially some form of off-peak pricing, has much in its favor. There are valid questions which can be raised regarding the welfare gains of price discrimination in one sector when the rest of the economy uses a single price. Nevertheless, some sort of price discrimination in the industry could be a useful way of reducing the costs of empty seats which are necessary for high schedule frequency and reliability. The stand-by half fare device is particularly attractive in this regard. The U.S. practice of giving servicemen available seats at one-half price has the important advantages of simple administration and difficult or unlikely ticket resale. The seasonal and directional price discrimination in the North Atlantic and the special rates during weekdays are useful and appropriate pricing schemes.

PRICING POLICY GIVEN THE CONTINUANCE OF SUBSIDIZED HIGH-COST CARRIERS. A final pricing question of a somewhat different order is posed by the prospect of continuing subsidies to inefficient carriers which will perpetually be high-cost firms. The question is: Whose marginal cost and break-even load factor should be the basis for price? A choice must be made between two basic alternatives. The industry has generally tended to set prices based on the marginal costs of the inefficient carriers. The result has been undesirable on all counts. High prices have resulted in lower demand; the break-even load factor for efficient carriers is reduced, leading to a tendency toward more empty seats and probably some additional incentive to bid costs up by service competition.

The alternative is to price at a lower level, based on the cost level of efficient firms; The break-even load factor would then be higher for all firms. (Passenger preferences are somewhat sensitive to realized load factors; if all other things are equal, higher load factors imply less likelihood of obtaining a seat on any given flight.) To the extent that inefficient carriers with the higher break-even load factors would have more difficulty realizing these higher levels, their losses would be relatively greater. Thus, maintaining prices at a low level, based on the costs of the more efficient firms, probably would put inefficient carriers under the greatest financial pressure. Their subsidy payments would be large relative to those of their competitors. The size of these costs could be a pressure toward exit from the market. In addition, lower fares and higher break-even load factors could tend to shift management attention more toward control over costs and away from costly service competition aimed at filling empty seats. Hence, while the commitment to subsidy produces an inefficient result, with distortions in both the "who" and the "how much" decisions, pricing based on the marginal costs of the efficient producers appears to be the best means of approximating an efficient outcome in these circumstances.

Capacity and Pricing Decisions in Various Possible Market Structures

In the subsequent examination of industry performance, it will not be necessary to formulate utility functions which differentiate in each market between the two alternative capacity and pricing policies of maximizing use versus maximizing schedule frequency. Maintaining IATA fares *above* the unitary elastic point is clearly non-optimal. Fares could be lowered to the unitary elastic point to the advantage of everyone, including the airlines. Only fare cuts *below* that point require a decision as to whether lower fares are desired at the expense of reduced average revenue and therefore of less capacity.

Application of the above model illustrates the likely character of pricing and capacity decisions in the various market structures which may exist. A monopolist would set the level of capacity and price at the point where the marginal change in average revenue per seat equals marginal cost. A revenue curve marginal to the A_1 curve would be the basis for the decision.

Competition, on the other hand, would result in price and capacity levels where average revenue per seat equals the marginal cost of additional capacity. In a market where prices are fixed but capacity adjustments are "competitive," each competitor would accept the prevailing price and load factors as given, and each would add (or reduce) capacity until realized load factors equaled the break-even load factor—that is, until prevailing average revenue just covered the marginal cost of capacity. Competitive adjustments of capacity to a given fare would therefore result in the largest capacity for which consumers would be willing to pay.

More generally, the fare (and hence the break-even load factor and the type of service) should also be regarded as variable. Some firms could be expected to compete by reducing fares, temporarily increasing their load factors until all other firms responded; a new equilibrium after that response would be reached at the point where average seat revenue equaled marginal cost, and where the break-even load factor would be higher if fares were reduced, and vice versa. The level of the equilibrium fare (or fares) and load factor will depend on the peaking characteristics of demand and the nature of the cost functions of competing carriers. The latter affect the extent to which carriers would choose to compete at lower fare levels, higher load factors, and a higher schedule frequency. With regard to fare levels, the demand characteristic most relevant to the outcome is the amount of business travel involved and hence the number of travelers who will pay for a higher-price, lower-load-factor type of service. In most markets a competitive equilibrium probably would require two fare levels. The most likely outcome would appear to be a basic fare for scheduled service at a load factor approximately that which prevails today and a charter type of service at much lower fares and higher load factors. This latter service would be for the occasional traveler, especially the tourist. Of course, there may be markets where there is insufficient demand to warrant any sort of special service at an especially low price and high load factor. The alternative of *all* service at a very high load factor seems unlikely, since most markets include a substantial number of people who value schedule frequency and the flexibility implied in being able to obtain a flight reservation for a departure time that is reasonably convenient.

Oligopoly market structures with few sellers (the expected environment in the airline industry) might produce prices close to or far from those of competitive markets and either capacity extreme discussed above. Restricting capacity jointly as a monopoly, either implicitly or explicitly by pooling agreement, is one possibility. There are other alternatives, depending on the preferences of passengers for each carrier and the assumptions that carriers make about the behavior of their competitors. One assumption is that the market share is divided in proportion to the capacity provided. Under these circumstances, and with no collusion, each carrier will add capacity until additional contemplated capacity cannot attract enough traffic from competitors to cover the costs of the added capacity. The resultant equilibrium situation would entail a capacity level above the break-even level reached by pure competition with many sellers. If some travelers have inherent preferences for particular carriers and will not switch in response to other carriers' schedule changes, the equilibrium load factor for such an oligopoly will be higher.

An alternative hypothesis is that large numbers of travelers use that airline with the greatest capacity because of its greater schedule convenience. In the extreme case where all travelers choose the carrier with the most capacity, the oligopoly may not be able to reach a stable equilibrium, and a single carrier could be expected to emerge as the winner of a "scheduling war."

An examination of capacity and pricing decisions in city-pair markets would reveal outcomes that variously conform with the above models. The smaller markets have elements of both sorts of oligopoly behavior outlined above. Where international travel is concerned, flag carriers of the two countries involved in a city-pair market probably have an important market share which they tend to divide according to their schedule frequencies if offered capacity is nearly the same. Otherwise, the market would be dominated primarily by one carrier if the other carrier chose not to match its competitor's schedule frequency. This explains why the two flag carriers at the origin and destination in many city-pairs often offer approximately equal service. This market will be somewhat secure from competition from third country flag carriers. In many such markets, of course, pooling agreements, explicit or implicit, have determined the capacity.

In larger markets able to support more carriers, the preferences of travelers for the flag carriers at origin and destination would be less significant for any single carrier in the market. All carriers would enjoy patronage by a few travelers who would prefer its service, but only carriers offering substantial capacity levels would earn a share of other traffic. If the relative schedule frequency of each is important only when each airline offers a fairly high absolute level of service, "scheduling competition" in the form of additional capacity would result, and the market as a whole would have a capacity level approaching a competitive one. This description seems illustrative of the North Atlantic market and many major city-pair markets where a number of carriers are present.

CHAPTER IX

Industry Performance

This chapter evaluates industry performance using economic efficiency as the criterion for judgment. Economic efficiency is important to the United States and to a few other countries, and it appears to be an objective which will assume increasing importance in policy decisions in the years ahead. The first part of the chapter uses the cost functions and the scheduling variables developed in Chapters IV and V to examine the cost performance of a sample of existing firms. The large cost variation which exists can be explained in part by differences in basic input scheduling. The second half of the chapter discusses performance of the industry in terms of judgments about pricing practices, product types, and investment standards.

Efficiency from a Static Comparative Advantage Viewpoint: Entry Considerations

Simple cost comparisons were shown in Chapter VIII to be sufficient to determine comparative advantage and thereby an efficient pattern of entry. The cost model developed in Chapter V can be useful in providing an approximate picture of the cost advantages and disadvantages which characterize existing entry.

The cost model provides an estimate of a firm's cost as a function of its route system, factor prices, and scheduling ability. If factor prices and scheduling are assigned values in the model equal to the industry average, the model describes costs solely as a function of the route system.[1] By inserting values describing each firm's route system into this equation, an estimate is provided of "expected costs" for each firm based only on its route system. Any differences in actual costs from these estimated "expected costs," representing average industry experience, reflect differences in factor prices, variation in input scheduling, and specification and estimation errors in the cost model. A negative residual indicates actual costs below those which would be expected of a typical firm with the same route structure.

The cost residuals for the 32-firm sample of carriers in 1962 appear in Table IX-1. The positive residuals of most long-haul carriers reveal one specification error, an overstatement of the cost advantages of longer stage lengths. Comparisons among firms of these residuals should therefore properly be confined to classifications by stage length.

Systematic effects of differences in relative factor prices or operating efficiency are important sources of "firm effects" giving rise to these residuals. Inadequate representation of the consequences of a firm's route system is another important source. There is some reason to expect that the former can partially explain the observed differences between actual firm costs and those predicted by the model; the model as an aggregation of equations for each cost component appears to be a good first approximation to route system effects. The cost residuals will therefore be interpreted below as at least partial evidence of "firm effects" on costs traceable to relative operating differences. Nevertheless, the underlying uncertainty involved in using the cost model in this manner must be noted. Making cost estimates for a particular firm is a step which places a considerably larger burden on the estimation process. There may be circumstances concerning a particular firm's route system which are not well represented in the cost functions, and the data describing each firm's operations are subject to error. In addition, the model was estimated only for the year 1962. The ensuing discussion of various firms' costs should be interpreted in the light of these limitations.

---

[1] This simplification of the cost model is as follows:

$$AC(\text{¢}/SM) = 0.6946 + 2.6751\ AC(d) - 502\ (1/d) + 0.00072\ (d) + 23{,}975{,}100$$
$$(n/SM) + 0.1599\ (K/SM) - 0.000102\ (h) - 0.108\ (d/h).$$

This equation yields an estimate of "expected costs" as a function only of route system.

TABLE IX-1. *Relative Operating Efficiency and Scheduling Abilities of International Air Carriers, by Stage Length, 1962*

Stage Length and Carrier	Cost Measure of Relative Efficiency	Flight Crew Scheduling		Capital Scheduling		Labor Scheduling	
		Crew Scheduling, S_c	Effect on Costs (cents per seat-mile)	Capital Scheduling, S_a	Effect on Depreciation Expense (cents per seat-mile)	Labor Scheduling, S_l	Effect on Labor Costs (cents per seat-mile)
	(1)	(2)	(3)	(4)	(5)	(6)	(7)
Stage length > 800 miles							
Trans World Airlines	0.026	0.994	−0.007	0.995	−0.002	1.248	0.324
Air-India	0.139	1.198	0.260	0.961	−0.021	1.181	0.112
Pan American Airways	0.234	0.942	−0.091	1.004	0.002	0.853	−0.195
British Overseas Airways Corporation	0.311	1.173	0.249	0.946	−0.029	1.123	0.114
Tasman Empire Airways	0.350	1.244	−0.335	0.771	−0.147	1.144	0.164
Pan American-Grace Airways	0.519	0.704	−0.378	1.055	0.035	0.809	−0.457
Air France	0.576	0.916	−0.141	1.030	0.017	0.783	−0.353
Thai International	0.602	0.950	−0.078	0.948	−0.028	0.814	−0.379
Qantas Empire Airways	0.890	1.441	0.614	1.170	0.121	1.467	0.354
Aerlinte Eireann	1.466	1.034	0.041	1.333	0.136	0.529	−0.385
Stage length: 500–800 miles							
Aden Airways	−2.632	0.715	−0.388	0.821	−0.092	0.911	−0.071
Canadian Pacific Airlines	−0.489	0.866	−0.242	0.875	−0.089	0.820	−0.174
Alitalia Airlines	0.104	0.909	−0.130	0.939	−0.031	0.664	−0.338
Japan Air Lines	0.199	0.830	−0.292	0.806	−0.124	0.561	−0.443
KLM Royal Dutch Airlines	0.815	1.530	0.811	1.057	0.041	1.375	0.374
Garuda Indonesian Airways	0.947	1.360	0.564	1.350	0.470	2.068	1.457
Stage length: 350–500 miles							
Royal Air Maroc	−1.389	0.810	−0.242	0.937	−0.030	0.492	−0.839
Iberia Airlines of Spain	−1.031	0.762	−0.348	1.251	0.094	0.655	−0.289
Air Canada	−0.936	0.581	−0.657	1.011	0.005	0.575	−0.994
South African Airways	−0.005	1.086	0.134	1.298	0.201	2.173	1.261
Sabena Belgian World Airlines	0.093	1.052	0.073	1.137	0.066	1.337	0.312
Swissair	0.500	1.189	0.269	1.012	0.007	1.212	0.214
Trans Royal Canadian Air Lines	0.546	0.951	−0.125	n.a.	—	0.750	0.140
Scandinavian Airlines System	0.872	1.397	0.560	1.008	0.004	1.262	0.241
Lufthansa German Airlines	1.077	0.741	−0.363	0.951	−0.030	1.089	0.096
Stage length < 350 miles							
Avianca Airlines	−1.389	0.673	−0.410	0.862	−0.030	0.930	0.045
Ethiopian Airlines	−1.230	1.040	0.054	0.782	−0.127	0.946	−0.158
Aer Lingus	−0.938	0.761	−0.299	0.982	−0.009	1.320	0.549
East African Airways	−0.859	0.910	−0.139	1.169	0.116	0.917	−0.077
Finnair	0.562	0.926	−0.119	0.976	−0.017	0.973	0.033
British European Airways	0.132	0.988	−0.025	1.200	0.164	1.109	0.152
Civil Air Transport (Formosa)	0.724	5.390	6.392	0.902	−0.049	0.911	−0.071

Sources: Figures in Cols. 1, 2, 4, and 6 are residuals generated by the cost model described on pp. 165–66. Figures in Cols. 3, 5, and 7 are derived from the model.
n.a. not available.

Relative Cost Position of Various Firms

The relative cost position of particular firms shows the big European carriers—British European Airways (BEA), Swissair, Royal Dutch Airline (KLM), and Scandinavian Airlines System (SAS)—ranking very low. (This relatively poor performance in terms of operating cost efficiency could well explain the financial difficulties experienced by these firms in recent years.) Of those carriers growing the most since World War II—Japan Air Lines, Alitalia, and Lufthansa—the first two seem relatively efficient, while Lufthansa still appears to be learning its lessons. BEA appears to be one of the highest-cost of all carriers serving short hops. The major U.S. and Canadian carriers—Pan American Airways (PAA), Trans World Airlines (TWA), Air Canada, and Canadian Pacific Airlines—rate high in terms of operating cost efficiency. (Later this is shown to be due to excellent scheduling.) Iberia and Avianca (because of low wages) also appear efficient in terms of operating costs.

Management quality and factor price differences are the two most important explanations of these cost differences, insofar as they represent "firm effects" rather than a mis-specification of route system effects. As indicated in Chapter IV, while the potential differences from factor prices appear substantial since factor prices vary so widely, in practice the cost differences are fairly small since high-wage firms have been better labor schedulers and have responded to relative factor price differences by altering their factor mix. What appears to be a major source of comparative advantage is largely mitigated and therefore fairly unimportant.

Cost Differences Due to Input Scheduling

The major explanation of the cost differences appears to lie in input scheduling. The measure of scheduling differences developed in Appendix A provides an indication of this effect on costs. The same qualification made above regarding the interpretation of cost differences applies to the quantitative interpretation of the effects of scheduling measures on costs. The scheduling measures are inherently more reliable in portraying an aggregated description of industry behavior than in describing particular firms. The scheduling measures were derived from average levels of input productivity in the industry; the extent of any firm's divergence from these standards depends on the accuracy and the relevance of this representation of that standard.

These qualifications aside, the scheduling measures do provide an explanation of some of the variation in the above cost differences. Table IX-1 reflects these scheduling differences and their expected effect on costs.[2] Aircraft scheduling is fairly closely correlated with relative cost differences for those carriers with stage lengths in excess of 800 miles. The numerical effect of scheduling on depreciation expense understates the total effects since utilization rates affect maintenance and insurance cost components as well. Flight crew scheduling is slightly correlated with the cost variance for carriers flying stage lengths averaging less than 800 miles. While the correlation of flight crew and labor scheduling with the cost differences is not close, these scheduling measures do suggest explanations for some of the firms with more extreme costs.

With some exceptions—for example, Japan Air Lines, Aerlinte, Aer Lingus, and Lufthansa—the cost effects of scheduling are fairly well correlated with the cost residuals in column (2). KLM, SAS, Swissair, and Qantas among the larger carriers all have excessive costs which can be explained largely by scheduling. A major rationale for labeling the cost residuals "comparative advantage" in the customary international trade sense thus lies in differing management abilities, presumably the underlying explanation of scheduling differences. The "comparative advantage" ranking in Table IX-1 is in effect an ordering which reflects how well carriers have been able to achieve certain levels of managerial skill in scheduling and in running the firm's operation. The difficulties which some of the major European carriers have had are noteworthy. It would appear possible for carriers of the less developed coun-

---

[2] S_c, S_a, and S_l are measures of flight crew, aircraft, and other labor scheduling derived in Appendix A. Values equal to one are average scheduling, while values greater than one indicate poor scheduling.

The cost impact of variations in crew scheduling is given by the effect on crew costs,

$$\left(\frac{S_c - 1}{S_c}\right) \cdot W_P \left(\frac{C}{SM}\right)_j,$$

plus the effect on total costs of S_c as indicated by its coefficient in the total cost equation, $\beta_p(S_a - 1)$. The effect of aircraft scheduling on capital consumption is given by

$$100[1 - S_a]\left(\frac{K}{SM}\right)_j.$$

The cost impact of labor scheduling is given by the residuals of actual labor costs per seat-mile from the labor requirements function,

$$\left(\frac{S_l - 1}{S_l}\right) \cdot W_L \cdot \left(\frac{L}{SM}\right)_j.$$

tries to achieve a satisfactory level of sophistication in managing their operation, as judged by the experience of Air-India and Avianca. Such favorable cases, however, appear to be the exception rather than the rule.

The above qualifications (about the significance of measuring a particular firm's costs or scheduling performance) aside, an important qualitative conclusion is evident. The industry includes a number of firms which provide service at a considerable cost disadvantage, and apparently at excessive cost levels. The variation in relative efficiency based on the cost model formulated is substantial. The "excess" seat-mile costs of this 1962 sample of 32 firms, as given by the sum of excess costs of firms with positive cost residuals, is 0.258 cent per available seat-mile, or 5.66 percent of total operating costs. Elimination of this excess could convert an industry which is just breaking even into one with reasonable profits. Profit-maximizing firms in a competitive market could not long exist with cost disadvantages of this magnitude.

Price and Product Dimensions of Industry Performance

The cost of inappropriate entry by inefficient carriers is no more important in an overall assessment of industry performance than a number of dimensions more dynamic in character. Industry pricing, about which little that is flattering can be said, is one such dimension. The International Air Transport Association (IATA) has maintained fares at such high levels that growth in demand has been delayed, as evidenced by the demand response to new classes of service at lower fares and the increase in demand when fares of established classes are reduced. The considerable price elasticity implies that fare cuts would raise average revenue. Fare reductions generally have had this effect. Though fare reductions appear valuable in developing markets, IATA has generally opposed pricing or marketing innovations. Until the 1964 fare cut, for example, North Atlantic fares had remained between 30 and 50 percent above transcontinental U.S. fares.

Effects of the Price Structure

The established high fares have also resulted in costly service competition and differentiation efforts. The level of passenger service, sales, and promotion expenses is much higher for international operations than for U.S. domestic operations. This premium on service has helped sustain many inefficient carriers, which often pay lower wages and thus have a comparative advantage in service competition.

The IATA fare level also has had effects on some of the problems associated with excess capacity. The present capacity problems in the Middle East, for example, might be quickly improved by a reduction of the very high fares prevalent in this region. To cite another example, when jets were phased in, fare reductions could have helped considerably in raising traffic to the new capacity levels. From 1958 until 1964, however, fare reductions were small. The large increases in capacity and accompanying financial requirements tended to make the airlines conservative in their pricing during this period. The possible benefits of a large fare reduction were by no means apparent to airline managements.

Pricing inflexibility has also had an indirect effect on capacity problems which have arisen in periods of re-equipment. Because of the absence of price competition, all carriers feel obliged to re-equip at once and in a very short time period (except when equipment restrictions are written into the bilateral agreements). This aggravates the peaking of capacity normally associated with new equipment. The shortened re-equipment period has also meant that low utilization, scheduling and maintenance problems, and other problems associated with the introduction of new equipment, have a proportionally greater cost impact than they would if the re-equipment process were more spread out. Thus, financial requirements weigh more heavily than they probably otherwise would.

More scope for price competition could somewhat alleviate these problem. Jets have both a cost and a marketing advantage in the long run over piston aircraft and hence are the superior equipment choice for most carriers. However, the ability to offer substantially lower fares on older equipment would provide firms which wanted to delay or spread out their equipment purchases an important option. Jet service was in fact sold at about a 10 percent surcharge in the North Atlantic until 1963 and still is today on Latin American routes. This price difference was insisted upon by smaller carriers which were not equipped with jets. The appropriate piston fare discount in view of the relative market demand for jet versus piston service, however, might have been much greater.

In addition, the internal subsidy via the fare structure has not only resulted in a transfer from travelers in the long-haul tourist markets to those in short-haul markets, but has also produced a subsidy which has benefited inefficient carriers. A number of inefficient carriers have managed to gain entry into profitable long-haul routes, particularly the North Atlantic. Aerlinte and KLM (neither is a model of efficiency) are examples of carriers which have earned a large share of their income in the North Atlantic. Efficient carriers of course have also profited from these markets, but presumably the inefficient have benefited more from the protection of internal subsidy.

Rate of Return on Investment

An efficient allocation of capital within a country requires that it be allocated to all industries so that each earns the same rate of return at the margin. Each industry should earn a return equal to the opportunity cost of capital, discounted for the appropriate degree of risk in the industry. The question of whether capital in the international airlines industry has earned its opportunity cost need not be concerned with a sophisticated determination as to what a "normal" rate of return would be for each country, since the industry has not earned anything approximating such normal rates. The operating results (operating revenues less expenses) for the industry are shown in Table IX-2.[3] The results do not connote a healthy rate of return, nor are they much improved by writing off the 1947–49 losses as a postwar learning experience. All International Civil Aviation Organization (ICAO) firms considered together earned 1.19 percent profit on operating revenues from 1950 to 1963 inclusive, 1.48 percent in 1962, 4.52 percent in 1963, 7.54 percent in 1964, and a preliminary estimate of 9.52 percent in 1965. With capital-output ratios slightly less than 1.0, the return on capital has been far below normal (1955–63, 1.2 percent; 1963, 1.9 percent; 1964, 9.1 percent, and 1965, 11.6 percent).

It is premature, however, to conclude that too much capital has been invested in the international airline industry relative to other industries. The rate of return is influenced by the cost level, which earlier was shown to be raised by product competition and also to be ineffec-

---

[3] The variety of forms of capital financing makes measurement of a rate of return on capital difficult. The customary use of long-term debt plus owner equity is treacherous. Profit rates on operating revenue are a much more reliable yardstick.

TABLE IX-2. *Aggregate Operating Revenue, Expense, and Profit of International Air Carriers, 1947–65*[a]

(In millions of dollars)

Year	Operating Revenue	Operating Expense	Net Profit
1947	1,044	1,158	−114
1948	1,324	1,397	− 73
1949	1,368	1,415	− 47
1950	1,521	1,501	20
1951	1,804	1,780	24
1952	2,050	2,063	− 13
1953	2,314	2,317	− 3
1954	2,560	2,528	32
1955	3,025	2,947	78
1956	3,510	3,426	84
1957	3,971	4,012	− 41
1958	4,122	4,107	15
1959	4,805	4,700	105
1960	5,400	5,358	42
1961	5,803	5,921	−118
1962	6,570	6,473	97
1963	7,215	6,889	326
1964	8,112	7,500	612
1965[b]	9,346	8,456	890

Source: International Civil Aviation Organization, *Digest of Statistics, Financial Data*, annual issues.
[a] Carriers reporting to International Civil Aviation Organization.
[b] Preliminary.

tive as a means of determining entry on the basis of efficiency. Profits are also reduced because of an irrational route system, which includes many politically-oriented routes, and by irrational pricing. The low rate of return therefore is not evidence of excessive investment, but rather is a result of investment by both efficient and inefficient operators and also of the general difficulties associated with rationalizing entry and pricing in a restricted market environment.

The welfare aspects of this low industry rate of return are not as dire as one might suppose. Failure to expand capacity as demand increased, plus inadequate modernization and product improvement, would be the expected outcome for an industry in these straits. However, the willingness of governments to subsidize their airlines has resulted in expansion as if profits were satisfactory; therefore the major consequence has been to create or to prolong a subsidy problem.

These industry data conceal considerable variation among individual firms. Table IX-3 presents data on the rate of return for a number of

TABLE IX-3. *Operating Revenue, Profit, and Rate of Profit of Selected International Air Carriers, 1957-64*
(Dollar amounts in millions)

Carrier	Operating Revenue			Profit			Profit Rate (percent)		
	1957-62	1963	1964	1957-62	1963	1964	1957-62	1963	1964
Aerolineas Argentinas	$ 98.435	n.a.	$ 24.478	$-39.381	n.a.	$-6.649	-40.01	n.a.	-27.16
Qantas Empire Airways	394.390	$ 94.650	110.935	17.809	$ 9.280	10.858	4.52	9.80	9.78
Cruzeiro (Brazil)	89.012	16.853	18.282	- 1.597	-2.915	-2.811	- 1.79	-17.27	-15.37
Sabena Belgian World Airlines	477.579	84.324	90.072	- 9.085	-1.006	0.303	- 1.90	- 1.19	0.33
Panair do Brasil	163.107	33.598	n.a.	-26.307	-3.588	n.a.	-16.13	-10.68	n.a.
Varig Airlines	175.351	45.561	49.305	- 5.466	-5.848	-2.598	- 3.12	-12.84	- 5.26
Canadian Pacific Airlines	210.754	52.099	57.251	-22.134	0.597	5.448	-10.50	1.15	9.55
Air Canada	852.145	184.466	n.a.	16.617	10.425	n.a.	1.95	5.65	n.a.
Civil Air Transport (Formosa)	37.417	8.655	8.728	- 0.020	0.002	-0.002	- 0.05	0.00	- 0.02
Ethiopian Airlines	50.013	13.829	16.811	6.809	-0.495	1.992	13.61	- 3.58	11.84
Finnair	65.800	24.060	22.205	1.981	1.110	-2.059	3.01	4.57	- 9.27
Karhumaki, Veljeksef	10.801	2.871	1.202	0.511	-0.139	-0.057	- 4.73	- 4.84	- 4.74
Air France	1436.569	333.655	298.320	-16.340	-4.411	6.161	- 1.14	- 1.32	2.06
Thai International	134.178	69.437	n.a.	1.873	4.728	n.a.	1.40	6.81	n.a.
Lufthansa German Airlines	430.477	142.530	172.450	-80.147	-0.808	5.965	-18.62	- 0.57	3.45
Air-India	205.005	56.029	62.695	11.723	8.030	7.558	5.72	14.33	12.05
Indian Airlines	161.284	40.499	n.a.	- 2.011	1.548	n.a.	- 1.25	3.82	n.a.
Garuda Indonesian Airways	98.947	15.048	32.344	11.913	2.200	5.754	12.04	14.62	17.79

Airline								
Aer Lingus	77.173	20.101	21.535	1.902	1.002	0.145	2.46	4.98	0.67
Aerlinte Eireann	40.790	16.390	19.650	− 2.254	2.400	3.308	− 5.53	14.64	16.83
Alitalia Airlines	419.140	152.390	174.368	14.270	8.300	7.073	3.40	5.45	4.05
Japan Air Lines	287.784	105.971	126.845	12.410	11.192	16.715	4.31	10.54	13.17
Middle East Airlines	84.202	27.579	30.792	− 1.132	2.326	2.234	− 1.34	8.44	7.25
Tasman Empire Airways	53.260	14.060	14.794	3.319	1.080	1.061	6.23	7.68	7.17
KLM Royal Dutch Airlines	849.050	152.720	168.652	−23.641	−11.540	2.912	− 2.78	− 7.56	1.72
Scandinavian Airlines System (SAS)	735.306	154.664	171.684	−12.845	9.172	17.238	− 1.75	5.93	10.04
South African Airways	184.001	43.507	147.362	12.295	8.368	4.394	6.68	19.23	2.98
Aviacion y Comercio	21.939	8.714	8.497	− 0.968	0.440	0.318	− 4.41	5.05	3.74
Iberia Airlines of Spain	162.150	60.955	79.687	8.061	6.329	7.123	4.97	10.38	8.93
Swissair	400.780	102.220	115.626	10.432	4.040	5.324	2.60	3.95	4.60
Tunis Air	19.394	5.148	5.225	0.687	0.767	0.705	3.54	14.94	13.49
Turk Hara Yollari	35.323	7.638	8.048	− 7.774	−2.757	−2.062	−22.01	−36.13	−25.62
British European Airways	722.840	167.420	183.757	34.663	16.460	11.665	4.80	9.83	6.34
British Overseas Airways Corporation (BOAC)	1288.810	293.250	322.575	8.324	23.200	46.894	0.65	7.91	14.53
Central African Airways	44.462	8.092	9.298	− 2.944	0.773	0.105	− 6.62	9.55	1.12
East African Airways	64.204	21.344	22.450	3.561	1.222	1.818	5.55	5.72	8.09

Sources: Annual reports of the airlines. Percentages are calculated from unrounded data.
n.a. Not available.

TABLE IX-4. *Operating Revenue and Profit of U.S. International Air Carriers, by Region of Operations, 1946–64*
(In thousands of dollars)

	Atlantic				Pacific				Latin America					
Year	Pan American Airways (Atlantic operations)		Trans World Airlines (all operations)		Northwest Airlines		Pan American Airways (Pacific operations)		Braniff International Airways		Pan American-Grace Airways		Pan American Airways (Latin American operations)	
	Revenue	Profit	Revenue	Profit	Revenue	Profit	Revenue	Profit	Revenue	Profit	Revenue	Profit	Revenue	Profit
1946	$30,335	$ -5,521	$16,860	$ -4,919	$ 720	$ 209	$ 7,350	$ -5,609			$10,888	$ -1,545	$54,351	$3,260
1947	52,081	-6,207	27,706	-3,550	4,543	-2,363	17,771	-6,080			12,746	-2,745	57,954	-520
1948	54,617	-8,147	31,633	-6,031	8,203	-2,382	24,313	-6,910	$ 566	$ -716	13,231	-1,572	55,055	-4,365
1949	56,345	-16,456	34,947	-2,614	8,611	-1,867	24,319	-7,484	2,439	-1,482	13,395	-1,225	53,276	-8,548
1950	54,322	-14,789	36,860	-1,965	10,956	-562	23,525	-5,309	3,779	-1,798	11,860	-1,408	54,350	-3,334
1951	53,470	-9,478	41,743	-1,217	13,863	-1,881	27,514	-2,060	5,696	-2,012	14,384	-100	59,281	-5,798
1952	62,640	-7,480	47,460	-45	14,931	-2,009	32,180	-3,880	7,092	-3,017	15,115	-615	61,129	-11,252
1953	67,316	-6,002	51,954	-492	14,239	-3,392	39,176	-2,048	7,060	-2,052	15,487	-608	62,741	-5,884
1954	78,127	-200	58,349	4,427	15,751	-1,833	47,601	333	7,251	-578	16,506	-632	65,438	-3,520
1955	98,734	7,206	60,820	1,526	21,312	-289	58,323	4,639	6,884	-877	17,921	849	72,769	-69
1956	120,474	10,482	65,842	-478	25,765	2,235	70,864	7,276	6,502	-161	20,004	1,587	83,434	-1,884
1957	133,156	11,996	67,164	505	28,938	4,994	79,197	5,524	8,003	115	20,157	718	93,855	-1,933
1958	142,985	6,258	75,056	-6,182	34,139	7,128	76,838	5,801	7,672	-521	18,463	-263	88,797	-4,549
1959	161,471	17,469	74,685	-7,815	38,822	5,220	91,324	5,557	8,065	-151	18,612	-794	98,129	-6,509
1960	186,367	16,593	100,958	17,096	35,986	937	117,729	18,672	10,799	-698	19,998	-997	101,460	-11,215
1961	208,384	4,468	83,271	-13,503	39,128	8,663	134,864	21,689	11,792	-1,134	22,821	454	109,673	-2,671
1962	227,489	12,489	102,118	15,270	49,902	11,068	146,740	30,965	9,895	-2,598	22,381	1,717	122,001	1,328
1963	257,750	33,272	133,088	23,352	58,973	15,483	162,815	38,815	10,987	-2,095	22,058	1,382	133,001	6,459
1964	275,996	26,150	155,361	34,625	71,604	24,258	175,867	34,993	13,648	71	22,761	1,469	144,835	3,886

Sources: Civil Aeronautics Board, *Handbook of Airline Statistics*, various issues; and International Civil Aviation Organization, *Digest of Statistics, Financial Data*, various issues.

carriers. The year 1964 was easily the most profitable up to that time, with many carriers reporting profits in excess of 5 percent; preliminary data for 1965 indicate even higher profits. The rate of return for an individual firm reflects both its route system and the efficiency with which it manages operations. There is a correlation between operating efficiency and the rate of return; carriers with inadequate rates of return generally are those which ranked low (see Table IX-1) in terms of comparative efficiency (for example, Aerlinte Eireann, Thai International, Air France, KLM, Lufthansa, SAS, Civil Air Transport, and Pan American-Grace Airways). There are some exceptions. A few carriers, although not efficient operators, earned reasonable profits because of a favorable system of long-haul routes, for example, Qantas, Japan Air Lines, and Garuda Indonesian Airways. There were also a few efficient carriers which lost money because of a poor route structure. The lowest rates of return have been experienced by a number of Latin American and European carriers with poor efficiency records.

Operating results for the major U.S. international carriers appear in Tables IX-4 and IX-5. From World War II until the middle of the 1950s, considerable losses were financed by government subsidy, an experience not unlike that of other nations' carriers during this period. Since 1956, U.S. carriers more closely resemble economic enterprises, although another period of losses was experienced when jets were introduced. At present the carriers are earning large profits, with the expectation of still higher profits over the next few years.

In the North Atlantic market, profits have been more than adequate since the middle 1950s. The Civil Aeronautics Board (CAB) has used this as a basis for its stand against higher fares; the rate of return in 1963 appears excessive and was, appropriately, the rationale for the CAB veto of the Chandler fares. The high profit rate in the Pacific— approximately 25 percent by PAA and Northwest in recent years— has invoked concern by the CAB over fares in this region. The Pacific has become especially lucrative as the longer-haul jets have made direct service feasible. The CAB has continually requested fare reductions, but has had little success. Fare reductions in these markets would have favorable consequences for carrier and traveler alike. Based on the assumption of high price elasticity, fare reductions from present levels should result in higher load factors and even greater profits. This is the effect of the 1964 fare reductions in the Atlantic.

The Latin American market, by contrast, is notorious because of con-

TABLE IX-5. *Operating Profit as Percentage of Revenue, U.S. International Air Carriers, 1956–64*

Carrier	Profit as Percentage of Revenue		
	1956–62	1963	1964
Trans World Airlines	0.86	17.55	22.28
Pan American Airways (total operations)	7.81	14.19	10.89
Atlantic operations	6.75	12.91	9.48
Pacific operations	13.31	23.82	19.89
Latin American operations	−3.92	4.89	2.68
Northwest Airlines	15.90	26.17	33.88
Braniff International	−8.21	−19.01	0.51
Pan American-Grace Airways	1.67	6.25	6.45

Sources: Civil Aeronautics Board, *Handbook of Airline Statistics*, various issues; and International Civil Aviation Organization, *Digest of Statistics, Financial Data*, various issues.

tinual losses. (See Tables IX-4 and IX-5.) The large European carriers and the local operators in this region have incurred losses comparable to those of U.S. carriers. Excessive capacity levels relative to the level and growth of income on the continent are a partial explanation. Lowering fares might produce some improvement, but the biggest boost probably would come from a relaxation of the many restrictions imposed on equipment and departure times. These restrictions have hampered rational development.

The Product Defined by Present Costs

The extent of entry and the level of capacity are important dimensions of product definition. While entry rights have been closely guarded, the industry does not suffer from inadequate capacity. The network of international air service has expanded rapidly—certainly as rapidly as market demand would suggest that economic operations can be conducted.

EFFECTS OF PRICING ON CAPACITY AND SCHEDULING. The level of service in particular markets has been affected by IATA rate regulations. In a fixed-price situation, maximizing schedule frequency is the best competitive means a firm has of assuring its present and future market share. This is an important motivation in view of the rapid growth in

Table IX-6. *Capacity, Costs, and Fares, All Scheduled Airlines, 1947–63*

Year	Tonne-kilometers Performed (millions)	Tonne-kilometers Available (millions)	Weight Load Factor (percent)	Cost (cents per tonne-kilometer available)[a]	Fare (cents per tonne-kilometer performed)[a]
1947	2,133	3,652	58.4	28.6	49.0
1948	2,509	4,552	55.1	29.1	52.8
1949	2,908	5,239	55.1	26.1	47.1
1950	3,544	6,006	59.0	25.3	42.9
1951	4,407	7,051	62.5	25.6	40.9
1952	4,922	8,109	60.7	25.3	41.6
1953	5,575	9,353	59.6	24.7	41.5
1954	6,278	10,525	59.2	24.3	41.1
1955	7,365	12,460	59.1	24.3	41.1
1956	8,568	14,267	58.1	24.6	41.0
1957	9,813	17,042	57.6	23.3	40.5
1958	10,203	17,816	57.3	23.1	40.4
1959	11,733	20,251	57.9	23.7	41.0
1960	13,062	23,373	55.7	23.1	41.3
1961	14,550	27,668	52.6	21.0	39.9
1962	16,776	32,034	52.4	20.5	39.2
1963	18,409	35,625	51.7	20.3	39.2

Source: International Civil Aviation Organization, *Digest of Statistics, Financial Data*, No. 115 (1964), p. 26.
[a] Average.

demand. Schedule competition in many city-pairs has driven load factors down to about 50 percent (see Table IX-6). Consumers have therefore been forced to take the cost reductions of new technology largely in this form, although specific markets have experienced some fare reductions. (In most noncompetitive city-pair markets, either pooling or capacity and schedule restrictions in the bilateral agreements have kept load factors higher.) Schedules appear, in general, to be convenient enough at present capacity levels that most consumers would probably prefer fare cuts if additional cost-reducing technology were introduced, and probably even if the fare reductions meant that capacity would be somewhat reduced.

The low profit rates of the industry periodically produce concern about excess capacity, and many industry spokesmen have argued in favor of capacity controls. The analysis here suggests that this problem has been far overemphasized. Efficiently run jet operations will cover costs if demand at the present level of fares yields a 50 percent load factor, and so will piston operations if the load factor is about 60 percent. (The exact figures depend on the stage length and density of the route in question.) The early 1960s was a period of some excess capacity since the added jet capacity pushed load factors down to 50 percent —below the level which would have covered costs of the mixed jet and piston fleets in operation at that time. However, fare reductions would have done much to offset this. Moreover, the effect on costs of increases in capacity was slight when compared to the effects resulting from the phasing in of new equipment and from learning how to use it. Aside from these few years, the industry should have earned an adequate rate of return on the capacity it has provided since 1950. Capacity levels are certainly not excessive at present, nor would they even appear so if IATA fares were not in the elastic range of the demand curve. In short, even the entry stimulus of external effects has not produced any significant capacity problems.

NEW TECHNOLOGY AND COSTS. A second important consideration of product definition concerns the nature of equipment used. The evolution of aircraft technology and its use in commercial aviation has been rapid, persistent, and always well received. The airline industry in the past received many of its technological improvements through government-financed research for military equipment, especially the development of four-engine aircraft during World War II and, in the next decade, the development of jet aircraft.

The incorporation of the various new technologies into successive commercial aircraft models has occurred rapidly. The importance of new equipment as a part of competitive strategy has been dominant in this decision-making. Often relatively small changes in design speed have proved very important in airlines' equipment choices. Much of this pressure for new equipment has arisen from the North Atlantic market. The advancement in equipment technology has been oriented toward development of long-haul luxury aircraft; application of this technology to shorter stage lengths has occurred only very recently. The IATA pricing regulation has been important in channeling aircraft technology in this direction.

The airline consumer has borne only a portion of the cost of this rapid advance. While the basic development costs involved in piston and jet technology have been government-financed, the cost of developing this technology into successive commercial aircraft models has been shared by many. Rapid rates of depreciation permitted by tax authorities have imposed some portion of aircraft development costs on the public. Successive piston models displaced by new equipment in the 1950s were sold for capital gains to U.S. local service and smaller trunklines; this represents a portion of the costs of the change in technology shared by trunkline and local-service travelers, and also by U.S. taxpayers in the form of subsidy support of local-service operations. The trunklines themselves have paid some portion of the costs, particularly for the last set of piston planes sold in the late 1950s. Finally, the aircraft manufacturers have paid some of the cost through low profits or bankruptcies.

Determining the rate at which travelers desire development of new equipment is very difficult. If more pricing flexibility were permitted in marketing older equipment, the demands of the traveling public for the latest technology might not be so strong as at present. Increasing tourist travel by people who are more price-conscious could reinforce this effect. The supersonic transport, of course, presents this problem in particularly acute form. The development costs and risks are far beyond the ability of commercial interests to assume, and public officials are faced with determining among other things how much people will pay for this technology. The U.S. government appears prepared to assume the initial development costs of about $5 million per plane; and while the economic future of supersonic aircraft is most uncertain at present, it is not beyond reason to expect this sort of development cost to be marketable in the future.

RESPONSIVENESS OF INDUSTRY TO CONSUMER PREFERENCES. A final consideration of product definition concerns the variety of the product. Although product competition has been considerable, consumers' preferences in product quality and in variety of services offered have not been heeded in many respects. The success of charter operations, special excursion and group fares, and Icelandic's cheaper propeller service is evidence that some consumers would prefer fare reductions and a more austere service. The success of higher-density seating classes adds to this evidence. Consumers are fairly begging for this sort of product change, which IATA and much of the industry have been reluctant to implement.

Summary

The economic performance of the industry has been mixed. Many of the weaknesses in the performance, however, are more apparent to the economist than to the traveling public. The willingness of governments to subsidize has produced a wide network of air service with high safety standards and reasonably convenient schedules. Air travelers have been forced to pay a somewhat higher price than would be necessary if the industry were rationalized, but most of the cost of the inefficiency has been paid for by general taxation via subsidies. The subsidies permit the widespread variation in operating efficiency noted above. More generally, the desire of governments to further the short-run interests of their carriers, even at the cost of entry restrictions and uneconomic pricing, has largely eliminated many competitive pressures toward rationality and has produced the performance described here.

CHAPTER X

The Relationship of Structure to Performance

THE THEORY OF INDUSTRIAL ORGANIZATION has suggested a number of relationships whereby industry structure, defined to include both technology and the regulatory environment, has an impact on performance. These relationships in the international airline industry have been described above.

There are several directions in which industry structure might be altered, with a variety of implications for industry performance. Less reliance on competition and more on the regulatory environment is one possibility. The development and implementation of additional political processes for making decisions on entry, capacity, pricing, etc., in the industry would, however, be a considerable task. Questions of administrative ease and effectiveness would be important in evaluating any such proposed change. More reliance on regulation would place additional burdens on regulatory processes and institutions, which already appear overtaxed. It would probably be difficult to institute additional nonmarket processes for decision-making, in an industry as complex and rapidly changing as this one, which would not produce further inflexibilities and rigidities in the industry's response to changing market conditions.

Conversely, more reliance could be placed on competition and the market place. The important issues are twofold: How will the oligopoly market structures which necessarily prevail in airline markets perform? Can state interests be suppressed sufficiently to make a more competitive market feasible? This chapter will argue that competitive airline markets would perform well. Unfortunately the political realities of vested national interests reduce considerably the number of structural changes in the market which are politically feasible. Apparently the industry must take on some form of limited competition.

This chapter will consider the expected performances of a variety of market structures, some more competitive and some more restrictive than the prevailing arrangement. The market structure which appears at present to be most feasible and efficacious is one in which as much pricing and marketing flexibility as possible is encouraged in an environment of regulated entry.

Open Competition

An environment of open competition has been suggested frequently and from a number of quarters, and the effects have been assessed variously as favorable or unfavorable. Unfortunately, the economic assessments have left something to be desired. Caves's analysis of the U.S. domestic airline industry[1] and possible de-regulation is the best starting point for considering a competitive model for the international industry.

Caves's Recommendations for U.S. Domestic Industry

The usual prediction for competitive airline markets is that cut-throat competitive behavior would result in sharply reduced public service. De-regulation in the U.S. domestic industry would ostensibly lead to a huge scramble for the profitable city-pairs now being served and to extreme instability in the form of scheduled capacity and prices. Safety concessions might also be made in the course of the competition. The eventual consequence would be virtual monopoly by the victorious firms.

Caves has effectively refuted this argument by pointing out that there is no economic reason for expecting such a reaction. Scale economies are not large, entry into and exit from both the industry and individual

[1] Richard E. Caves, *Air Transport and Its Regulators* (Harvard University Press, 1962).

markets are relatively easy, capital-output ratios are low, most costs are variable, and there is some opportunity for product competition. All of these conditions are inconsistent with predatory price cutting that would drive out competitors and create a monopoly position. Caves suggests that de-regulation of the major city-pairs (of sufficient demand to sustain more than one carrier) would have favorable results. It would enable firms to shift capacity and enter markets so as to rationalize their route system in terms of service with their available equipment. He suggests that some city-pair markets would be served both by large trunklines offering through service and by specialist firms with equipment suited to the particular turn-around service. Ease of entry and the appearance of specialist firms would help to reduce the recognized interdependence and the resultant parallel action that somewhat restrains competition in the present industry; therefore increased product and market innovation would probably occur. Caves concludes that there is no reason to believe that either a sporadic or an excess level of capacity would be provided, with capacity decisions resulting in losses in the major markets and high profits in all smaller markets; nor, he concludes, is there reason to believe that excessive investment in new capacity would be made. Rather, the additional marketing competition and flexibility should improve the performance of the markets.[2]

Arguments Against Open Competition in the International Industry

A not dissimilar dialogue has taken place among analysts of the international industry. Wheatcroft[3] has presented the latest and most succinct version of the arguments advocating the necessity and desirability of regulation. Wheatcroft observes that some of the benefits accruing to a country from national airline service—national defense, prestige, stimulus to the country's domestic aircraft industry, and contribution to social overhead capital—are external effects. Private decision-making processes, therefore, may not lead to an optimum decision. Wheatcroft argues further that the "natural economic characteristics" are such that unregulated airline markets will not achieve desired policy objectives. The size of markets is such that oligopoly necessarily ex-

[2] *Ibid.*, pp. 378–87, 447–48.
[3] Stephen Wheatcroft, *Air Transport Policy* (London: Michael Joseph, Ltd., 1964), pp. 46–65.

ists, and it is an oligopoly which will not reach a stable equilibrium. The absence of scale economies and the inability of any existing airline to differentiate its product mean that there are no significant economic barriers to entry.[4] This inability to compete on the basis of product plus the ease of entry means to Wheatcroft that price competition by both existing firms and new entrants would be severe; disastrous price wars would be a likely outcome.

In the absence of these barriers to new entry it is unlikely that an un-regulated air transport industry would achieve the stable equilibrium that has been attained in other oligopolistic industries. It is much more likely that there will always be newcomers who, in order to establish themselves in a new market, will offer lower rates than those of the existing operations. This action is almost certain to precipitate a rate war because, without the protection of a clearly differentiated product, the established operators are certain to retaliate. Such price wars can be ruinous for all competitors.[5]

Finally, he points out that the decrease in unit costs as a carrier's passenger volume in any city-pair increases is such that service by more carriers rather than fewer carriers is likely to raise operating costs.

Arguments for Strong Industry Competition

Some questions can be raised concerning this interpretation by Wheatcroft. Leaving aside for the moment the role of public subsidy and state intervention—the importance of which Wheatcroft quite properly points out—the economic characteristics of the industry do not appear to lead to the poor performance he suggests. It has been shown above that economic structural traits exist in the international airline industry similar to those Caves noted in the U.S. domestic industry: no significant economies of scale, easy entry, relatively low fixed costs, and a steady and rapid growth in demand. The fairly large number of firms, many of which have substantial "staying power" in the event of a price war in any given city-pair, would discourage attempts at predatory action aimed at establishing a monopoly. In addition, ease of entry would not permit a monopoly or a stable oligopoly to maximize joint profits. Moreover, it does not follow that easy entry necessarily leads to excessive entry since there are no *economic* grounds for firms to enter if profits are below competitive levels. There would appear to be no

[4] *Ibid.*, pp. 55–56.
[5] *Ibid.*, pp. 56–57.

economic basis for the result of easy entry to be an irrational pattern of entry or unstable service to the public.

There are additional features of the international airline industry which would tend to improve performance in a competitive environment (assuming for the moment that governments could allow pricing and entry decisions as in a competitive market). One is the increased scope for product differentiation. There is an increasing number of plane types available, and the different nationalities of the carriers allow more differences in cabin service. Moreover, different carriers would have an advantage in different types of services because of wide differences in relative factor prices, a difference which is potentially the source of considerable product variety. In an environment without International Air Transport Association (IATA) restriction on price or product, a much wider product variety, in both service and price, would be available—a variety which would more nearly correspond to consumers' dictates. There is also evidence that, in addition to the established carriers, a number of specialist firms would quickly appear. Icelandic is one such example already in operation. The nonscheduled carriers in the North Atlantic and elsewhere also appear eager to expand their operations. Additional applications by would-be charter operators are continually being refused. A very dense market (Paris to London, for example) would almost surely attract a specialist firm operating a closely scheduled turn-around service; performance in this type of market would surely be an improvement over the performance of the present two-firm monopoly pool.

The likelihood of more entrants which would emphasize charter and special product types points up another characteristic of the international industry that would help to make competition effective—the large number of firms. Over the next decade there will probably be at least two dozen carriers which will be important operators in the long-haul markets and many more which will become important regional operators. Although the level of demand in particular city-pair markets is such that only one or a few carriers can profitably exist, there is a high likelihood that any firm will face different rivals in many of its different markets; this is in contrast to the U.S. domestic trunklines, which tend to compete with the same firms in many of their important markets. This characteristic of the international airline industry would tend to make collusion more difficult. (It would also make predatory price or scheduling competition difficult, since a considerable coincidence of route structures would be necessary for a firm to conduct effective "economic warfare.") The diversity of vested national interests would have a similar effect. When combined with ease of entry, it would appear that joint profit maximizing, yielding abnormal returns, would not be a likely outcome, and if it did occur, it probably would not long persist. Price or marketing competition, or both, appears more likely. In short, the economics of airline operations do not lead to any obvious necessity for regulation.

The market size which is large enough to sustain more than one firm —without imposing significantly higher unit costs on each firm as traffic density decreases—can be determined empirically. The decline in costs was made explicit in Chapter V. There are certainly large numbers of city-pair markets of sufficient density that service by more than one carrier will not significantly raise unit costs for all. The market size "sufficient" to support more than one carrier and yet not have significantly higher unit costs is not unambiguously defined. The static cost comparison of one large firm versus several smaller carriers must be weighed against the expected favorable dynamic effects on market performance of competition among firms.

Unfortunately the interests of governments mean that a competitive market in the customary sense of the word is infeasible, probably as politically infeasible today as in 1944. While there are more carriers able to compete on a fairly equitable basis than in the immediate postwar years, there are still many firms which would be unable or unwilling to compete in an open market. Many of the developing countries' carriers, for example, have inferior equipment and technical skills. Furthermore, the bilateral entry process is now firmly entrenched; many nations would not be anxious to give up their share of "traffic of national origin" in order to bring about open entry. The commitment to subsidy also appears well entrenched. Open competition, although an attractive industry structure on many counts, is therefore largely an academic issue. Analysis of open competition is useful, however, since it suggests ways in which the present limited competitive market structure might be altered to improve performance.

Totally Regulated Industry Structure

The other extreme in possible market structures would be strict determination of capacity and prices by an international authority, which either owned and operated the aircraft or dictated decisions to state-owned carriers. The major advantages of this ostensibly would be provision of coordinated schedules and better utilization of equipment. Presumably these could result in lower fares.

Such systems are also politically infeasible for a number of reasons, the most important being the unwillingness of nations to entrust such an authority with the requisite power. It also seems unlikely that nations would be able to agree on a set of objectives to be used in the decision-making. These problems prevailed in 1944, and they persist today.

An alternative to such a system would be one in which capacity, schedules, and prices were determined by means of bilateral or multilateral agreements among carriers. Such an international cartel could presumably achieve the scheduling and utilization advantages that have been cited above.

Whatever appeal exists for these sorts of cartel arrangements is more than offset by associated disadvantages. In the context of the present jet technology, the absence of scale economies, the cost savings made possible by spares pools, and the high utilization of equipment achieved by many small carriers suggest that firms acting as a cartel would not perform more efficiently on a unit cost basis. Nor is schedule duplication serious in any but the smaller markets. A reduction in the governmental commitment to subsidy and an environment of increased competition probably would do far more to increase firms' internal efficiency than agreements among firms on schedules or capacity. Perhaps most important in this assessment of the predicted outcome is the general failure of cartel-dominated markets to achieve high performance. Cartel arrangements do not generally lead to fare or marketing experimentation. A cartel arrangement therefore does not appear to be an economically desirable structure.

Looking somewhat ahead to the advent of the supersonic transport, its high fixed cost and large capital requirements will preclude entry, at least initially, by many carriers. Arguments favoring a cartel arrangement, perhaps entailing joint ownership, pooling agreements, schedule coordination, or revenue sharing, will have their advocates. Such a change is unwarranted. The basic management problems of supersonic service do not appear much different from those of subsonic operations. The problem of high capital costs, which will put a premium on equipment utilization and scheduling, is similar (in kind if not in degree) to that of present jet operations. The same problem will exist for airlines using jumbo jets in the next decade since the capital investment per seat will be nearly as large as for the supersonic planes. Nor does the marketing problem appear significantly different for the supersonic aircraft. Pooling or cartel arrangements would probably sacrifice marketing innovation for little or no gain in scheduling or equipment utilization.

Limited Competition

An environment of limited competition includes a range of possible industry configurations. The present restricted environment is one such possibility, but there are alternative types of market environment which hold the promise of improved industry performance. The extent to which they are realized depends in large part on nations' evaluations of the roles of their own flag carriers and on the degree of protection they maintain. Both the need for protection and the propensity to maintain it will decline in some countries in the future, while protective policies will be retained in others. It is important that the market structure of the industry be shaped so that the tendencies toward less restriction can exert their influence. The opportunity for rationalization of the industry within the context of this mix of restrictive and competitive policies is discussed below.

Possibilities for Changes in Attitude Toward Subsidy

One of the most serious deviations from competitive conditions—and one unlikely to change in the immediate future—is the commitment to subsidy. Government attitudes concerning external effects, "infant carrier" needs, and the necessity to support a flag carrier (whether efficient or inefficient) in its competition with other chosen instruments, will surely persist.

It is difficult to estimate how much subsidy nations would be willing to pay in support of their flag carriers, or would be willing to pay if they participated in a market free of entry and price restrictions. In the long-haul markets, removal of entry restrictions would probably lead to excess entry and capacity. As a practical matter, however, any price or scheduling war leading to large losses would constitute a dispute which would quickly reach diplomatic levels. Subsidy wars are far less expedient than a denial of access rights and a breakdown of any multilateral agreements which were the foundation of the competition. The biggest cost of the commitment to subsidy and support of flag carriers is the restriction bred by concern over the amount of subsidy to be drawn from public treasuries. If nations are ever to forego restrictive policies, a change in attitudes with regard to subsidy support of flag carriers must occur first.

Little can be done at present, apparently, to discourage the commitment to subsidy or to achieve agreement among nations concerning what constitutes a rational subsidy plan. The one beneficial step available to nations favoring industry rationalization is to insure that the subsidy burden falls on the inefficient carriers and on the countries committed to subsidy. A rational fare structure eliminating geographical cross-subsidization and the implicit subsidization resulting from excessive service competition would be a proper step in this direction.

Possibilities for Changes in Entry Restrictions

Entry conditions are the most intractable part of market structure. The proper economic advice is to keep entry as free and flexible as possible. Such advice, however, is not likely to be followed; the bilateral entry process is deep-rooted, and virtually all countries are unwilling to give up their control over access rights. Nations have, if anything, grown more restrictive over time. This tendency applies not only to the newest carriers of the developing countries trying to establish themselves, but also to U.S. carriers hoping to retain a large share of traffic generated in the United States. Only a far more liberal attitude than the prevailing one, by all governments, will lead to an easing of entry restrictions.

Nations can be restrictive in three ways, listed in order of decreasing desirability: by being very careful in awarding access, though still following Bermuda principles of no capacity restrictions; by including capacity and frequency restrictions in the bilateral route agreements; or by creating pooling agreements. None of these restrictive methods is desirable from an economic point of view. Pooling agreements appear the least desirable, since they create a common interest which seriously undermines competition. A pool which controls capacity and shares revenue is not likely to encourage innovation in the form of service or price changes. Detailed specification of capacity, frequency, departure times, or plane choice in bilateral agreements is probably next, for such restrictions considerably complicate bilateral negotations. They have in many cases produced such severe constraints on a route as to make economic operations impossible. Frequencies and departure times may have important effects on the ease of equipment maintenance and the ability to achieve satisfactory utilization rates. Decisions made in the bilateral bargaining process that are such an integral part of a firm's operation tend to make management's job far more difficult.

Bermuda-type agreements with no restrictions are the entry procedure which would be most conducive to improving performance. A policy of careful route granting can, of course, be very restrictive. Presumably a policy of careful Bermuda grants would mean that each nation would make its route agreements after weighing estimates of traffic to be gained and lost. With such a system, there may be cases where no mutually acceptable concessions can be found (perhaps no single-carrier market exchanges are available), and hence no entry occurs. For example, it may be difficult for the United States to find a route concession by a small nation that it feels is compensatory for access to a city in the United States servicing international routes. In these circumstances, such an impasse resulting in no entry is an outcome probably preferable to an agreement which permits the foreign carrier access to New York only a few times a week or in some other way restricts operations.

Perhaps the best justification for recommending that the industry restrict entry by making careful route grants along Bermuda lines, rather than by making detailed capacity restrictions in all agreements, is that entry is already widely extended. In these circumstances, careful route grants would appear wiser than added entry subject to many restrictions. The geographical entry pattern resulting from nations bargaining on these terms might not produce route systems which lead to excessive additional costs. As a matter of perspective, the geographical pattern of a route system created by the economic market potential of particular cities does not always lead to the most convenient pattern for scheduling airline service. Careful bargaining among nations on the basis of Bermuda principles might not, in short, produce route systems that are overly costly, especially relative to the other methods of restriction which are available.

Possibilities for Price and Capacity Flexibility

It may still be possible to reach efficient solutions in terms of price and capacity. Many major markets have several carriers participating, and even two carriers can be sufficient competition if price collusion or pooling is avoided. Even within the industry's restricted entry system, price flexibility would pay huge benefits. The benefits of rationalized fares were discussed in Chapter IX. Rationalized fares that eliminated cross-subsidization would, in turn, remove a significant source of motivation for entry restrictions aimed at market protection.

FREE PRICING. IATA rate setting is the one area of industry structure which is amenable to change and which could make the regulated competition more effective. The most radical recommendation would be complete freedom in pricing. Even in the context of limited entry, free pricing would produce a much closer approximation to rational pricing than the present IATA method. New marketing strategies could be tried, and competition could be oriented to price rather than service. Certainly the long-haul, dense markets would experience some price reductions. The large number of firms in the international airline industry would make collusion difficult, and it certainly seems unlikely that any collusion which occurred could result in higher prices than the present IATA system produces. There appear to be enough carriers of sufficient importance in the industry which could reduce and rationalize fares (especially if those airlines were sufficiently prodded by their governments) to make a flexible price policy worthwhile.

The degree to which prices would approach rationality would depend essentially on the cooperation of governments—specifically, on the extent to which they refrained from the use of subsidies or entry rights to promote irrational prices. Price competition by the efficient carriers could imply losses for many others, which is, of course, the reason for opposition from many quarters to competitive pricing. Realistically, subsidies would be paid to many carriers to sustain their position, and state action with regard to access rights (as a coercive means of influencing price) would be induced. In short, free pricing is a rather radical structural change which would not be easy to implement at present, and its success would depend on a changed and more enlightened attitude by many governments. It is therefore worthwhile to consider what can be recommended within the general framework of IATA.

DEFENSE OF PRESENT IATA POLICY. There are industry spokesmen who argue that the present IATA framework is doing a satisfactory job. Wheatcroft is one advocate of IATA; he feels that it achieves a satisfactory balance between private and public interests and that the resultant rates have been quite satisfactory:

> Whatever criticisms may be made of the rate agreements arrived at by IATA it cannot reasonably be said that they represent the decisions of a private cartel.[6]
> . . . the IATA system of international rate-making incorporates special features which tend to produce agreements that represent a reasonable compromise between the interests of the traveling public and the economic health of the airlines; and this is the delicate balance with which public regulation is constantly concerned. It will not be suggested that the IATA system never results in fares which are higher than might have been charged without price fixing. But one of the aims of a system of economic regulation is to secure stability in the industry, and price levels below the costs of most, if not all, operators would not be conducive to this objective.[7]

Wheatcroft offers several explanations as to why firms have not priced at monopoly levels. First, IATA is not permitted to discuss capacity so it is not possible for carriers to agree to capacity restriction. Output restriction and monopoly profits are therefore not possible. Second, carriers fear that their failure to produce a desirable fare structure will mean a transfer of this responsibility to intergovernmental negotiation; this fear has made the carriers quite public-spirited. Third, the requirement for unanimous agreement gives minorities a strong position, and there is an asymmetry in the bargaining which favors the advocates of low fares since they would stand to gain in an open fare situation. Finally, governments not only approve final fare agreements but continually advise their carriers in the bargaining process. In short, Wheatcroft argues that IATA achieves a fine balance between the countervailing powers of airlines and governments and that IATA, when working at its best, produces a desirable outcome.[8]

Wheatcroft places the blame for any IATA shortcomings on governments which at times have taken actions which have disturbed this

---

[6] *Ibid.*, p. 77.
[7] *Ibid.*, p. 80.
[8] *Ibid.*, pp. 80–84.

system of checks and balances. There have been occasions, for example, in which a majority of airlines have blocked the acceptance of lower fares, and their governments have let it be known that they would not permit a minority to introduce lower fares. On the other hand, he believes the unilateral action taken by the U.S. government to lower fares in the Chandler crisis was also improper. In general,[9] he argues that unilateral action by one government to impose its own interpretation of the public interest on all airlines is hardly likely to be successful, even if that interpretation is impeccably correct. What is needed, Wheatcroft argues, is a better understanding by governments of their role in order that both of the above extremes can be avoided. In particular, he suggests that governments need to agree on the general circumstances under which they would allow fares to be decided in an open-fare situation.

CRITIQUE OF PRESENT IATA POLICY. Wheatcroft has properly identified the role of governments as crucial in the achievement of rational rates. His analysis of past IATA proceedings and the "system of checks and balances," however, is more optimistic than that suggested in the present volume. The entire basis of any check on IATA lies in governmental influence, which unfortunately in the past has been largely unsuccessful. Nations other than the United States have generally not taken an interest in any broad interpretation of the public welfare. Government approval has been readily given to IATA decisions, not because the resultant fares are a desirable compromise of airline and public interests but because governments generally have had no wider objective than the short-run welfare of their own carriers. With the exception of the CAB "unilateral actions," IATA has behaved as an uncontrolled private cartel.

The existence of an asymmetry of power favoring the low fare advocate in the bargaining is also questionable. The right of government disapproval can be used by advocates of either low or high fares; the European stand in favor of the Chandler fares exemplifies the denial of opportunity for low fare advocates to win their case in an open-rate situation. In general, fare cuts have not been arrived at by the action of a low fare advocate in an open-rate situation. Neither PAA nor the CAB has been able to force its low fare proposals on others in the North Atlantic by open-fare situations. The market pressures on fare changes have worked only very subtly.

[9] *Ibid.*, p. 85.

There is no evidence that carriers have assumed a particularly public-spirited attitude in their pricing decisions. The information available indicates that IATA bargaining and the resultant fares have been a compromise of carrier interests, with each carrier's position reflecting its profit-maximizing choice on the basis of its own demand and cost curves. There is no reason to expect otherwise. Efforts at joint profit maximization appear to have been made in many routes operated by pools. Although IATA cannot control capacity, this does not preclude pricing to maximize joint profits, or at least profits above competitive levels. The pricing experience in the North Atlantic is relevant to this judgment about IATA procedures. It is the one market where there are enough sellers (and ostensibly enough interested governments) that IATA bargaining should perform well, if it is to perform well in any market. The slow rationalization of the fare structure in this market has been noted.

Recommendations for Improvements in Price Negotiations Within the IATA Setting

The means to improved performance in the area of pricing is increased attention and participation by governments. Governments must be encouraged to address themselves to the public interest construed on broader terms than the short-run success of their own carriers. This public attention should be directed toward reducing rates, rationalizing the fare structure, and fostering additional pricing and marketing flexibility. The cross-subsidization implicit in the present fare structure exemplifies the problem. A major drawback of present IATA procedures for establishing prices is the tendency to disguise the consequences of cross-subsidization and hence to remove price negotiations from the political arenas where they should properly be reviewed. Public attention to the level and structure of fares needs to be more explicit than the very loose control over IATA rates which currently prevails.

The CAB, acting for the U.S. government, has made a small but positive contribution through its attempts to influence pricing decisions. The statements of "pricing objectives" made by the CAB to American carriers prior to IATA meetings are issued to convince both foreign and American carriers of U.S. objectives and resolve. Only the occasional vetoes by the Board have had much weight, however, since PAA has almost always initiated proposals for fare reductions long before the

Board has stepped in. In the last analysis, the most important successes have occurred only as other governments have consented. In the three major fare cuts in the North Atlantic market (1952, 1958, and 1964) a change in position by European governments was the turning point in the fare negotiations. This is to be expected in an industry where political considerations have been important, but it also rather pointedly indicates the location of any hope for the future. At least several nations which represent important international air markets must assume genuine interest in fare rationalization. Without such an interest, the particular mechanics of any fare-setting procedure will be dominated by restrictionist policies; conversely, given that interest, the means for inducing changes can be worked out fairly readily.

The future of intergovernmental bargaining over the details of fares is not bright, and certainly nothing appears to be gained by substituting government bargaining as the sole means for setting fares in place of the present conference procedure of carriers. The airlines themselves are best suited to this task. Governments, however, should be included explicitly in the IATA bargaining process. If all governments were to send representatives to attend and participate in IATA meetings, the sessions could become even more cumbersome than they are now, necessitating an overhaul of the bargaining mechanics. On the other hand, there would appear to be no substitute for governmental attention to the public interest if a conference procedure is to be retained. Since governments presently can veto fares, no additional inflexibility would be introduced by making their positions explicit in the negotiating process. It would also help to solve the particular U.S. problem created when CAB objectives differ from those of private U.S. carriers.

The recent experience in determining fares in the Middle East is a relevant bit of encouragement for the aforementioned recommendations. An open-fare situation technically prevailed after April 1, 1965, because previous IATA fares expired on that date, and no new agreement had been reached. The airlines tacitly agreed upon previous IATA rates for the most part, which they filed with governments for approval. However, the fare from the Middle East to New York was reduced. The El Al Israel Airlines group fare of $535 (New York to Tel Aviv) had long been contested (the offering of an unrestricted group flight of this type was questionable under IATA rules). United Arab Airlines in April 1965 led a number of carriers in the region in a move to obtain equal rights. This carrier filed a fare of $535 for group flights from New York to Cairo; the United Arab Republic government, furthermore, indicated that other carriers and states should comply with this rate.[10] TWA applied for a group fare at the same rate, which was accepted by IATA, and all other carriers subsequently followed. This is one instance in which concerted carrier and state action brought about a significant reduction in fares. Hopefully such an outcome could be realized in other circumstances in which governments take an active interest in fares and in fare rationalization.

A similar development occurred in late 1966. El Al, apparently prompted by the Israeli Government Tourist office, announced that it would offer charters to groups of 80 or more during the winter at a $399 round trip price, rather than at the $535 level. Pan Am immediately seized the opportunity, claiming that this action of the Israeli government amounted to a denunciation of the IATA agreement and offered a new set of inclusive tour fares for small groups (10 or more) over short periods (14 to 21 days) at sharply lower levels. Other carriers quickly matched these fares.[11] IATA subsequently agreed on a set of inclusive tour excursion rates at levels comparable to PAA's proposal. Marketing aggressiveness in response to a seasonal peaking problem, coupled with government action, has thus produced a favorable change in IATA fares.

Recommendations for Charter Operations and for Non-IATA Airlines

A structural improvement related to the one outlined above is the recommendation to encourage that element in the industry which conducts specialized, nonregulated operations. This includes charter operations and non-IATA participants such as Icelandic. These elements contribute important flexibility to the industry and often produce market innovations that the industry needs.[12] The nonscheduled charter operators in the Atlantic have served this function, having initiated the growth of a considerable market. Similarly, Icelandic's contribution in the North Atlantic market should not be underestimated. The permis-

---

[10] *Air Travel* (May 1965), p. 69.

[11] Paul J. C. Friedlander, "A Subjunctive Review of the Atlantic Air-Fare Caper," and David Gollan, "The $230 Non-Blackout Ticket to Europe," *New York Times*, December 4, 1966, Section XX, p. 5.

[12] Caves has suggested that market innovation in the U.S. domestic airline industry has tended to come from small, "disadvantaged" firms. Caves, *op. cit.*, pp. 425–26.

sion granted to SAS to match Icelandic's propeller rates is a proper encouragement of this sort of marketing innovation. These non-IATA-controlled services provide an important check on the level of IATA fares, partially offsetting the maintenance of high fares and low load factors. As noted earlier, schedule frequencies in most of the large markets are such that this sort of nonscheduled service with lower fares and a higher load factor would seem to be recommended.

This endorsement of charter operations must answer the charge that charter operations and other promotional fares will undermine scheduled operations and thus result in chaotic service. The argument is that charter service will force scheduled service to reduce its fares, and since average revenue per seat can be maintained only if load factors increase proportionately with the fare reductions, it may be necessary to reduce schedule frequencies. Reduced schedule frequencies will then reduce the service gap between scheduled and nonscheduled operations, further aggravating the problem for the scheduled operator.

This is an unrealistic view. Problems for the scheduled operator may occur in extremely thin markets (service once or twice per week), but in the great majority of routes even considerable reductions in schedule frequencies to meet charter competition would not markedly reduce the service differential between the two. It is inconceivable that charter operations could seriously disrupt scheduled service in international markets of average and above average density; the North Atlantic clearly faces no serious threat along these lines.

The likely outcome of unrestricted entry and pricing for charter operations would be, first, a reduction in the price difference between scheduled and nonscheduled service as IATA fares are forced down and, second, a moderate penetration by the charter operators in the denser, tourist-oriented markets. Much of this market consists of only occasional travelers. Charter operations would not be an important drain on passengers of scheduled operations in the markets of lesser density.

It is important, of course, that charter operators not be subsidized lest this undermine scheduled operations. Since many governments are reluctant to permit charter operations and would be concerned about subsidized operators, there might be some hope for a multilateral agreement on the terms of subsidy to such carriers. An agreement limiting subsidy in this area might gradually have an impact on government attitudes with regard to all subsidies.

Recommendations on Mergers

A final aspect of industry structure concerns mergers. Since World War II there has been a definite trend toward merger in the industry. This trend may have diminished in the last five years, but it has been supplemented by a great increase in intercarrier cooperation through pooling agreements. In general, the merger trend has gone sufficiently far in the industry that there apparently are no significant gains to be realized from further mergers; this is especially true in the nations with the largest carriers, which already have undergone a considerable period of rationalization via the merging of smaller carriers. The justification for this position against further merger is based on the general conclusion that cost reductions resulting from merger are not large, while the increased market concentration could reduce competitive incentives. Significant scale economies are not present, and pooling arrangements in the form of spares pools and subcontracting can produce nearly all of the cost savings of merger. Even quite small firms can compete with the aid of such arrangements.

In recent years a number of mergers have been proposed involving some of the industry's largest carriers—PAA and TWA, BOAC and BEA, and Air Canada and Canadian Pacific Airlines. Fortunately none has been consummated. In the latter case, it was realized that the Canadian markets are sufficient in most instances to sustain competition. The TWA-PAA merger likewise appeared to be an unnecessary creation of market power without significant cost savings. The BOAC-BEA merger was dropped for a number of reasons: the carriers did not operate a common set of plane types, had little route or station duplication, and were so large already that no saving in overhead costs would result from merger.[13] In each of these cases a merger would have created a colossus in size but would not have eliminated much common overhead expense.

The most important merger proposal still pending is that of "Air Union," a proposed consolidation of Air France, Lufthansa, Alitalia, and Sabena. KLM, originally a participant, withdrew when it could not agree to the terms, but subsequently re-expressed interest in joining. Luxair is also a possible member. The proposal is to pool all equipment

[13] Wheatcroft, *op. cit.*, pp. 118–27.

and sales efforts, to fly all schedules at agreed frequencies, and to divide revenues according to an agreed proportion: Air France, 34 percent; Lufthansa, 26 percent; Alitalia, 20 percent; and Sabena, 10 percent. The argument offered in favor of the merger is that it would reduce sales costs and would provide better schedules with less excess capacity. However, since the carriers have such a large variety of equipment, technical cost savings from the pooling of equipment are questionable. The end result would be an unfortunate reduction of competition in Europe.

The political problems are such that a successful merger seems remote. The governments involved have never fully accepted the scheme. It took considerable effort in the airlines themselves to agree upon the original percentage shares, since this involved reconciling different cost levels, market shares, and market growth rates. It now appears that another reconciliation effort is needed since the recent growth of Alitalia and Lufthansa has made these carriers discontented with the original division of revenues. Nor have the political issues of national sovereignty been resolved. France has indicated concern over loss of her identity in such an arrangement and has also requested that Air Union buy only Common Market aircraft, which essentially means French aircraft. Alitalia objects strongly to this. It would appear that Air Union is a long way from consummation.

The overall economic effects of further merger in the industry do not appear beneficial. Mergers would not be a quick and easy solution to the political influences which have produced inefficient performance. The political reconciliation necessary for merger is such that agreements could be reached only by carriers with similar motives: for example, by a number of European carriers striving to protect their share of intra- and through-Europe traffic, or by a number of carriers of less developed countries, anxious to show the flag. Mergers of these types would not suddenly convert a political entry process into one that is economically rational. There is no reason to believe that a merger of inefficient carriers following protectionist policies will produce a single carrier which is any less restrictionist.

An exception to this stand against mergers should be noted regarding certain regional carriers in the less developed nations in Latin America and Africa, where some additional consolidation could be beneficial. Air Afrique, a consolidation of the airlines of eleven former

French colonies, is one good example of a beneficial merger. Air Afrique has made a rational beginning in that it has taken over French routes and is leasing equipment and receiving aid from Air France and Union de Transports Aériens until it can afford its own. This is in sharp contrast to those African carriers, such as Ghana Airways or Nigerian Airways, which have embarked on very ambitious undertakings and appear to be extending themselves irrationally into the long-haul jet markets.[14]

Summary

Political considerations make a purely competitive environment an infeasible alternative to the present industry structure and also render somewhat dubious the ability of competition to produce economically efficient performance. At worst, the commitment to subsidy would result in a breakdown of free access rights; at best the industry would probably persistently operate at excess capacity and with small losses.

While an environment of limited competition is unavoidable, the industry could do much better than it presently does. The structure which will yield the best performance is one in which as much price and marketing flexibility as possible is forced into the existing system of restricted entry. The right of governments to control access is not one which will be given up in the foreseeable future. On the other hand, it would seem possible to introduce more rational pricing than that which emerges from IATA at present. Governments should take a more active role in supervising IATA rate setting, with the objective of encouraging and expanding the latitude for price competition. Price competition should result in prices more nearly in conformity with marginal costs than they are at present. Rational pricing also would eliminate the cross-subsidization of inefficient carriers. There would still be natural monopoly markets and monopolies by collusive agreement which would enjoy excessive profits; this situation, however, would be no different from that arising from IATA control, where collusion is very easy.

[14] See the discussion of Air Afrique in Anthony Vandyk, "Air Afrique, New 11-Nation Airline," *Airlift*, Vol. 26 (April 1962), pp. 19–20.

CHAPTER XI

Recommendations for U.S. Policy

INTERNATIONAL AVIATION POLICIES of the United States have been examined from time to time, usually as the result of some outcry by the public or by a carrier. The Smathers investigation of entry agreements in 1956 was mentioned earlier. The latest and by far the most substantial review was undertaken by an Interagency Steering Committee appointed by President John F. Kennedy in September 1961 "to determine whether U.S. air policies developed since 1944 can adequately serve U.S. interests in the future." The committee's "Statement on International Air Transport Policy" was approved by the President in April 1963.[1] This examination was in part a response to increasing pressure for policy changes and especially for a more protectionist position. The pressure arose because of the diminishing market share of U.S. flag carriers in the late 1950s and early 1960s. The study and resulting approved statement enunciated a much clearer conception of U.S. objectives than had been developed before and indicated a greater degree of coordination among the various interests and the responsible agencies within the government.

Present Policy Objectives

The 1963 "Statement on International Air Transport Policy" included a recommendation for industry rationalization. It concluded that

[1] Press release, April 24, 1963, from the office of the White House Press Secretary. Members of the Steering Committee were N. W. Halaby (FAA),

203

A well reasoned policy . . . will carry us far toward the primary objective of U.S. international air transport policy: to develop and maintain an expanding, economically and technologically efficient international air transport system best adapted to the growing needs of the Free World, and to assure air carriers of the United States a fair and equal opportunity to compete in world aviation markets. . . .[2]

The U.S. policy statements essentially opposed all restrictions. Support was voiced for the bilateral entry system, and in particular for the Bermuda principles of no capacity restrictions. The statement also supported the International Air Transport Association (IATA) fare machinery, but asked Congress to grant the Civil Aeronautics Board (CAB) authority to set rates and also to veto rates which it considered unreasonable. The policy, in short, was antiprotectionist. The major aspects of this policy statement are given in the following excerpts:

The world air transport system . . . must be as free from restrictions as possible, whether these be imposed by government or through intercarrier agreements. Any policy of arbitrarily restricting capacity, dividing markets by carrier agreements, encouraging high rates or curtailing service for which a demand exists, would be harmful to our national interests. Such a policy would not be in accord with our basic attitudes toward private enterprise. . . .[3]

The U.S. policy for air transport includes the following principles:

1. *Basic Framework.* The U.S. will maintain the present framework of bilateral agreements by which air routes are exchanged among nations and the rights to carry traffic on them are determined according to certain broad principles. The substitution of a multilateral agreement seems even less feasible or acceptable today than when first attempted at the Chicago Conference in 1944.

This framework of agreements . . . rejects as completely impractical unregulated freedom of the skies, and recognizes that the exchange of routes is a useful tool in building sound and economic growth of air transport. On the other hand, this framework rejects the concept that agreements should divide the market or allocate to the carriers of a particular country a certain share of the traffic. The latter concept would surely restrict the growth of international aviation and would result in endless bickering among nations as to their proper share of traffic. It is totally foreign to our basic trade policies. . . .[4]

---

chairman, K. R. Hansen (Bureau of the Budget), executive secretary, A. S. Boyd (CAB), Hollis B. Chenery (AID), Griffith Johnson (Department of State), C. D. Martin (Department of Commerce), and F. K. Sloan (Department of Defense).

[2] "Statement on International Air Transport Policy," The White House, April 24, 1963 (mimeographed), p. 14.

[3] *Ibid.*, p. 2.

[4] *Ibid.*, p. 7.

2. *Air Routes and Services.* Our policy is to provide air service where a substantial need therefor develops . . . an expansion of the present route structures must be approached with caution.

. . . Neither the interests of a sound transportation system nor of the countries involved are served when a route with little traffic is burdened by a number of carriers greater than is economically justifiable. The demand for swift, safe passage, not forced flag flying, should determine the services offered.[5]

3. *Capacity Principles.* The United States supports the "Bermuda" capacity principles which flexibly govern the amount of service individual carriers may offer to the world travelling and shipping public. . . . They prohibit predetermined limits on capacity, but permit capacity restrictions on certain categories of traffic, known as secondary justification traffic, on the basis of *ex post facto* review of traffic carried.[6] [The U.S. desires a "reasonable and fair" interpretation of what constitutes fifth freedom traffic.]

5. *Rates.* International air transport rates are now recommended by the carriers, acting through . . . the International Air Transport Association (IATA), and approved by the governments concerned. This multilateral mechanism . . . should be maintained. . . . To provide for more effective governmental influence on rates, Congress should adopt legislation which would give to the Civil Aeronautics Board authority, subject to approval by the President, to control rates in international air transport to and from the United States.[7]

9. *Aviation Assistance to Less Developed Countries.* More intensive consideration shall be given in the foreign aid program to the contributions that internal and regional aviation programs can make to economic development in the less developed countries. Where aviation assistance proposals are proposed for political or national security reasons, they must be subjected to the same rigorous justification that applies to other projects competing for scarce resources.[8]

The economic basis for this objective of a rational industry free of restriction should be clear from the discussion of structure and performance throughout this study. The expected improvement in performance of a rational industry has been discussed. An economically efficient industry will best serve the interests of U.S. travelers abroad. In addition, it has been shown here that the U.S. carriers are among the most efficient and would therefore assume an important place in a rationalized market. The fact that U.S. carriers would not need protection in a rationalized industry has undoubtedly made it easier for the United States to advocate rationalization.

[5] *Ibid.*, pp. 7–8.
[6] *Ibid.*, pp. 8–9.
[7] *Ibid.*, pp. 10–11.
[8] *Ibid.*, p. 14.

Entry Policy Recommendations

These objectives suggest that the appropriate long-range goal of the United States should be the gradual development of freedom of entry, or at least prevention of increased restrictions in this area. The United States is both a large generator of traffic and an efficient operator, and therefore should continue to occupy a major place in the industry. The opposite policy—freezing present market shares by introducing restrictions in renegotiated bilaterals or pooling arrangements—is both inconsistent with basic U.S. objectives of free trade and free markets and unnecessary if progress can be made toward a rationalized industry.

Promotion of Freer Entry Through Route Grants

The improving profit levels and excellent prospects for the immediate future present a good environment for pursuing freer entry and other objectives aimed at industry rationalization and increased competition as well. The financial recovery of many carriers and the large growth in markets should help eventually to reduce protectionist tendencies. The United States should try to convince other nations of the wisdom of easier entry. Its biggest influence, of course, will be by example. Negotiation of unrestricted bilaterals and abstention from market-sharing pools in the many important markets in which U.S. carriers participate would be influential.

While striving for a more liberal entry environment, the United States should not sacrifice its own carriers' commercial position by liberal route grants while other countries remain restrictive. The best means available to the United States for leading the way toward a more liberal entry policy is through selective use of route grants (within the framework of the Bermuda principles). This selectivity should consider the adequacy of the existing level of capacity as well as the traffic to be gained and lost by each new entry agreement. As noted in Chapter X, the alternative restrictive policies with regard to entry—that is, specifying capacity and frequency limitations or entering into pooling agreements—appear to be much less flexible and to limit competition unduly. Moreover, any tendency which the United States might show toward restriction would tend to reinforce restrictionist thinking abroad. In all aspects of international aviation policy, the

United States must make every effort to assume a liberal position whenever possible, in opposition to any market restrictions.

"Fifth Freedom" Problems

While careful Bermuda grants are the recommended policy, the difficulties of applying Bermuda principles and especially the problems associated with preventing competitors from carrying excessive fifth freedom traffic have been noted. The best procedure for enforcing Bermuda principles concerning intermediate traffic is not apparent. Although Bermuda-type agreements indicate that an *ex post facto* review is to be held, in practice no such review has led to a mutually acceptable interpretation of fifth freedom rights.

Considerable debate has taken place within the United States as to whether this country should engage in capacity controls on fifth freedom traffic, specifically by expanding the control power of the CAB.[9] One proposal would have allowed the CAB to act as an "enforcer" of the U.S. position concerning fifth freedom traffic. All carriers would submit origin and destination traffic statistics to the Board for review, which in turn could suspend operations if excessive fifth freedom traffic were being carried. The Board's power would thus be greatly enhanced; its licensing authority would in effect be used to force acceptance of the U.S. interpretation of Bermuda principles.[10]

The protagonists of such a plan have argued that such capacity controls do exist elsewhere, that the United States has been unsuccessful in achieving a fair interpretation of Bermuda principles, and that the CAB would not abuse its new power. There are, however, important reasons for questioning such a role for the CAB. First, the argument that such restrictions already exist is exaggerated. As was noted earlier, the major aviation powers do not impose such restrictions on the United States. Those European nations which do impose restrictions are relatively few. Most of the restriction arises in Latin America,

[9] *Foreign Air Transportation*, Hearings before a Subcommittee of the House Committee on Interstate and Foreign Commerce, 87 Cong. 2 sess. (1962); Investigation of the Terms, Conditions, and Limitations of Foreign Air Carrier Permits, CAB Docket No. 12063, Order E-16288 (August 27, 1962). See also Nicholas H. Kittrie, "United States Regulation of Foreign Airlines Competition," *Journal of Air Law and Commerce*, Vol. 29 (Winter 1963), pp. 1–13.

[10] Investigation of the Terms, Conditions, and Limitations of Foreign Air Carrier Permits, CAB Docket No. 12063, Order E-16288 (January 18, 1961).

where the carriers involved need the protection of restrictionist policies and the local political environment is willing to provide this protection. It would appear unlikely that these states could be coerced into lessening restrictions. In general, the claim that foreign government control severely hampers U.S. carrier operations has not been substantiated.[11]

A more important question concerns the overall efficacy of such an expansion of CAB power. Several major European carriers (BOAC, KLM, SAS, Swissair, and Sabena) have objected to the proposed extension of CAB authority on the grounds that it amounted to unilateral control vested in a national administration and was therefore inconsistent with international bilateral agreements. Such an objection appears well taken. Unilateral CAB authority to interpret the Bermuda agreements is inconsistent with the spirit of those agreements. This sort of power vested in an aviation administration in the United States would mean that the CAB would assume responsibility equal to or stronger than that of the Department of State. Foreign governments would necessarily be forced to negotiate with both parties. Even such CAB authority, however, would not allow the United States to further its position unilaterally. The likely response would be considerable retaliation abroad in the form of capacity restrictions and encouragement to the entire airline industry to move further in this direction. Unilateral interpretation by national authorities is not the manner in which agreement is best achieved on what constitutes legitimate fifth freedom traffic under the Bermuda agreements.

Following debate within the CAB and in Congress, the proposal was dropped. The basic conclusion was that such action was largely unjustified and would precipitate serious retaliation abroad. This policy conclusion is strongly supported here; the United States must avoid all temptations to use capacity restrictions.

There is, furthermore, some question as to how hard the United States should press for an interpretation of the freedom classification. The various efforts to reach agreement on both a precise definition of the various freedoms of traffic and a statistical procedure for data collection have been fruitless in the past, and agreement seems unlikely in the future. Moreover, agreement on a strict definition is probably not in the best long-run interest of the United States or of the industry. A worldwide network by a single carrier necessarily requires fifth freedom traffic if it is to be viable. A rigid definition of how to allocate

[11] Recommendations of Hearing Examiner (June 21, 1962), in *ibid.*, p. 66.

traffic to third, fourth, and fifth freedom classes might steer the industry farther toward strict national claims.

The best long-run policy for the United States probably is to strive to settle disputes over fifth freedom traffic on a case-by-case basis. Arbitration has been used in the industry in recent years (for example, in the dispute between the United States and France over cargo rights under the existing bilateral agreement)[12] and may be a good means of settling fifth freedom questions. In this or in any other means of settlement, the United States should not press its claims concerning fifth freedom traffic any harder than the other major aviation powers, because any nationalist claim could delay or reduce the chance for progress toward more open entry.

The recommendation of firmer bilateral bargaining was implicit in the 1963 White House policy statement and has been pursued by the United States since that time. Cautious granting of entry through Bermuda-type agreements is the best strategy for the United States to follow, given its already well extended route system. To be denied further access rights is no great cost, and certainly is a small price to pay if existing routes can be kept from becoming any more restrictive. The obvious corollary is the relatively greater need of a number of foreign carriers which still have considerable ambitions in the form of route extensions. In these circumstances, the United States should not underestimate the value of its route grants and should bargain hard.

Moreover, it may be possible for the United States to achieve, with route grants, objectives other than merely increasing its own route network. Granting of access rights might be exchanged for cooperation in rationalizing fares or in removing protectionist capacity restrictions. Similarly, fifth freedom concessions might be used in bargaining for cooperation on rates and related questions of product type. Inclusion of these other features explicitly in the bilaterals would overly complicate the language, but informal agreements at the diplomatic level during negotiations might yield worthwhile dividends. Additional grants by the United States in some of its denser routes might not be a large price to pay in view of the high rate of growth in demand in many of these markets. Such a policy might be of relevance in solving the problems of excessive fares in the Pacific, for example. The United States

---

[12] "International Arbitration for the Interpretation and Implementation of Air Transport Bilaterals—the Example of Arbitration between the United States and France," *ITA Documents 66/2-E* (Paris: Institut du Transport Aérien, 1966).

and Japanese governments could eventually dictate fares in the Pacific if necessary. It might have been possible (in the 1965 U.S.-Japan negotiations) for the United States to use its access grant to Japan in the North Atlantic market to win Japanese support in reducing fares. (Such a proposal, or others, might have been discussed; the bargaining transcript is not public information.)

Pricing Policy Recommendations

The United States should take a stronger position regarding fares and the process of negotiating fares. This recommendation is consistent with the concept that more government attention is needed. The White House policy statement recommended that steps be taken toward rationalizing fares, but progress has been slow. The United States should strongly oppose higher IATA rates. However, caution must be exercised, since either overt disapproval of the IATA machinery or any U.S. action which might appear as an effort to dictate fares would be unfavorably received abroad. Europe's faith in IATA and distrust of U.S. motives have been noted. Even Canada, often allied with the U.S. in many fare disputes in the past, has reacted strongly against the harsh criticism and threats directed toward IATA by the CAB. W. Gordon Wood, Vice President of Air Canada, remarked in February, 1965:

. . . [No government], not even Boyd [CAB Chairman], can dictate fares and rates, and there is no evidence that inter-government negotiations would be more effective. . . . There is no reason to believe travelers of the world who have reaped benefits of lower fares in an era of rising costs, thanks to IATA's collective efforts, should be handed over to the hazards of the politically-minded U.S. Board which now appears anxious to control our affairs.[13]

Opposition to IATA and attempts at reform, therefore, should be handled in such a way that strong adverse reaction will not be aroused abroad.

CAB Rate-Setting Authority Not Recommended

One proposed policy change which has been the subject of much debate involves granting the CAB the authority to set fares on routes to

[13] "Air Canada VP Replies to CAB Criticism of IATA," *Interavia Air Letter*, No. 5694 (February 25, 1965), p. 1.

and from the United States. The White House policy statement advocated such a change, and the CAB itself has continually asked Congress for legislation granting this authority. The Congress, however, has not seen fit to enact such legislation. Such a change in CAB authority is also opposed here.

Under present legislation the CAB has the power to prevent discriminatory rates and to approve or disapprove rates proposed either by U.S. or by foreign carriers, but has no power to set rates. The Board has argued that in cases where no bilateral agreement exists there is no control over rates except disapproval, since no means exists to have carriers propose a proper fare, and that fare setting legislation would correct this. The Board also feels that rate-setting authority would redress an imbalance of power in the bargaining process which exists because other aeronautical authorities can set rates. Lack of such power by the CAB has reputedly hampered U.S. carriers' bargaining position in IATA. Finally, the CAB feels that the United States is at a disadvantage in a fare dispute such as the Chandler crisis, because the CAB lacks authority to set rates.[14]

In determining whether granting this authority to the CAB is in the best U.S. interest, it must be kept in mind that there is no room for unilateral expansion of one nation's power in the field of international aviation. Governments have shown a continued strong interest in their own positions and hence undoubtedly would not be willing to accept decisions or rates made by the CAB. The 1946 Bermuda Agreement reflected this fact of national sovereignty when it set up the IATA conference procedure. The same symmetry of state interests and authority over entry and price exists today and cannot be altered by any action by Congress. The important question concerning the CAB request, therefore, is whether granting the CAB authority to set rates is the best means of furthering the U.S. position in fare negotiations, in the context of a multilateral bargaining arrangement. The United States should presume that other nations will, if they so choose, assume the same rate-setting power.

Given the continuance of the IATA conference method, rate-setting by the CAB does not appear to be the best procedure for the United States. Other governments do not have authority comparable to that requested by the CAB. Granting such authority to the CAB would

[14] *International Air Transportation Rates,* Hearing before the Senate Committee on Commerce, 88 Cong. 1 sess. (1963), pp. 102–23.

probably precipitate similar legislation in other nations, at which point IATA negotiations would face a considerable job of reconciliation. Because there does not appear to be any ready substitute for some sort of conference procedure, no action should be taken which will introduce additional inflexibility. An advisory role for governments would appear sufficient as a means of government participation; it is hard to conceive of any advantages to the bargaining process which would accrue from each nation having power to "determine" a fare for its own carrier. Governments should, of course, retain their veto power over IATA fares. Such a veto power is as strong a unilateral step as can be taken. Furthermore, the power to set rates is no real additional benefit since a rate unacceptable to other countries would be vetoed.

The argument that the United States is at a bargaining disadvantage, especially in the case of a dispute in which IATA fares are not accepted, is likewise questionable. Bilateral agreements to which the U.S. is a party provide that rates be agreed upon by IATA and approved by each government; in the event that governments do not accept IATA fares, or IATA is unable to reach an agreement, the process of fare determination reverts back to government bargaining. When an acceptable IATA agreement has not been reached and U. S. and foreign carriers then apply for different rates, the disagreeing countries are to try to reach a negotiated settlement within thirty days. If at the end of the thirty-day negotiation period the dispute remains unresolved, one of the two alternative procedures for resolution provided by the Bermuda Agreement can be implemented.[15] Paragraph (f), Annex II, states that if a nation's aeronautical authority does not have rate-setting authority, it may suspend service offered by either a flag or a foreign carrier at an objectionable rate, pending settlement by arbitration.[16]

[15] "Air Services Agreement between the United States . . . and the United Kingdom . . . and Final Act of the Civil Aviation Conference Held at Bermuda January 15 to February 11, 1946," *Treaties and Other International Acts Series*, No. 1507 (1946); hereinafter cited as the Bermuda Agreement. Two alternative provisions were included in the Bermuda Agreement because the United States at the time had not yet determined whether the CAB should have statutory powers to set rates on international routes to and from the United States.

[16] (f) . . . If one of the Contracting Parties is dissatisfied with any new rate proposed by the air carrier or carriers of . . . the other Contracting Party, it shall so notify. . . . It is recognized that if no such agreement can be reached prior to the expiry of such thirty days, the Contracting Party raising the objection to the rate may take such steps as it may consider necessary to prevent the inauguration or continuation of the service in question at the rate complained of. (Bermuda Agreement, Annex II, par. [f].)

The arbitration, to be conducted by ICAO, is to be binding. To date, no fare dispute has reached this arbitration stage. The alternative procedure for a settlement, paragraph (e), can be put into effect if a nation has rate-setting authority. In this circumstance a nation gives up its right to suspend operations.[17] The difference, in essence, is that the CAB would lose the right to suspend operations of foreign carriers if the CAB had rate-setting authority. Other nations with similar authority would be similarly affected.

The CAB has felt that the United States is at a disadvantage when paragraph (f) is applicable. Under provision (f), both nations can suspend operations at any proposed rate. On the other hand, under section (e), countries yield their rate suspension power; a dual rate could therefore exist while the dispute was being arbitrated (for example, if rates were proposed by both the United States and IATA). The Board has argued that since U.S. carriers with lower costs will generally be proposing the lower rate, they would have an obvious advantage. The market success of the lower rate would serve as a considerable advantage in the arbitration process; time itself would be on the side of the one proposing the lower rate.[18]

This argument—that rate setting by the CAB might produce a dual rate situation which would be resolved in the United States' favor—is not well taken. First, it is very improbable that foreign governments would allow a dual rate situation to exist and thus let the market alone dictate the lower rate. Low fare advocates have not won out via market pressures in an open fare situation in the past. Europe was quick to suspend landing rights in the Chandler crisis, and there have been other cases where governments have stood ready to bar access. Governments have suspended or restricted access when bilateral negotiations have gone against them or when they were unable to force an acceptable interpretation of their traffic rights. This effect of political considerations on market pressures is such that the latter as a policy instrument,

[17] (e) . . . If one of the Contracting Parties . . . is dissatisfied with the new rate proposed by the air carrier or carriers of the other Contracting Party, it shall so notify . . . If agreement has not been reached at the end of the thirty-day period . . . , the proposed rate may, unless the aeronautical authorities of the country of the air carrier concerned see fit to suspend its operation, go into effect provisionally pending the settlement of any dispute in accordance with the procedure outlined in paragraph (g) below. (Bermuda Agreement, Annex II, par. [e].)

[18] International Air Transportation Rates, Hearing before the Senate Committee on Commerce, 88 Cong. 1 sess. (1963), pp. 102–23.

though by no means irrelevant or useless, must be subtly and discriminately employed. Market pressures have the inherent limitation that badly disadvantaged nations might suspend entry.

Second, it does not appear that the United States is in an unfavorable bargaining position vis-à-vis European nations because the CAB lacks rate control. This sort of argument was loudly voiced following the Chandler crisis, an incident so disconcerting from the U.S. point of view that considerable pressure for an increased CAB role was exerted. It appeared to many that the United States lacked authority comparable to that of the British government. This, however, was not the case. The source of difficulty for the United States was an overall lack of coordination between the CAB and the U.S. State Department and the absence of a unified position on the issue. At the time of the incident, neither the CAB nor the State Department felt it had the statutory power to force suspension. The CAB took a firm stand in the dispute, but was later reversed at the height of the crisis by the State Department. On the other hand, the British suspension of landing rights appears improper under the provisions in the Bermuda Agreement for settling fare differences; the British, however, were little interested in a legal interpretation and were suspending operations based on any government's right to deny landing. This right of suspension is inherent in all international aviation negotiation. The United States, in the Office of the President, had an equal right.[19]

In hindsight, of course, the subsequent compromise which resulted in the 1964 fare reduction was such a large step forward for the industry that it is difficult at this point to criticize seriously the overall manner in which the United States represented itself. The State Department at the time felt that any further extension of the direct confrontation could perhaps work against the basic goal of compromise. The United States, of course, should improve coordination of its efforts lest it be badly prepared for any future dispute.

In summary, CAB rate-setting authority would not appear to be the best means of furthering the United States position in fare negotiation.

[19] For an excellent discussion of national authority over rates or landing rights in the context of domestic and international law, see a letter by Steptoe and Johnson, attorneys at law, November 25, 1960, "Memorandum re Presidential Control over Foreign Air Carrier Rates," in *International Air Transportation Rates,* Hearing before the Senate Committee on Commerce, 88 Cong. 1 sess. (1963), pp. 57–74.

While the Bermuda Agreement and subsequent bilaterals have included provisions whereby both countries are permitted to set fares but forego the right of suspension, this sort of rate determination has not occurred and does not seem likely. Conference rate making has been the custom and will persist. CAB rate authority would not apparently make any contribution to this procedure and is not needed to redress any imbalance of power.

The United States Should Bargain Firmly for Lower Rates Where Justified

Of policy recommendations within the present IATA framework, the first and most obvious is for the United States to take a firmer bargaining stand. The United States should be more aggressive in attempting to bring about reduced fares where such a change is economically rational and should use the veto power if necessary. The White House policy statement in 1963 indicated that the United States will veto "unreasonable" rates if necessary. (The Chandler incident was the first example of this). While the United States has faced considerable criticism for its action, the uncertainties and trauma did produce a large fare reduction. This fare cut has proved so successful that it eventually became popular with most carriers.

Specifically, further government attention is required in the Pacific and soon will be needed in the Atlantic if IATA disputes (for example, over movies) continue to delay fare reductions. The United States is in a relatively strong bargaining position to pursue its goal in these two areas. No nation is anxious for a suspension of traffic which eliminates the U.S. tourist dollar or channels it in another direction. If a fare dispute in the North Atlantic, for example, reached an impasse and traffic rights were suspended, it would be necessary for all of Europe to unite behind a proposed "European" fare. Suspension of the United States-to-London route would be more serious to the British than to the United States if American tourists could still reach Europe by alternative routes—that is, if some European countries did not bar access. This sort of lack of unity almost developed in May 1963. While the right of traffic suspension should not be employed indiscriminately, the costs of suspension to other countries relative to costs to the United States are such that this country should pursue its bargaining vigorously.

The United States Should Encourage Charter Operations

Another means toward fare rationalization that the United States might pursue is to encourage services offered at less than standard IATA rates. This includes all excursion and promotional fares, special services such as those offered by Icelandic, and most importantly, charter operations. The absence of any significant control by IATA makes charter operations potentially quite useful. Encouragement of charter operations by the United States could help fill the gap of much needed lower priced service and also could provide pressure on IATA to reduce its fares. Indeed, the latter possibility should not be underestimated. A competitive step of this nature may place protectionist countries in a difficult position, since the retaliatory measures available to these countries might not be subtle enough to be justifiable under the circumstances. Such a carefully and rather narrowly defined market pressure cannot be easily construed by other countries as sufficient cause, for example, to suspend entry to U.S. carriers, in view of the difficulties of such a diplomatic confrontation with the United States.

U.S. POLICY IN THE ATLANTIC REGION. U.S. policy with respect to charter operations has in the past been reasonably "permissive" in that licenses generally have been granted upon request. European countries likewise have granted licenses reasonably freely. The first confrontation over charters occurred in the Atlantic market in 1961, when the CAB denied licenses to a British independent, Cunard Eagle, for a large expansion in its charter operations. The CAB had in the past limited off-route charter operations of the U.S. scheduled carriers to 10 percent of their scheduled passenger-miles. It used the same rule of thumb in determining whether foreign carriers should be given charter authority. In this instance, Cunard's request exceeded the 10 percent limit, and therefore the CAB denied access. The British immediately responded by threatening to limit or suspend charter operations of U.S. supplemental carriers. Fortunately the crisis was averted when Cunard merged with British Overseas Airways Corporation (BOAC).

The United States decided in 1963 that its carriers should be encouraged in the charter market. The CAB therefore granted temporary five-year certificates to serve the North Atlantic to two supplemental carriers—Capitol Airways and Saturn Airways—effective April 30, 1964.[20] The Board felt that a continued interest and identity in the market, rather than the ad hoc basis of the past in which many carriers had participated, would provide these two carriers with a better chance of effective operation. Since that time the CAB has increased the number of U.S. charter operators; three carriers were given special permits for the 1965 peak season,[21] and a year later they were given five-year certification in the North Atlantic. At the same time the Board sharply curtailed off-route charters of U.S. scheduled carriers in the Atlantic—Trans World Airways (TWA) and Pan American Airways (PAA). The limit of 2½ percent *quarterly* of the previous year's total was replaced by an *annual* limit of 2 percent.[22] This restriction on the charter operations of PAA and TWA was intended to aid the U.S. supplemental carriers. Since this restriction on PAA and TWA off-route operations in the entire Atlantic market still allowed unlimited concentration in any particular city-pair, the Board subsequently further curtailed PAA and TWA charter operations by creating limitations on a city-pair basis.[23]

As a consequence of entry into the charter market by both European and U.S. firms, the North Atlantic charter market has become extremely competitive. The scheduled European carriers committed themselves in the early 1960s to obtaining a share of the peak tourist market by charters, and recently a number of non-IATA foreign-flag carriers appeared.[24] PAA and TWA have subsequently expanded their efforts in the charter area.

[20] Transatlantic Charter Investigation, CAB Docket No. 11908, Order E-20776, April 30, 1964, and Certificate of Public Convenience and Necessity for Supplemental Air Transportation.

[21] CAB, Order E-22045, April 16, 1965 (Overseas National Airways, American Flyers, World, and Trans International Airlines), and Order E-22260, June 2, 1965. Although American Flyers was an applicant to the original order, its permit was not granted until June 2, 1965. Overseas National Airways' application was dismissed November 23, 1965, because of financial problems.

[22] CAB, ER-419, issued September 18, 1964, to be effective October 26, 1964.

[23] CAB, ER-443, issued September 2, 1965, to be effective October 10, 1965.

[24] Reopened Transatlantic Charter Investigation Case, CAB Docket No. 11908, Brief filed by TWA (September 13, 1965), pp. 14–18. In 1963, only one such carrier, Caledonian Airways, Ltd., held a permit. Later Caledonian was joined by four others: British Eagle International Airlines, Kar-Air, Sudflug, and Adria Airways. Output of this group increased from 8,200 passengers in 1963 to 33,961 in 1965. There are many more potential applicants. Icelandic has indicated plans to enter more actively into charter operations.

The large increases in charter operations by the European carriers have implicitly defined charter flights as grounds upon which they are willing to compete. The United States should meet this competition, on the expectation of benefits to the less affluent traveler, the airlines, and perhaps to our effort to attain "reasonable" rates. A sharp increase in charter operations might convince those opposed to fare cuts that fare reductions would stimulate demand still further. The huge growth in charter operations in 1961 seemingly had this sort of effect, for the success of the charters at that time was construed as evidence of a demand for lower priced group flights and thus led to the adoption of group fares.

The means to encourage this competition, in particular the granting of entry rights, necessarily raises some difficult issues, many of which tend to be very political in nature. The Board continually finds itself weighing the economic fortunes of particular companies in its domestic route decisions,[25] and this would also be true in decisions on international route grants or entry. Indeed, the Board's decisions about what additional domestic carriers will be granted entry in the Pacific—and there is a huge list of hopefuls spurred on by the pricing deadlock and the possibility of large profits—will be one of the most influential decisions of the Board of recent years with regard to the future of various carriers.

Civil Aeronautics Board policy which regulates the charter market continually involves a weighing of equity considerations among U.S. supplemental and scheduled carriers. For example, it was frequently suggested that Board policy which protected supplemental charter operators at the expense of restricting TWA and PAA operations was overly conservative (with regard to the potential of the charter market) and reduced the chances to further encourage fare rationalization. The restrictive policy has certainly helped Capitol and Saturn to become established, but its continuance might well have aided these particular U.S. supplemental carriers at the expense of broader objectives.[26] The

[25] Richard E. Caves, *Air Transport and Its Regulators* (Harvard University Press, 1962), pp. 192–231.

[26] The very substantial profits which some of the supplementals have earned have recently attracted public attention. World Airways, Capitol, and Trans International, three of the largest supplementals licensed in the transatlantic, earned a higher rate of return on stockholders' equity for the year ended June 30, 1967, than did the scheduled carriers. Transatlantic licenses apparently were the turning point in these carriers' financial fortunes; all made huge profits during

scheduled carriers, as most capable competitors, must be encouraged in the charter market. For these reasons, the 2 percent limit on the off-route operations of PAA and TWA was recently relaxed.[27] The economic position of the supplementals was deemed much improved, principally because large military contracts have left them short of capacity. In addition, large numbers of charter passengers which PAA and TWA could not serve because of the restrictions arranged for charter flights with foreign carriers, hence producing a balance of payments loss.

The role of the CAB in promoting inclusive tour operations has involved the same questions. In 1966, the Board took a major step toward opposing the IATA fare structure by licensing U.S. supplementals in the trans-Atlantic to offer inclusive tour charters.[28] This amounted to a big marketing step, since most IATA charters had been based on "affinity" rules which define a group. The operator for the inclusive tour must sell the total package for at least 110 percent of the regular air fare, but the price between agent and carrier for the aircraft service is a matter for negotiation. IATA, after an initial outcry protesting the CAB action in licensing such cut-rate charter competition,[29] responded at the December meeting in Rome by sanctioning inclusive tours at much lower rates.[30] Again, CAB pressure appears to have been successful, but at the possible expense of placing the smaller supplementals in the charter market in a hard competitive struggle with the larger scheduled carriers.

U.S. POLICY IN THE PACIFIC REGION. In the Pacific, the charter position is somewhat different. Charter operations in this region have been carried on almost solely by U.S. carriers (both scheduled and supplemental), which receive licenses on a case-by-case basis. In September 1964 the

---

the 1965–66 tourist season and have continued to do so since that time. On the other hand, supplementals which did not receive this favorable route license have not done as well. James P. Wooley, "Meanwhile, on the Supplemental Airline Scene," *American Aviation*, Vol. 30 (February 1967), pp. 23–24; Fred S. Hunter, "Top Supplementals Make Top Money," *American Aviation*, Vol. 31 (February 1968), pp. 61–63.

[27] CAB, Reg. ER-482, issued January 13, 1967, effective January 18, 1967.

[28] CAB, Reg. ER-475, adopted March 11, 1966, to be effective November 26, 1966.

[29] Eric Bramley, "New Rights May Prove a Million-Dollar Plum for Supplementals," *American Aviation*, Vol. 30 (November 1966), pp. 35–36.

[30] "$165 to $230 to Europe?" *New York Times*, January 1, 1967, Section XX, p. 1.

CAB licensed the first charter operator in the Pacific—World Airways, Inc.[31]—and subsequently licensed Trans International Airlines, Inc.[32] U.S. scheduled carriers in the Pacific have naturally opposed these grants. While encouraging charter operations is a proper method of competition in the Atlantic, this position must be moderated in the Pacific. Licensing several new U.S. charter operators might produce undesirable results. First, foreign carriers in the Pacific have not made much of an effort to sell charter operations; their relative difficulty in competing with the United States might lead them to restrict landing rights. Bilateral negotiations with Japan and the Philippines, always difficult, might also be hindered. In general, more care must be taken by the United States in dealing in the Pacific because of the smaller number of gateways, the smaller number of firms, and the relative "youth" of these firms. The Pacific carriers tend to be more restrictive and less receptive to U.S. efforts at rationalization. A consensus by countries in the Pacific region to suspend landing rights or otherwise restrict U.S. operations appears more likely than in the Atlantic, for example, because of the relatively small number of foreign carriers and the limited diversity of their interests. Expansion of charter operations by the existing U.S. flag carriers might be a safer means of bringing pressure to bear on fares.

[31] CAB Docket No. 15254, Order E-21304 (September 21, 1964).
[32] CAB Docket No. 15594, Order E-21574 (December 9, 1964).

CHAPTER XII

The Industry in the Future

THE INTERNATIONAL AIRLINE INDUSTRY will continue to change dramatically in the coming years as the industry grows and new technology evolves. In Western Europe especially, more and more people will be able to afford air travel. New technology offers the potential of fare reductions, which will further contribute to the industry's growth. There is no end in sight to the very high growth in demand for the services of the industry.

The ever-increasing level of demand is the factor which has probably contributed most toward alleviating the problems of the transition to jets and toward making the industry commercially viable. Nevertheless, public policy will continue to have a marked effect on the industry's future performance. The challenges remain large, especially those of making successful use of the evolving technology. If they are handled poorly, the industry could again take on the appearance of a struggling "infant industry." This chapter briefly outlines these challenges.

The Prospects for Rationalization

Many countries stand to gain from a rationalization of the industry. The United States is by no means the only country suffering from the existing restrictive industry structure and resultant performance, nor are U.S. carriers the only efficient operators. The comparative cost disadvantages faced by many large European carriers were shown to be due to scheduling difficulties rather than to any inherent disadvantages in factor endowments or technology. Briefly, comparative advantage in airline operations requires access to capital for jet equipment and a management skilled enough to achieve certain levels of input utilization and other internal efficiencies. Thus, a number of carriers which are not efficient at present have the potential of becoming so, and would benefit from industry rationalization. It is not unreasonable to hope for progress toward that goal.

If rationalization is to be achieved, nations must be willing to risk their carriers' fortunes in a less restricted environment. Many countries are not so inclined, some with quite good reason—their carriers can expect to suffer from more competition. The flag carriers which are heavily dependent on internal cross-subsidization are in this category. Many governments, however, appear to be advocating restrictionist policies even though they have little cause for alarm—perhaps because of their previous historical position requiring protection or because of a lack of confidence in a rationalized outcome.

There are good reasons why countries other than the United States may find rationalization to be in their own interests. The growing number of economically efficient carriers represents a vested interest in avoiding further restrictions on entry or pricing. The recent profit levels experienced by a number of carriers, including some of the larger European carriers which are not particularly efficient, also should encourage rationalization. The recent level of profits raises questions as to the need for further subsidies and ought to influence governments to discontinue their present policies of underwriting losses. In addition, as more and more European nationals travel abroad there will be an increased pressure for a wider interpretation of the public interest; European governments should become more interested in their traveling citizens and less concerned about their flag carriers. Promotion of tourism is most easily achieved by a reduction in air fares. This step is frequently in conflict with protectionist policies supporting a flag carrier. The overall growth in travel and the prospect of large balance of payments earnings are making the promotion of tourism increasingly important to many countries. Governments should gradually respond to these pressures by taking more and more interest in a rationalized industry.

There is even some evidence that such a trend is underway. Considerable increases in crew and aircraft productivity occurred from 1962 to 1964. A number of carriers with mediocre records in the jet transition phase appear now to have made progress toward rationalizing their operations. In recent years, a number of large European carriers have looked critically into their operations and have taken steps to improve their operating efficiency. British Overseas Airways Corporation adopted the "Guthrie" plan to reduce the number of its employees from 20,600 in 1964 to 17,300 in 1966.[1] The firm's losses have aroused opinion in Britain; apparently the public does not feel that the company should employ unnecessary personnel as a means of providing jobs. KLM Royal Dutch Airlines also went through a considerable management and operating shakeup and in 1964 dropped 1,100 employees from the payroll, despite some expensive job termination settlements.[2] Scandinavian Airlines System and Air France also made an effort in 1964 to improve their operations.

Implications for the Less Developed Countries

The assessment of benefits and costs in determining international aviation policy by the developing countries differs from that used for advanced countries. As indicated earlier, the benefits of regional air service can be substantial. Linking a nation with its neighbors and with the long-haul network increases accessibility and can aid in attracting trade, tourism, private investment, and foreign aid. Regional air service may provide a number of other external benefits. In cases where economical operations are not possible, the benefits to development are such that the state may have to provide the service itself. On the other hand, the benefits of entry into the long-haul jet markets are less tangible; the political benefits of showing the flag and of advertisements abroad are the major considerations. These must be weighed against possible operating subsidies and foreign exchange costs, both of which can be substantial.

Subsidy and foreign exchange costs depend upon the efficiency with which a firm operates and the nature of the route system involved. Less developed countries must consider their relative factor prices carefully when making operating decisions, both on ground op-

[1] *Air Travel* (January 1965), p. 27.
[2] KLM annual reports.

erations and on plane choice. Aircraft scheduling is important in determining the appropriate plane choice; input scheduling is also an important determinant of all cost levels and therefore of resultant subsidy costs. Successful, efficient operations require a certain level of sophistication in handling basic scheduling problems.

Many of the less developed countries appear quite capable of participating efficiently in regional markets. On the other hand, efficient entry into the long-haul jet markets is more difficult because of higher capital requirements and increased competition. Some carriers (for example, El Al Israel Airlines and Air-India) have done well in the long-haul jet markets, but most have not been successful. Foreign exchange difficulties have been encountered by long-haul carriers of most of the less developed countries. Route extensions have often been made at the expense of lower utilization rates and in circumstances where capital constraints make it impossible to schedule flights at frequencies which compare favorably with those of the better-equipped established carriers. Moreover, successful entry may not become any easier in the future. The major routes promise to become more competitive, as many of the established European carriers extend their operations.

In areas where jet technology appears to be the proper choice for the regional operations of less developed countries, this would be the logical starting point for any expansion plans. Lessons learned in a regional jet operation might then be applied to long-haul operations in the future. Probably the two most important considerations relevant to a nation's decision to enter the long-haul market are the availability of outside financing and the opportunity to negotiate favorable bilateral route grants.

Special consideration in the world capital market can be very helpful. Often U.S. aid money is available for technical assistance and for financing jet purchases. With respect to entry considerations, nations located on important long-haul routes can negotiate for access to important markets. Examples of carriers belonging to countries favorably situated on or near long-haul routes include El Al Israel Airlines, Air-India, and Pakistan International Airlines. If carriers can gain access to sufficient fifth freedom traffic in long-haul markets and can achieve the needed level of technical skill, such expansion can be profitable. Spares pools and maintenance subcontracting arrangements with larger carriers can also be helpful.

The overall policies of the various developing countries with regard

to restriction or nonrestriction on entry, pricing, pools, etc., are important. Presumably those nations with relatively efficient carriers should
be inclined toward policies which lead to industry rationalization. Unfortunately for the industry, the carriers of most developing nations are
inefficient and will continue to be so, especially in the long-haul markets, and will want the protection of restrictionist policies. The less
developed nations on the whole, therefore, will probably oppose the
gradual move toward industry rationalization.

The Promise of New Technology

The jet revolution of the last decade has been spectacular, but continuing advances in jet technology and the advent of the supersonic age
will be equally so. The evolving subsonic technology will produce some
definite improvements, as outlined in Chapter V. The Boeing 727 and
Douglas DC-9 at present are producing cost economies at shorter stage
lengths; and, as turbine engine technology develops, additional cost
savings will accrue to these three- and two-engine planes. In the next
decade "stretched" versions of the DC-8, 727, and DC-9, and the jumbo
jets, will reduce costs well below today's levels.

The supersonic transport (SST) has the potential of providing dramatic time savings. For example, flight time from New York to Los Angeles will be two hours, as compared with five hours for present jets.
The severity of the sonic boom is still a major unknown; public reaction to the sonic boom will condition decisions on whether the plane
will be scheduled over densely populated areas and also on how much
additional cost must be incurred because of choices about flight pro-
files, altitudes, and subsonic operating speeds that attempt to reduce
the boom. Even if sonic boom problems are such that the plane cannot
be scheduled over populated areas, about 50 percent of the international markets over 700 miles can still receive supersonic service. It
therefore appears that substantial savings in travel time will be available for a modest price. In the longer-haul markets the supersonic
plane is expected to be essentially competitive with the stretched DC-
8s, and its projected costs are only silghtly above the costs of the
jumbo jets. The large time savings of the SST in long stage lengths
may well make it the dominant aircraft by 1990 in these markets if the
SST demand density is high enough to sustain load factors of about 60

percent and utilization rates on the order of nine to ten hours per day.

Realization of this potential will depend in part on the ability of the airlines to handle scheduling and other problems associated with the transition to this new equipment. These transition problems are fundamentally important for management attention. Realization of the SST potential also depends on the ability of the airlines to finance what has become a huge and very rapidly growing capital investment. Finally, the nature of pricing and scheduling policies ultimately determines the extent to which cost reductions are passed on to the traveler—in the form of lower fares, greater schedule frequency, or greater attention to service. In view of the considerable governmental influence in the market environment, the performance of the international airline industry is the responsibility of the public as well as of the airlines.

It was argued earlier that a more open entry environment than that existing today would be beneficial in the future—this is especially important to the success of supersonic transport. If the restricted market environment experienced during the switch from piston to jets also prevails during the SST transition period, the results could be very costly in view of the scheduling requirements for economic operation of the SST. The prestige associated with supersonic operations will be highly valued by many countries and could breed such protection. However, the economic stakes will be very high; the technical, management, and scheduling sophistication needed and the capital investments required will be so great that perhaps premature SST entry by uneconomic operators—and particularly by large numbers of developing countries—can be avoided. Given a reasonably rational entry pattern into supersonic operations, the motives for excessively protective policies will be less strong. A rational entry pattern and unrestricted choice of equipment are important objectives in the decade ahead if the SST is to realize its full potential.

While there are no a priori arguments which indicate the appropriate mix of fare reductions, service improvements, and increased schedule frequency that should result from the coming cost reductions, consumer tastes seem to suggest that fare reductions are desired more than improved service or scheduling. The operating costs of the stretched jets ought to be the basis for "standard" tourist fares in the decade ahead, which means that tourist rates would be 10 to 15 percent lower than they are now. The use of jumbo jets may result in further fare reductions as passenger densities permit. Aircraft of the present jet technology probably will continue to be used, because of their excellent performance to date in terms of durability and low maintenance costs. Existing jet equipment probably will still be competitive for some time through price depreciation. The earliest jets will be almost entirely written off in ten years' time and will be sold on the used market at prices reduced sufficiently to make them competitive with stretched jets. These older jets will be the equipment used by entrants with high capital costs.

The importance of fare reductions as costs are decreased in the industry cannot be overemphasized. The U.S. domestic airline industry has enjoyed considerable prosperity in recent years as the replacement of piston aircraft by jets has sharply lowered unit costs. This trend toward lower costs will continue as the latest three- and two-engine jets are put into service on the shortest stage lengths. Fare reductions during this period have been relatively small, primarily selective reductions in the off-peak period given to special classes of travelers—family discounts, nonweekend rates, and excursion fares of one sort or another. This kind of off-peak pricing and promotional fare cutting has much in its favor and for the airlines is a particularly popular way of cutting fares. However, this fairly limited rate reduction and the high profits made recently by the major airlines have stimulated debate concerning the appropriate rate of return for this regulated industry. High capital requirements for re-equipment have been set forth as an appropriate reason for permitting high cash flows and high internal rates of return.

The international airlines will go through this same experience in the immediate future and will need to resolve these same questions. The airlines will surely use selective fare reductions on group or tour flights and charter operations as the first means of satisfying public pressure to cut fares. This sort of price cutting is the most likely result of present International Air Transport Association (IATA) procedures. Participants, including carriers and governments, will be quite attentive to the capital demands of new equipment which loom in the future— first for stretched versions of the present jets and subsequently for the jumbo jets and supersonic transport. The very sharp losses the industry has sustained in the recent past, regardless of the reasons for the losses, will not be forgotten. Considerable pressure to generate high internal profits will surely prevail, both to recover these past subsidy losses and to help finance new equipment.

The appropriate decisions concerning internal versus capital market financing and concerning the role of excess profits in this financing are not easily made. There are, however, some important arguments to be made against relying on high profits as a source of internal funds. First, the capital market for the airlines is much different now from the market in the 1950s, when sensitivity of demand to business conditions and inability of the industry to sustain profits over any period of time made capital investment or loans appear somewhat risky.[3] The high growth in demand and the cost reductions resulting from jet technology have converted airline operations into a rapidly growing and prosperous industry; capital is now available via bonds, convertible or otherwise, or new issues of stock. While the capital outlays for jumbo jets and supersonic equipment will be large, world capital markets will be more than up to the task; capital probably will be readily available at rates comparable to those offered other types of corporations at that time. Unusual capital requirements do not appear to be a convincing argument in favor of monopoly profits over the coming years as a source of internal funds.

Unless the IATA price cartel is made more responsive to rational pricing objectives, the considerable cost reductions which will arise with the stretched and jumbo jets may be lost to the traveling public, either through excessive profits to the carriers, through expenditures on service competition and advertising, or through poor internal control by airline management. The stretched and jumbo jets are especially suited to marketing a "mass travel" service if appropriately priced, but they could be used by the airlines in an exploitative fashion if prices are not, in fact, reduced.

A rational fare structure in the important international markets in 1975 will almost certainly consist of a dual set of fares—tourist and first class services—with the latter employing supersonic equipment where possible. The much faster supersonic equipment will allow the airlines to offer a first class service which will be genuinely different from the alternative tourist service (a real change from the present!). A dual fare structure will be necessary if the subsonic jet equipment is appropriately priced.

Some industry skeptics have suggested that the considerable invest-

[3] The fact that this risk was more apparent than real has been described by Caves in his analysis of the U.S. domestic airline industry. See Richard E. Caves, *Air Transport and Its Regulators* (Harvard University Press, 1962), pp. 398–402.

ments by governments in financing the development of the SST and eventually in financing the equipment itself could result in government opposition to fare reductions for service using subsonic technology, lest these undermine the market for supersonic service. Large reductions in subsonic fares could perhaps make inroads into the market expected for supersonic flights, but this view is regarded by this writer as somewhat extreme, based in part on a more optimistic forecast of the market for the SST for long-haul flights than the skeptics anticipate, and in part on the expectation that the governments involved will not rate the economic results of their supersonic investments so highly that they will advocate this sort of cross-subsidy. The IATA price system and the airlines themselves appear to be the more likely sources of opposition to fare reductions which will be made possible by the evolving subsonic equipment, rather than the governments in the countries where air service is in greatest demand. Airlines which are not well equipped because of capital constraints or which want a luxury-oriented service may continue to oppose fare rationalization.

Appendixes

Scheduling and Factor Substitution in the Production Function

$P_{\text{RODUCTION}}$ TECHNIQUES FOR INTERNATIONAL AIRLINE SERVICE and the inputs used appear relatively homogeneous for all firms. This makes the industry particularly well suited to international comparison. There is one important exception—differences in ability to schedule certain inputs. These differences are revealed by some simple cross-section comparisons of input productivity levels, after appropriate adjustment for the effects of plane choice and route system on input productivity. These differences, especially that of scheduling equipment, appear to reflect differences in management.

The production function itself is characterized by variable proportions, with the possibility of considerable input substitution. There are certain fixed coefficients relating fuel, crew, and other inputs for each plane type. However, the choice of planes involves possible substitution of capital for labor, or vice versa. The jets are a capital-intensive choice, but are economical with respect to fuel, labor, and maintenance costs. Similarly, more or less labor can be used in baggage handling, reservations, and sales functions. Passenger services on board also can be simple or lavish, the latter type generally requiring more labor.

Factor substitution has often been postulated in production studies, but empirical documentation has been difficult. Intra-country data do not typically exhibit much variation in factor prices or factor proportions. The widely differing factor prices in an international industry are such that a wide range of input combinations often exists. This sample variation is necessary if the extent to which input substitution is possible is to be empirically determined.

The international airline industry in the early 1960s, with its transition period from piston planes to jets, is particularly well suited to observing and

232

parameterizing such factor substitution. During this period the structure of operating costs of piston and jet aircraft was such that carriers with differing factor prices, especially in the costs of capital and foreign exchange, reacted in very different ways to the opportunity to use jets. Those carriers least constrained by capital costs were the first to purchase the jets. Other characteristics of the international airline industry help to minimize problems which often plague empirical production studies of input substitution: the production function is relatively homogeneous, the stock of aircraft as the capital input is variable in the fairly short run, and the existence of a relatively perfect market for used aircraft permits a reliable measure of the amount of real capital actually employed. The discussion below will focus first on scheduling or input productivity differences and then on the factor substitution which occurred during the jet transition period.

Input Scheduling

Aircraft Scheduling

Aircraft scheduling is the dimension of input scheduling which probably has the greatest effects on costs. Differences in daily utilization rates affect the productivity of a firm's aircraft fleets and hence unit costs of depreciation, as well as some portion of maintenance costs.

The explicit scheduling measure developed below is based on differences in daily aircraft utilization rates. The industry average daily utilization rates for each plane type are used as a standard for comparison, after appropriate adjustment for route system effects. Interpretation of aircraft utilization rates is complicated by the fact that carriers are often in the process of phasing equipment in or out. In the period under observation here, the transition from piston to jet planes was occurring. Some carriers probably did not attempt to schedule their piston aircraft as intensively as their jets since the former represented standby equipment. Low utilization rates for piston aircraft in these circumstances, of course, need not necessarily reflect any serious management weakness. Treating piston equipment as a standby fleet tends to lower the average utilization of piston equipment for the industry. At the same time, jet utilization rates may be affected by the tendency for a firm to sustain low utilization rates temporarily when adopting new equipment. The time required to raise these utilization rates to levels comparable to the utilization rates of its competitors may be fairly short or quite long. Of interest here are the more persistent differences in aircraft utilization realized by different firms.

An initial comparison was made of each firm's fleet productivity with that which would have been achieved if the firm's utilization rates had been equal to the industry average. The fleet productivity ratio, R_j, is given by

$$R_j = \frac{\sum_i (n_{ij} \cdot s_i \cdot u_i)}{\sum_i (n_{ij} \cdot s_i \cdot u_{ij})},$$

where:

n_{ij} = number of planes of type i in the fleet of firm j,
u_{ij} = utilization rate of plane type i (hours per day) for firm j,
s_i = average productivity per hour, in seat-miles, for plane i for the industry, and
u_i = average utilization rate of plane type i (hours per day) for the industry.

R_j denotes the fleet productivity ratio for all aircraft; R'_j denotes the same measure based on only the jet portion of each firm's fleet. Realized utilization of the inherently more productive aircraft—the jets—has a greater effect in the above summations for R_j. A value of R_j greater than unity denotes that the fleet of firm j was not as productive (available seat-miles flown) as if the firm had realized daily utilization rates comparable to the average for the industry.

This measure of relative productivity depends on the interpretation of the industry's average utilization rates. The mean utilization level is a numerical average of all international carriers; as an average it does not reflect desired or efficient levels. (And, as shown in Table A-1, some of the mean levels are not high.) In addition, smaller carriers which rely primarily on piston aircraft—and hence schedule them more frequently than those carriers which count piston planes as standby capacity—will tend to receive a "higher score" in the above fleet productivity ratios.

The daily productivity of the fleet of firm j—

$$\sum_i (n_{ij} \cdot s_i \cdot u_{ij})$$

—reflects its choice of plane type, its scheduling or realized utilization rates for those aircraft, and the firm's route system. With regard to the route system, stage length affects the ease with which equipment can be scheduled and therefore affects the utilization rates, all other things equal. Stage length also should affect hourly productivity of each aircraft because of the effect of stage length on average speed. This latter effect is subsumed in the assumption of a single industry average for hourly productivity of each aircraft type, s_i. Rather than derive functional relationships for each firm's hourly plane productivity and utilization based on the firm's particular route system, a single equation was derived which should appropriately adjust the productivity ratios, R_j, for these effects of the route system on productivity. This is a simplification necessitated by practical considerations; insufficient information is available about the scheduling problems associated with particular plane types and route systems to proceed on a more disaggregated basis.

The route system variables postulated as appropriate to explain fleet productivity (independent of scheduling differences among firms) were firm size, route density, and stage length. In the 1964 sample the effect of stage length was statistically significant in explaining variation in R_j. Shorter

TABLE A-1. *Productivity and Capital Costs of Selected Models of Aircraft, 1964*

| Aircraft Make and Model | Productivity Factors[a] | | | Capital Costs | | |
	Seats	Speed (miles per hour)	Utilization (hours per day)	Market Price (thousands of dollars)	Future Life (years)	Capital Cost per Day, d_i (dollars)
Jet						
Boeing 707	144	470	9.52	6,000	11	1,494
Douglas DC-8	144	470	9.33	6,200	11	1,544
Boeing 720	115	460	8.67	4,800	11	1,196
Convair 990	105	465	6.93	5,400	10	1,479
Convair 880	105	465	7.42	5,200	11	1,295
Tupolev TU-104	90	460	...	4,500	9	1,370
Comet 4	85	450	7.80	4,500	9	1,370
Caravelle	84	450	6.08	3,000	9	913
Boeing 727	94	440	7.05	4,500	11	1,121
Trident	88	440	3.40	4,500	11	1,121
Turboprop						
Canadair CL-44	148	250	9.18	3,300	9	1,005
Britannia 300s	109	260	4.33	1,000	8	342
Britannia 100s	109	260	...	1,000	8	342
Vanguard	132	300	6.13	3,000	8	1,027
Electra	80	300	6.83	1,500	10	411
Viscount V-800s	64	220	5.72	700	7	274
Viscount V-700s	52	220	5.85	500	7	196
Herald	44	200	4.00	400	6	183
Fairchild F-27	40	200	6.03	900	10	247
Piston						
Lockheed 1649	86	275	1.80	100	6	46
Douglas DC-7s	90	265	6.47	150	6	68
Lockheed 1049	86	265	3.98	150	6	68
Lockheed 749	74	215	3.52	100	5	55
Douglas DC-6B	84	245	5.78	250	7	98
Douglas DC-6A	84	245	5.78	250	7	98
Douglas DC-6	84	245	...	250	7	98
Douglas DC-4	56	225	3.83	75	5	41
Heron	14	220	2.13	100	6	45
Convair 440	44	195	5.83	125	6	57
Convair 340	44	195	5.83	100	5	55
Convair 240	40	185	5.70	75	4	51
Curtiss C-46	52	180	4.12	40	5	22
Martin 404	40	175	5.10	60	4	41
Douglas DC-3	28	150	3.15	40	5	22

Sources: Figures for number of seats and speed are based on author's assumptions, given the stage length. Utilization data are averages reported by ICAO carriers in 1964; see International Civil Aviation Organization, *Digest of Statistics, Fleet and Personnel*, No. 116 (1964), pp. 26–31. Market price and future life of aircraft are author's estimates based on prices as reported in trade journals.

[a] Figures are the numerical average of all international carriers.

stage lengths decreased aircraft productivity, presumably because of more frequent turn-arounds and necessary minimum down time. The equations for the 1964 fleet productivity ratios were as follows:

(1) Total fleet

$$R_j = 1.1552 + 0.0918(1/d) - 0.1616 AC(d) \qquad R^2 = 0.3404$$
$$\quad\quad\quad (0.0245) \qquad\quad (0.1096)$$

(2) Jet portion of total fleet

$$R'_j = 1.2826 + 0.2254(1/d) - 0.3412 AC(d) \qquad R^2 = 0.3856$$
$$\quad\quad\quad (0.0571) \qquad\quad (0.1476)$$

where d is average stage length and $AC(d)$ is an estimate of direct costs as a function of plane choice and stage length.

In the 1962 sample examined, none of these variables proved to be statistically significant in explaining variation in the productivity ratios. The inherent scheduling difficulties for a transition period when a new plane type is added or substituted for old equipment, and the varying ability with which managements cope with these problems, apparently have resulted in a large enough variation in fleet productivity to conceal any underlying route system effects.

The effect of scheduling differences on fleet productivities net of route system effects for firm j is simply the ratio of the actual productivity ratio, R_j, to the "expected" ratio, R^e_j, as given by the above equations: $S_{aj} = R_j/R^e_j$. S'_{aj} denotes the same measure for the jet portion of the fleet of firm j. Since in the 1962 sample no equation was found as an appropriate reflection of route system effects on fleet productivity, the fleet productivity measure for 1962 also is the scheduling measure of the effect of aircraft utilization rate differences $(S_{aj} = R_j)$.

The aircraft scheduling data appear in Tables A-2 and A-3. The figures for 1962 exhibit the larger variance and to a greater extent reflect the transition from piston to jet planes than the figures for 1964. There are no apparent explanations of the scheduling differences in 1962 in such variables as firm size, wage levels, or the labor scheduling measures derived below. Scheduling differences are influential in explaining a particular firm's capital costs and are a partial explanation of the cost measures of relative efficiency. (This is discussed in Chapter IX.) The fact that route system effects are discernible in the 1964 fleet productivity ratios lends more support to the 1964 figures. High-wage firms were the superior jet aircraft schedulers in 1964, as evidenced by the inverse correlation (-0.2518) of S'_{aj} with labor's wage. At the same time the wage was inversely correlated with the scheduling of the piston portion of the fleet, reflecting the fact that many high-wage carriers were phasing out and selling off their piston fleets.

With regard to particular firms, the measures of aircraft scheduling for the two years were positively though not highly correlated. Notable in the changes in the ranking of particular firms are the records of four of the largest carriers—PAA, TWA, BOAC, and Air France; in each case these carriers received a significantly "lower" score for scheduling in 1964 than

TABLE A-2. *Fleet Productivity and Scheduling Ratios, Selected Air Carriers, 1964*

Carrier[d]	Daily Opportunity Cost of Capital for Aircraft Fleet, $\sum_i (d_i n_i)$ (dollars)	Fleet Productivity, $\sum_i (n_i s_i u_i)$ (millions of seat-miles)	Fleet Productivity Ratios[a]		Aircraft Scheduling Ratios[b]	
			Total Fleet, R_j	Jets, R'_j	Total Fleet, S_{aj}	Jets, S'_{aj}
Trans World Airlines	130,137	52.722	1.050	1.058	1.042	1.059
Pan American Airways	71,682	50.102	1.021	0.975	1.027	1.015
British Overseas Airways Corporation	78,481	26.235	0.933	0.935	1.031	1.006
Air France	77,096	26.921	1.041	1.042	1.021	1.013
Northwest Airlines	38,464	18.331	0.901	0.879	0.933	0.990
Air Canada	55,969	17.267	1.059	1.106	1.040	1.057
Alitalia Airlines	38,242	14.947	0.918	0.918	0.892	0.883
KLM Royal Dutch Airlines	32,235	14.076	0.985	0.914	0.975	0.900
Lufthansa German Airlines	19,397	9.070	0.892	0.900	0.854	0.837
British European Airways	49,697	11.565	1.037	1.146	1.009	1.060
Scandinavian Airlines System	27,058	10.509	0.937	0.990	0.942	1.004
Braniff International	19,238	9.265	1.050	1.059	1.017	0.968
Japan Air Lines	28,747	11.576	1.019	1.070	0.996	1.041
Swissair	23,047	7.763	0.894	0.887	0.856	0.826
Qantas Empire Airways	21,192	9.507	0.962	0.951	0.981	1.028
Iberia Airlines of Spain	18,617	6.737	1.081	1.092	1.067	1.071
Canadian Pacific Airlines	10,084	5.521	0.819	0.748	0.774	0.671
South African Airways	7,261	3.371	1.038	1.007	1.047	1.037
Sabena Belgian World Airlines	18,716	7.003	1.079	0.974	1.067	0.976
Aerolineas Argentinas	9,023	2.039	1.310	1.253	1.171	1.203
Pakistan International Airlines	7,264	2.689	0.879	0.899	0.856	0.862

Footnotes to table appear on p. 238.

TABLE A-2—*Continued*

Carrier[d]	Daily Opportunity Cost of Capital for Aircraft Fleet, $\sum_i (d_i n_i)$ (dollars)	Fleet Productivity, $\sum_i (n_i s_i u_i)$ (millions of seat-miles)	Fleet Productivity Ratios[a]		Aircraft Scheduling Ratios[b]	
			Total Fleet, R_j	Jets, R'_j	Total Fleet, S_{aj}	Jets, S'_{aj}
United Arab Airlines	11,008	2.915	0.989	1.035	0.989	1.045
Philippine Air Lines	4,795	2.331	0.731	0.791	0.797	1.100
East African Airways	5,046	1.436	0.806	0.814	0.751	0.745
Pan American-Grace Airways	6,448	2.809	1.118	1.014	0.891	1.045
Aerlinte Eireann	3,886	1.446	1.079	1.079	1.094	1.150
Finnair	6,183	1.224	1.375	1.508	1.203	1.171
Aer Lingus	3,914	1.006	0.975	—[c]	0.901	—[c]
Tasman Empire Airways	1,233	0.770	0.637	—[c]	0.523	—[c]
Austrian Airlines	3,901	0.926	1.134	1.039	1.081	0.929
Royal Air Maroc	2,893	0.920	0.898	0.864	0.878	0.835
Aviacion y Comercio	547	0.436	1.240	—[c]	1.125	—[c]
Caribair	517	0.329	1.302	—[c]	0.824	—[c]
Sociedad Aeronautica Medellin	208	0.257	1.048	—[c]	1.017	—[c]
El Al Israel Airlines	7,900	3.238	0.993	0.986	1.013	1.055
Aerotransportes del Litoral Argentino	110	0.840	0.781	—[c]	0.615	—[c]
Karhumaki, Veljeksef	243	0.125	1.368	—[c]	1.085	—[c]

[a] See text, pp. 233–36.
[b] See text, p. 236.
[c] No jets in the fleet.
[d] For data on aircraft utilization and fleet size of each carrier, see International Civil Aviation Organization, *Digest of Statistics, Fleet and Personnel*, No. 116 (1964).

1962. These carriers were well into the jet transition by 1962. Between 1962 and 1964 they saw their competitors make the transition, improve their fleet utilization, and thus close the scheduling gap. Carriers making the biggest improvements in equipment scheduling over the two-year period in this sample were Alitalia Airlines, Qantas Empire Airways, Swissair, Braniff International, Pan American-Grace Airways, Iberia Airlines of Spain, South African Airways, Pakistan International Airlines, United Arab Airlines, and East African Airways.

TABLE A-3. *Fleet Productivity Ratios, Selected Air Carriers, 1962*

Carrier[c]	Daily Opportunity Cost of Capital for Aircraft Fleet, $\sum_i (d_i n_i)$ (dollars)	Fleet Productivity, $\sum_i (n_i s_i u_i)$ (millions of seat-miles)	Fleet Productivity Ratios[a]	
			Total Fleet, R_j	Jets, R'_j
Trans World Airlines	78,400	43.556	0.995	1.002
Pan American Airways	36,218	41.686	1.004	0.983
British Overseas Airways Corporation	34,361	24.626	0.946	0.937
Air France	27,002	23.045	1.030	0.994
Northwest Airlines	36,665	12.938	1.017	1.033
Air Canada	19,507	14.960	1.011	1.079
Alitalia Airlines	11,404	11.212	0.939	0.947
KLM Royal Dutch Airlines	14,733	14.225	1.057	1.022
Lufthansa German Airlines	8,054	8.544	0.951	0.997
British European Airways	19,185	10.356	1.200	1.368
Scandinavian Airlines System	11,124	10.174	1.008	0.943
Braniff International	16,717	6.540	1.094	1.266
Japan Air Lines	7,831	9.858	0.806	0.872
Swissair	8,278	7.582	1.012	0.984
Qantas Empire Airways	7,761	6.776	1.170	1.117
Iberia Airlines of Spain	5,268	4.500	1.251	1.327
Canadian Pacific Airlines	4,676	4.759	0.875	0.804
South African Airways	3,229	2.776	1.298	1.210
Sabena Belgian World Airlines	7,223	6.043	1.137	0.997
Aerolineas Argentinas	8,627	2.330	1.141	1.197
Pakistan International Airlines	8,847	3.216	1.110	0.932
United Arab Airlines	10,837	2.303	1.136	1.224
Philippine Air Lines	4,073	1.660	0.911	1.225
East African Airways	1,889	1.004	1.169	0.972
Pan American-Grace Airways	2,275	2.471	1.055	0.981
Aerlinte Eireann	4,488	1.031	1.333	—[b]
Finnair	1,736	1.341	0.976	1.050
Aer Lingus	1,478	1.020	0.982	—[b]
Tasman Empire Airways	750	0.599	0.771	—[b]
Austrian Airlines	1,762	0.527	0.977	—[b]
Royal Air Maroc	844	0.761	0.937	1.003
Aviacion y Comercio	2,790	1.131	1.861	1.119
Caribair	268	0.253	1.346	—[b]
Sociedad Aeronautica Medellin	255	0.369	0.812	—[b]
El Al Israel Airlines	9,622	2.865	1.066	1.033
Aerotransportes del Litoral Argentino	135	0.119	0.700	—[b]
Karhumaki, Veljeksef	539	0.305	0.976	—[b]

[a] See text, pp. 233–36.
[b] No jets in fleet.
[c] For data on aircraft utilization and fleet size of each carrier, see International Civil Aviation Organization, *Digest of Statistics, Fleet and Personnel*, No. 102 (1962).

Crew Productivity

A similar scheme was developed to measure flight crew scheduling, essentially comparing the realized crew productivity of each firm's pilots, co-pilots, and other flight personnel (engineers, navigators, and radio operators, but not stewardesses) to the industry average.

As before, adjustments had to be made for each firm's choice of equipment. An estimate was made of the number of crew members required for each plane type. (All planes of one type are designed for the same size crew.) In the analysis below a four-man crew was assumed for jets, a three-man crew for four-engine piston planes and turboprops, and a two-man crew

TABLE A-4. *Aircraft Classified by Crew Size, 1964*

Four-Man Aircraft (Jet)	Three-Man Aircraft		Two-Man Aircraft (Two-Engine Piston)
	Turboprop	Four-Engine Piston	
Boeing 707, 720, 727	Canadair CL-44	Douglas DC-7s, DC-6s, DC-4	Curtiss C-46
Douglas DC-8	Britannia 100s, 200s, 300s	Lockheed 1649, 1049, 749, 049	Martin 404, 202
Convair 880, 990	Vanguard		Convair 340, 440
Tupolev TU-104	Electra	Argonaut	Douglas DC-3
Comet 4	Viscount V-700s, V-800s		Heron
Caravelle	Herald Armstrong- Whitworth 650 Fairchild F-27		Miscellaneous one- and two- engine aircraft

Source: See text.

for all two-engine planes. Any crew size greater than this (essentially the legal minimum) appears as "poor scheduling." The crew size data are shown in Table A-4. When using piston aircraft over long flight stages, the concept of a fixed "crew requirement" per piston-aircraft hour may not be strictly appropriate. An extra man or even an entire extra crew may be carried to provide relief for the trip of ten to twelve hours required to cross the North Atlantic in a DC-6 or DC-7. The alternative is to provide extra time off the day after a North Atlantic flight, hence implying a trade-off between bivouacking crews at a layover station. The appropriate "crew requirement" is thus not

TABLE A-5. *Flight Crew Employment and Scheduling Ratios, Selected Air Carriers, 1962 and 1964*

Carrier	1962			1964		
	Flight Crew, C_j (number of employees at mid-year)	Required Crew Hours, $\sum_i c_i h_{ij}$ (thousands)	Flight Crew Scheduling Ratios, S_{cj}	Flight Crew, C_j (number of employees at mid-year)	Required Crew Hours, $\sum_i c_i h_{ij}$ (thousands)	Flight Crew Scheduling Ratios, S_{cj}
Trans World Airlines	1,092.9	1,988	0.994	1,346.9	2,181	1.011
Pan American Airways	1,031.1	1,777	0.942	1,152.2	1,966	1.066
British Overseas Airways Corporation	690.2	1,481	1.172	667.0	1,382	1.294
Air France	756.2	1,267	0.916	683.2	1,286	1.170
Northwest Airlines	482.7	625	1.255	546.1	696	0.796
Air Canada	602.0	640	0.581	596.3	644	0.674
Alitalia Airlines	324.7	540	0.909	450.9	610	0.845
KLM Royal Dutch Airlines	510.5	1,429	1.530	437.4	1,084	1.548
Lufthansa German Airlines	378.9	514	0.741	392.3	582	0.926
British European Airways	494.5	894	0.988	592.2	920	0.970
Scandinavian Airlines System	342.3	875	1.397	363.9	885	1.519
Braniff International	388.9	501	1.198	369.3	74	0.834
Japan Air Lines	267.2	432	0.884	195.6	476	0.845
Swissair	217.0	472	1.189	247.2	491	1.240
Qantas Empire Airways	183.2	483	1.441	221.6	575	1.620
Iberia Airlines of Spain	200.2	280	0.762	261.8	317	0.755
Canadian Pacific Airlines	143.3	227	0.866	150.2	218	0.906
South African Airways	127.8	254	1.086	149.5	229	0.956
Sabena Belgian World Airlines	254.5	490	1.052	249.0	468	1.174
Aerolineas Argentinas	159.8	333	0.878	189.7	336	1.106
Pakistan International Airlines	135.4	350	0.692	138.0	431	1.950
United Arab Airlines	103.1	147	1.284	123.3	200	1.013
Philippine Air Lines	168.5	149	2.069	203.9	207	0.634
East African Airways	74.5	124	0.910	88.4	140	0.988
Pan American-Grace Airways	58.6	76	0.704	58.9	77	0.816

Source: See text, pp. 240–41.

TABLE A-5—*Continued*

Carrier	1962			1964		
	Flight Crew, C_j (number of employees at mid-year)	Required Crew Hours, $\sum_i c_i h_{ij}$ (thousands)	Flight Crew Scheduling Ratios, S_{cj}	Flight Crew, C_j (number of employees at mid-year)	Required Crew Hours, $\sum_i c_i h_{ij}$ (thousands)	Flight Crew Scheduling Ratios, S_{ej}
Aerlinte Eireann	29.6	56	1.034	33.8	73	1.346
Finnair	72.0	122	0.926	85.6	120	0.874
Aer Lingus	92.6	129	0.761	96.2	148	0.960
Tasman Empire Airways	31.2	71	1.244	39.3	85	1.349
Austrian Airlines	44.0	483	1.441	55.0	59	0.669
Royal Air Maroc	38.7	51	0.810	31.9	49	0.957
Aviacion y Comercio	66.3	81	1.499	70.3	91	0.808
Caribair	30.1	63	1.195	33.0	60	1.134
Sociedad Aeronautica Medellin	29.8	43	1.031	29.4	56	1.187
El Al Israel Airlines	67.1	138	0.890	108.4	143	0.824
Aerotransportes del Litoral Argentino	23.5	75	0.897	12.9	26	1.259
Karhumaki, Veljeksef	30.7	58	0.970	16.7	47	1.748

obvious as a standard for measuring a firm's performance. However, neglecting these subtleties probably has little bearing on performance measures developed here since the total amount of such long-haul piston service in the sample was empirically fairly small.

The productivity measure used was the output per employee of "required pilot-hours" derived from a firm's fleet by plane type.[1]

Let:

c_i = number of required pilots, co-pilots, and engineers in a crew of plane type i,

h_{ij} = number of hours flown by plane type i for the jth firm in a year,

$c_i h_{ij}$ = number of man-hours required, given the mix of plane-hours flown,

C_j = number of pilots, co-pilots, and other flight personnel employed by the jth firm at mid-year, and

$\sum_i c_i h_{ij} / C_j$ = required man-hours of output per employee for the jth firm.

---

[1] A measure similar to this was developed by Robert J. Gordon (when examining crew scheduling in the U.S. domestic industry). See Gordon's "Airline Costs and Managerial Efficiency," in *Transportation Economics* (Columbia University Press for National Bureau of Economic Research, 1965), pp. 70–75.

The mean of required flight hours of output per employee, λ, for the reporting firms for 1964 was 624.8 hours compared with 546.5 hours in 1962. A measure of the quality of crew scheduling is given by comparing each firm's output per employee with this industry mean. The crew scheduling quality ratio for firm j, denoted by S_{cj}, may therefore be expressed as follows:

(3) $$S_{cj} = \frac{\lambda \cdot C_j}{\sum_i c_i h_{ij}},$$

where $S_{cj} = 1$ for a firm obtaining just 624.8 hours from each employee in 1964 and $S_{cj} < 1$ for better crew scheduling than the industry average.

The crew productivity ratios for a number of firms appear in Table A-5. There is considerable similarity in the records for particular firms for the two years. No correlation existed between this measure of pilot scheduling and stage length or route density, although on a priori grounds one might suppose short stage lengths would have an effect. S_c was inversely correlated with pilot's wage (correlation, $r = -0.2669$), indicating that high-wage firms were better pilot schedulers. S_c was also correlated with "all other labor" scheduling ($r = 0.2564$), a measure discussed below.

"Nonflight Crew" Labor Productivity

The final measure of scheduling involves "all other labor," which refers to all labor except the flight crew. The following "labor-requirements" function—relating labor per seat-mile to the wage, the nature of the equipment employed, and the route system—was estimated cross-sectionally for 1962:

(4) $$(L/SM) = 0.7885 + 0.5640AC(d) - 91.8(1/d)$$
$$(0.2022) \qquad (37.5)$$
$$+ 1,700,000(n/SM) + 50.10(1/W_L) \qquad (R^2 = 0.5851)$$
$$(1,000,000) \qquad (15.80)$$

where

L = labor in man-years,
n = stations,
d = average stage length,
W_L = labor's wages in dollars,
SM = seat-miles in millions, and
$AC(d)$ is an estimate of direct costs as a function of plane choice and stage length (see Appendix B).

$AC(d)$ is a decreasing function as d increases and acts as a proxy in this equation.

The presence of stage length and route density in the labor-requirements function is as expected. Longer stage lengths and denser routes spread the fixed cost of ground personnel and also raise cabin crew input productivity through the economic use of larger aircraft, often jets. There are three possible explanations for the presence of labor's wage in the equation. One explanation is that firms paying higher wages are able to reduce the labor input by factor substitution. Another possibility is that higher wage labor is more productive. A third related possibility is that firms facing higher wages are better labor schedulers and hence get more output per laborer. While there is no means available to distinguish between these possibilities, the presence of labor's wage in this equation has been assumed here to reflect, at least in part, factor substitution in response to relative factor prices.

The quantity W_L appears in the equation in inverse form. The residuals of the equation are not correlated with either the wage or labor per seat-mile, suggesting that this particular specification of the equation was reasonable. This form for the labor-requirements equation implies that labor costs per seat-mile are independent of the wage and that differences in wages can be offset by substituting capital. This is consistent with actual industry experience, since actual labor costs per seat-mile are uncorrelated with the wage.

Deviations from this function can be considered labor scheduling abilities, with positive residuals indicating an excessive amount of labor employed. The ratio of actual to expected labor requirements—L_j/L_j^e—provides a measure of labor scheduling denoted by S_{lj} for the jth firm, which has taken into account both factor substitution and the nature of the route system (stage length and route density). This measure of labor scheduling is independent of the wage. The results of the labor scheduling calculation for a number of airlines appear in Table A-6. This measure of labor scheduling was correlated with flight crew scheduling but not with capital scheduling.

Factor Substitution through Aircraft Choice

Aircraft choice provides an important opportunity for firms to substitute inputs, a choice which is especially relevant to the developing countries. The structure of input requirements and costs—fuel, pilots, maintenance, etc.—varies with plane type. These differences are revealed by examining direct operating costs disaggregated into each input component. Data describing the breakdown of direct costs by component for each aircraft in the total domestic operations of U.S. carriers is available. (This breakdown will reflect the stage length over which the equipment was used, though the variation in the cost breakdown due to stage length will be only marginal.)

An important additional source of differences in the structure of costs by component is that of differing factor prices or input productivity. As suggested, the effects of different factor prices may be so great that the optimal or least-cost aircraft varies in different countries.

To illustrate the effects of differing factor prices on aircraft cost structures, two illustrative cases are compared—factor prices and costs for a carrier in the United States or Western Europe with relatively low capital costs, high

TABLE A-6. *Nonflight Crew Employment and Scheduling Ratios, Selected Air Carriers, 1962*

Carrier	Nonflight Crew, L_j (number of employees at mid-year)	Nonflight Crew Scheduling Ratios, S_{Lj}
Pan American Airways	21,660	0.853
British Overseas Airways Corporation	20,780	1.123
Air France	24,560	0.783
Air Canada	11,470	0.575
KLM Royal Dutch Airlines	15,850	1.375
Scandinavian Airlines System	11,100	1.262
Alitalia Airlines	6,470	0.664
British European Airways	15,540	1.109
Lufthansa German Airlines	11,860	1.089
Trans World Airlines	18,720	0.844
Swissair	7,200	1.212
Japan Air Lines	4,300	0.561
Sabena Belgian World Airlines	8,210	1.337
Qantas Empire Airways	6,120	1.467
Canadian Pacific Airlines	2,320	0.820
Iberia Airlines of Spain	4,360	0.655
Air-India	5,670	1.181
Avianca Airlines	5,370	0.930
Union de Transports Aériens	1,730	0.682
South African Airways	3,420	2.173
Pan American-Grace Airways	1,110	0.529
Transportation Corporation of America	280	0.750
East African Airways	2,120	0.917
Finnair	1,470	0.973
Garuda Indonesian Airways	4,590	2.173
Aerlinte Eireann	240	0.639
Aer Lingus	2,940	1.320
Tasman Empire Airways	1,000	1.144
Ethiopian Airlines	1,060	0.857
Royal Air Maroc	600	0.492
Civil Air Transport (Formosa)	1,020[a]	0.911
Aden Airways	650	0.855

Source: Labor data are from International Civil Aviation Organization, *Digest of Statistics, Fleet and Personnel*, No. 102 (1962), various pages. Labor scheduling derivation is described in the text, pp. 239–42.
[a] Year-end figure.

wages, and high labor productivity; and factor prices and costs for a typical carrier of a developing country with higher capital costs, lower labor costs, and lower labor productivity. These two cases are meant to be illustrative only, essentially as a means of describing the general trade-off in factors implicit in aircraft choice under different circumstances. Direct operating and capital costs were calculated for 1962 and 1965 for a selection of plane types. The resultant costs are discussed in Chapter IV, where the implications for equipment choice are developed.[2]

With regard to labor wages and productivity, the assumption was made that flight crew costs for the "developing country carrier" are approximately three-fourths those of the carrier with assumed costs equal to U.S. domestic operations. The basis for this assumption with regard to crew costs is the common experience in the developing countries that large pilot wage differences—often on the order of four to one—are largely offset by scheduling or crew productivity differences. This generalization, of course, conceals a huge variation in actual performance on a unit-cost basis. An examination of a sample of Latin American carriers in 1964 showed that Costa Rican and Colombian carriers reported direct operating costs roughly one-half those of U.S. operators employing comparable equipment, while Brazilian and Venezuelan carriers incurred costs at least as high as, or higher than, the U.S. carriers. The Colombian carriers reported flight crew and maintenance labor costs roughly one-third of U.S. costs because of nearly equal crew and labor scheduling and productivity, while wage levels were roughly one-fourth U.S. wage levels. The crew and labor scheduling for the Brazilian carriers was far inferior, low enough to more than offset any potential cost advantage of lower wages.[3]

With regard to maintenance, the assumption was made that lower labor costs in the developing countries do not produce any maintenance savings. There is, of course, the suggestion of possible savings in piston aircraft maintenance because of the high labor requirements. However, much of the maintenance on piston planes does not come cheaply in the developing countries.[4] In many cases parts must be bought at very high prices, and sometimes part of the aircraft fleet is cannibalized to obtain needed parts (which results in lower utilization and therefore higher capital costs). The

[2] The author discusses further these cost trade-offs and their implications for the choice of an appropriate air technology in the developed countries in "Air Passenger Technology and Public Policy in the Developing Countries" (paper prepared for delivery at the Transportation Research Forum, Kansas City, September 5, 1968).

[3] Mahlon Straszheim, "The Choice of an Optimal Air Technology for the Developing Countries," Discussion Paper No. 28 (processed; Harvard Research Project, 1966), pp. 6–9.

[4] Lockheed, for example, found maintenance costs on the C-47 and the C-54 in Argentina to be almost equal to U.S. maintenance costs for the same planes. See Argentine C-130, *Economic Justification Reports* (Buenos Aires: Lockheed-Georgia Company, April 27, 1962), pp. A1–A3.

Brazilian carrier Varig, for example, has often had 30 percent of its piston fleet on the ground because planes have been cannibalized for spare parts. Nor have maintenance costs for jets in use in the developing countries generally been any lower than these costs for U.S. carriers.

Fuel and insurance costs were assumed the same for the two types of carrier. Depreciation expenses were based on actual market prices, with 6 percent interest rates used for the U.S. carrier and 10 percent for the "typical" carrier in a developing country. The resulting structure of costs by plane type is shown in Tables A-7 through A-11.

Summary: Scheduling Differences and Factor Substitution

The effects of scheduling differences and factor substitution in the industry can be summarized by examining capital, labor, and output data for the 1962 sample. Essentially, firms can substitute capital in the form of aircraft for labor (all labor excluding the flight crew) in response to different relative factor prices. Capital in the form of aircraft (measured in an opportunity cost sense, using prevailing aircraft market prices) is a proxy for all capital that is variable. Labor's wage is used as a proxy for relative factor prices perceived by the firm. Capital cost data would be desirable but are not easy to estimate since, as noted, capital for the industry comes from such diverse sources. While real opportunity costs of capital probably vary widely, the relevant cost in examining factor substitution is the perceived cost to the firm; the willingness of most countries, including the less developed ones, to subsidize their carriers implies that the variation in this perceived cost is much less than the differences in the real social cost of capital among nations.

The capital-labor trade-off implicit in aircraft choice is most directly evident in flight crew costs. Actual flight crew costs are positively correlated with the pilot's wage ($r = 0.2037$). However, there is an inverse correlation of flight crew requirements per seat-mile with pilot's wage ($r = -0.3348$), indicating that higher wage firms are choosing equipment with lower crew requirements. In addition, higher wage firms are better flight crew schedulers (S_c inversely correlated with W_p: -0.2669). Actual pilot costs therefore understate the extent of the potential cost differences among firms due to pilot wage differences; adjusting actual costs for scheduling differences produces a correlation of required flight crew costs with pilot's wage of 0.4123. In short, high-wage firms have reduced, but not eliminated, an inherent flight crew cost disadvantage both by their plane choice and by better crew scheduling.

Output-capital ratios are also positively correlated with labor's wage (0.2460), but the explanation for this positive correlation lies in aircraft scheduling. Aircraft capital scheduling was correlated with factor prices (S_a correlated with W_L: -0.2518), indicating better scheduling by the larger capital users. Observed capital-labor ratios are also affected by these scheduling differences and thus overstate the chance for input substitution. After adjusting capital consumption to reflect these scheduling differences ($K_j^0 = K_j/S_a$), capital consumption per seat-mile is not correlated with labor's wage. In short, aircraft scheduling rather than relative factor prices is the relevant explanation of capital-output ratios; S_a is correlated with actual capital cost per seat-mile ($r = 0.4251$) and with reported depreciation expense ($r = 0.3854$), while labor costs are not correlated with either.

The trade-off of capital and labor is also illustrated in labor-output and capital-labor ratios, after adjusting observed labor inputs for the effects of differences in route systems. The labor-requirements function estimated earlier indicates that labor per seat-mile is correlated with labor's wage after the effects of the route system are accounted for. The labor-requirements function can be used to eliminate route system effects. Labor requirements for each firm can be computed on the basis of its wage level (but independent of its route system) by substituting the firm's appropriate wage level into the labor-requirements function, $L/SM = f(x_1, \ldots, x_n, W_L)$, and by substituting values describing the route system for the average firm in the industry. The ratio of this labor requirement to the labor requirement as determined by the firm's *particular* wage level and route system is the effect of the route system on the firm's labor force independent of factor substitution. Multiplying the labor employed by each firm j by this ratio shows the variation in labor employed solely as the result of wage level differences:

$$(5) \qquad L_j^* = L_j \left[\frac{f(\bar{x}_1, \cdots, \bar{x}_n, W_L)}{f(x_1, \cdots, x_n, W_L)} \right].$$

A bar over a variable indicates that it has been assigned a value equal to the industry mean. This measure of labor, L_j^*, can be used to illustrate the input substitution; the evidence is the positive correlation of wages to the adjusted capital-labor ratio, K_j^0/L_j^*, of 0.3858, and the positive correlation of adjusted labor/output, L_j^*/SM, with labor's wage of 0.2670. Assuming a constant elasticity of substitution production function,[5] the substitution for capital in the 1962 sample implies an elasticity of substitution of about 0.8 for the industry.[6]

[5] Kenneth J. Arrow and others, "Capital-Labor Substitution and Economic Efficiency," *Review of Economics and Statistics,* Vol. 43 (August 1961), pp. 225–50.

[6] The details of this production function estimation appear in the author's "Efficiency in the International Airline Industry" (Ph.D. dissertation, Harvard University, 1964). The result here adds one more piece of evidence to the observation of B. S. Minhas that production generally occurs under conditions which allow less input substitution than in the Cobb-Douglas model. Minhas's study of 19 countries as observations on 24 industries produced estimates for the elasticity of substitution ranging from 0.72 to 1.01. See Bagicha Singh Minhas, *An International Comparison of Factor Costs and Factor Use* (Amsterdam: North-Holland Publishing Co., 1963).

TABLE A-7. *Comparison of Direct Operating and Capital Costs of Four Aircraft Models in an Advanced Country and in a Developing Country, Stage Length 750 Miles, 1965*

(In cents per available seat-mile)

Cost Component	Costs in Advanced Country[a]				Costs in Developing Country[b]			
	Boeing 720	Electra L-188	Douglas DC-7B	Douglas DC-6	Boeing 720	Electra L-188	Douglas DC-7B	Douglas DC-6
Crew	0.239	0.397	0.530	0.583	0.179	0.297	0.397	0.437
Fuel and oil	0.369	0.278	0.492	0.461	0.369	0.278	0.492	0.461
Insurance	0.039	0.019	0.008	0.006	0.039	0.019	0.008	0.006
Maintenance and overhead	0.458	0.658	0.950	0.901	0.458	0.658	0.950	0.901
Depreciation and opportunity cost of capital								
Aircraft	0.350	0.290	0.050	0.100	0.390	0.340	0.060	0.110
Spare parts	0.066	0.055	0.010	0.019	0.074	0.064	0.011	0.021
Ground equipment	0.035	0.029	0.005	0.050	0.039	0.034	0.006	0.011
Jet crew training	0.028	0.031	0.000	0.000	0.031	0.000	0.000	0.000
Total costs	1.584	1.757	2.045	2.120	1.579	1.690	1.924	1.947
Total costs when interest rate is 20 percent	—	—	—	—	1.825	1.887	1.947	1.991
Total costs when utilization is 20 percent less than basis for above figures	1.694	1.819	2.061	2.162	1.713	1.799	1.943	1.982

Sources: For assumptions as to crew, fuel, maintenance, and insurance, see pp. 246–47. For derivation of capital costs, see pp. 75–77, and Table IV-5b, p. 77.

[a] Figures are for costs calculated in terms of U.S. factor prices and labor productivity. Depreciation costs are based on actual market prices; an interest rate of 6 percent is used.

[b] Figures are for costs calculated in terms of the lower relative labor costs and reduced labor productivity assumed to be characteristic of developing countries. Depreciation costs are based on actual market prices; an interest rate of 10 percent is used.

TABLE A-8. *Comparison of Direct Operating and Capital Costs of Four Aircraft Models in an Advanced Country and in a Developing Country, Stage Length 500 Miles, 1965*

(In cents per available seat-mile)

Cost Component	Costs in Advanced Country[a]				Costs in Developing Country[b]			
	Boeing 727	Electra L-188	Douglas DC-7	Douglas DC-6	Boeing 727	Electra L-188	Douglas DC-7	Douglas DC-6
Crew	0.360	0.419	0.549	0.609	0.240	0.314	0.412	0.452
Fuel and oil	0.384	0.294	0.510	0.481	0.384	0.294	0.510	0.481
Insurance	0.043	0.020	0.009	0.006	0.043	0.020	0.009	0.006
Maintenance and overhead	0.438	0.695	0.984	0.941	0.438	0.695	0.984	0.941
Depreciation and opportunity cost of capital								
Aircraft	0.430	0.320	0.060	0.100	0.510	0.370	0.060	0.120
Spare parts	0.082	0.060	0.010	0.019	0.097	0.070	0.011	0.022
Ground equipment	0.043	0.032	0.006	0.010	0.051	0.037	0.006	0.012
Jet crew training	0.034	0.000	0.000	0.000	0.041	0.000	0.000	0.000
Total costs	1.814	1.840	2.128	2.166	1.804	1.800	1.992	2.034
Total costs when interest rate is 20 percent	—	—	—	—	2.126	2.014	2.015	2.081
Total costs when utilization is 20 percent less than basis for above figures	2.021	1.995	2.147	2.198	1.979	1.919	2.011	2.072

Sources: For assumptions as to crew, fuel, maintenance, and insurance, see pp. 246–47. For derivations of capital costs, see pp. 75–77, and Table IV-5b, p. 77.
[a] Figures are for costs calculated in terms of U.S. factor prices and labor productivity. Depreciation costs are based on actual market prices; an interest rate of 6 percent is used.
[b] Figures are for costs calculated in terms of the lower relative labor costs and reduced labor productivity assumed to be characteristic of developing countries. Depreciation costs are based on actual market prices; an interest rate of 10 percent is used.

TABLE A-9. *Comparison of Direct Operating and Capital Costs of Six Aircraft Models in an Advanced Country and in a Developing Country, Stage Length 250 Miles, 1965*

(In cents per available seat-mile)

Cost Component	Costs in Advanced Country[a]						Costs in Developing Country[b]					
	Douglas[c] DC-9	Electra L-188	Douglas DC-7B	Douglas DC-6B	Convair 340/440	Fairchild F-27	Douglas[c] DC-9	Electra L-188	Douglas DC-7B	Douglas DC-6B	Convair 340/440	Fairchild F-27
Crew	0.492	0.476	0.626	0.677	0.829	0.636	0.363	0.357	0.457	0.507	0.607	0.459
Fuel and oil	0.393	0.333	0.582	0.535	0.478	0.410	0.393	0.333	0.582	0.535	0.478	0.410
Insurance	0.065	0.023	0.010	0.007	0.020	0.074	0.065	0.023	0.010	0.007	0.020	0.074
Maintenance and overhead	0.598	0.789	1.123	1.047	1.101	0.948	0.598	0.789	1.123	1.047	1.101	0.948
Depreciation and opportunity cost of capital												
Aircraft	0.300	0.360	0.060	0.110	0.140	0.710	0.360	0.420	0.070	0.130	0.160	0.830
Spare parts	0.057	0.068	0.012	0.020	0.028	0.014	0.068	0.080	0.013	0.025	0.030	0.158
Ground equipment	0.030	0.036	0.006	0.011	0.014	0.071	0.036	0.042	0.007	0.013	0.016	0.083
Jet crew training	0.024	0.000	0.000	0.000	0.000	0.000	0.000	0.000	0.000	0.000	0.000	0.000
Total costs	1.959	2.085	2.419	2.407	2.610	2.863	1.883	2.044	2.262	2.264	2.412	2.962
Total costs when interest rate is 20 percent	—	—	—	—	—	—	2.138	2.287	2.289	2.316	2.475	3.443
Total costs when utilization is 20 percent less than basis for above figures	2.061	2.201	2.488	2.442	2.655	3.062	2.085	2.179	2.284	2.306	2.463	3.229

Sources: For assumptions as to crew, fuel, maintenance, and insurance, see pp. 246–47. For derivation of capital costs, see pp. 75–77 and Table IV-5b, p. 77.
[a] Figures are for costs calculated in terms of U.S. factor prices and productivity; an interest rate of 6 percent is used.
[b] Figures are for costs calculated in terms of the lower relative labor costs and reduced labor productivity assumed to be characteristic of developing countries; an interest rate of 10 percent is used.
[c] DC-9 data are for the period of October 1, 1965, to September 30, 1966.

TABLE A-10. *Direct Operating and Capital Costs of Four Aircraft Models in a Developing Country, Stage Lengths 750 Miles and 500 Miles, 1962*

(In cents per available seat-mile)

Cost Component	Stage Length and Aircraft Model							
	750 Miles				500 Miles			
	Boeing 707	Electra L-188	Douglas DC-7	Douglas DC-6	Boeing 720	Electra L-188	Douglas DC-7	Douglas DC-6
Crew	0.150	0.212	0.240	0.315	0.182	0.212	0.243	0.315
Fuel and oil	0.449	0.294	0.451	0.479	0.551	0.294	0.467	0.479
Insurance	0.449	0.128	0.107	0.142	0.430	0.658	0.709	0.809
Maintenance and overhead	0.159	0.658	0.684	0.809	0.261	0.128	0.111	0.142
Depreciation and opportunity cost of capital								
Aircraft	0.390	0.340	0.060	0.110	0.410	0.370	0.060	0.120
Spare parts	0.074	0.064	0.011	0.021	0.098	0.070	0.011	0.022
Ground equipment	0.039	0.034	0.006	0.011	0.041	0.037	0.006	0.012
Jet crew training	0.032	0.000	0.000	0.000	0.033	0.000	0.000	0.000
Total costs	1.742	1.730	1.559	1.887	2.006	1.769	1.607	1.899
Total costs when interest rate is 20 percent	2.011	1.927	1.582	1.931	2.244	1.983	1.630	1.946
Total costs when utilization is 20 percent less than basis for above figures	1.901	1.839	1.578	1.922	2.126	1.888	1.626	1.937

Sources: For assumptions as to crew, fuel, maintenance, and insurance costs, see pp. 246–47. For capital costs, see pp. 75–77 and Table IV-5b, p. 77. An interest rate of 10 percent is used.

TABLE A-11. *Utilization, Stage Length, and Aircraft Operating Costs in U.S. Domestic Operations, 1962*

Item	Aircraft Model				
	Boeing 707	Boeing 720	Electra L-188	Douglas DC-7	Douglas DC-6
Utilization (hours per day)	8.48	7.31	5.57	5.06	5.32
Average actual stage length (miles)	754	630	260	270	203
Associated costs (cents per available seat-mile)	1.56	1.49	2.26	2.72	2.55
Percentage distribution of costs, average actual stage length					
Flight crew	12.8	14.3	15.7	14.6	20.6
Fuel and oil	28.8	31.9	16.0	20.5	23.5
Maintenance and overhead	30.3	24.9	35.8	31.1	39.7
Insurance and miscellaneous	10.2	15.1	7.0	4.9	7.0
Depreciation	17.9	13.8	25.5	28.9	9.2
Total	100.0	100.0	100.0	100.0	100.0
Total costs, stage length 750 miles (cents per available seat-mile)[a]	1.56	—	1.84	2.20	2.04
Total costs, stage length 500 miles (cents per available seat-mile)[a]	—	1.73	1.94	2.28	2.13

Source: Federal Aviation Agency, *Direct Operating Costs and Other Performance Characteristics of Transport Aircraft in Airline Service, Calendar Year 1962* (1963) pp. 16–19.
[a] Author's estimate.

A Model of International Airline Costs

AN EMPIRICAL DETERMINATION of cost functions for the international airline industry can be made using cross-section data.[1] The cost model estimated below relates average cost for each functional component of costs to variables describing the route system, aircraft and labor inputs employed, their scheduling, and labor's wages. The amount of labor employed and the capital expense of aircraft are determined both by the route system and by the particular firm's scheduling abilities. Sorting out these separate effects is fundamental to obtaining an accurate representation of the effects of the route system on costs.

As noted, the differences in production functions and factor prices among the international airlines imply that there are differences in cost functions among firms. Moreover, these differences, especially in input scheduling, are not distributed randomly throughout the industry. Many of the firms paying higher wages, with managements which have proved to be very capable at scheduling crew and aircraft and which have achieved high input utilization rates, are also operating over longer-haul, denser-route systems. Care must be exercised, therefore, in parameterizing a cost function relating costs to route system characteristics, lest differences in wages or scheduling obscure the relevant relationships.

One possible approach in handling this heterogeneity among firms is the

[1] The basic exposition of statistical costing is by John Johnston, *Statistical Cost Analysis* (McGraw-Hill, 1960). For a discussion of the applicability to transportation see John Meyer and Gerald Kraft, "The Evaluation of Statistical Costing Techniques as Applied in the Transportation Industry," *American Economic Review*, Vol. 51 (May 1961), pp. 313–34. For applications, see George H. Borts, "The Estimation of Rail Cost Functions," *Econometrica*, Vol. 28 (January 1960), pp. 108–31; or John R. Meyer and others, *The Economics of Competition in the Transportation Industries* (Harvard University Press, 1959), Chapter 3, pp. 32–63.

use of panel surveys, pooling cross-section data over a period of years;[2] such an expansion of the sample may yield estimates of the differences, or "firm effects." The estimation described below used only one cross section. It was therefore necessary to determine what were the differences in the parameters of the cost functions for the various firms involved; by incorporating these firm effects into the equation, a single cross-section fit was significant.

As shown earlier, the important difference in production techniques is scheduling, and the important difference in factor prices is that of labor's wages. The incorporation of these differences into the cost model is based on the discussions in Chapter IV and Appendix A. Labor inputs in the cost function were weighted by the appropriate wage and the scheduling index for that firm. Both scheduling and factor price differences were thus represented by a multiplicative weighting of the particular input as it appeared in each equation. The scheduling differences derived earlier were defined so that they are exact representations of the impact of input scheduling on costs. Separate equations were estimated for the level of input variables as a function of the route system, and independent of scheduling differences across firms.

The effect of omitted variables or omitted "firm effects," such as omitted or misrepresented effects of scheduling differences, is subsumed in the error term in each equation. Unbiased estimates will result if the error term and the exogenous variables are independent. While such independence cannot be tested directly, the wage and scheduling measures derived here are probably closely related to true firm effects; the former were not highly correlated with the independent variables used in the equations, and hence the chance of misrepresentation is reduced. The difficulties of pooling data from different cost functions in order to estimate costs from a single cross-section sample would therefore seem to be well handled by these adjustments.

Average cost was the dependent variable, with equations estimated for eight functional cost components. The variables used in the equations are the following:

n/SM = number of stations per seat-mile (route density)

h = average passenger hop (miles)

d = average flight stage length (miles)

d/h = average flight stage length per average passenger hop (miles)

$AC(d)$ = expected average direct operating cost per seat-mile, as a function of the plane choice and flight stage length

S_l = nonflight crew scheduling

S_c = flight crew scheduling

S_a = aircraft scheduling

C/SM = flight crew (in man-years) per seat-mile

K/SM = capital expenses (cents) per seat-mile

L/SM = all other labor (man-years) per seat-mile

W_P = pilot wage (dollars per year)

W_L = wage of all other labor (dollars per year)

[2] Edwin Kuh, *Capital Stock Growth: A Micro-Econometric Approach* (Amsterdam: North-Holland Publishing Co., 1963).

The sample was from 31 firms in the International Civil Aviation Organization (ICAO) in 1962; the data and sources appear in Tables B-1 and B-2. The sample was relatively small because many ICAO firms do not report complete data. The sample was also limited (with a few exceptions) to those carriers who operate at least two-thirds of their seat-miles internationally. First, route density was known only for international operations; this variable could take on a substantially different value for carriers operating a domestic network of any significant size, since the route structure of the two is likely to be dissimilar. Second, since the ICAO data include only international flights in the sample of routes, the data for seat-miles by plane type and stage length [used to define the variable $AC(d)$] become rather sketchy approximations in those cases where domestic operations are large.

The sensitivity of direct operating costs to the type of plane and the stage length over which it is flown poses one of the most difficult problems in developing a cost model. Costs of operating different plane types are shown in Tables B-3 to B-6, and a graph relating costs to stage length (for U.S. domestic operations) in 1965 was portrayed in Chapter V. Unfortunately, data are not readily available on the direct operating costs of international carriers using particular plane types over particular route systems. Accordingly, the cost experience of U.S. domestic carriers was used to approximate the relationships between costs, plane type, and route system for international operations.

International carriers describe their entire route structure and the type of plane they flew in each city-pair in the March and September traffic surveys conducted by ICAO. Using this description of each firm's route system, a variable "expected direct operating costs" was defined—a weighted average of estimated operating costs as a function of stage length. The weights were the number of seat-miles of each plane type flown. "Expected direct operating cost" is defined as follows:

$$AC(d) = \frac{\sum_i SM_i AC_i(d)}{\sum_i SM_i},$$

where AC = average cost (by aircraft type) as a function of stage length, d, SM = seat-miles, and i = runs over seven aircraft groups. The estimate of operating costs for each plane was derived from cost curves by plane type for the U.S. domestic trunklines for the sample year, 1962. Values for $AC_i(d)$ are read from cost curves for each plane group as shown in Figure B-1. Each cost value is that which is appropriate for the average distance flown by the particular plane type for that firm. This weighted average direct cost variable thus reflects both the plane type and the stage lengths over which these planes were flown.

Rather than grouping aircraft, it would be most desirable if the $AC_i(d)$ curves were defined for each plane type, in the spirit of the Air Transport Association method discussed in the text, and for each particular route over which the aircraft was scheduled. However, the representation of direct

TABLE B-1. *Route System Characteristics, Thirty-One International Air Carriers, 1962*

Carrier	Seat-Miles Flown (millions)	Average Direct Operating Cost,[a] $AC(d)$ (cents per seat-mile)	Route Density, n/SM[b]	Ratio of Average Flight Stage to Average Passenger Hop, d/h	Average Flight Stage, d (miles)
Aden Airways	58	2.58	0.255	0.490	815
Civil Air Transport (Formosa)	142	2.20	0.062	1.211	342
Royal Air Maroc	180	2.26	0.107	1.807	471
Tasman Empire Airways	233	1.75	0.047	0.844	1,350
Aer Lingus	287	2.78	0.110	1.143	224
Aerlinte Eireann	293	1.55	0.010	1.428	2,158
Finnair	310	2.46	0.086	1.472	199
East African Airways	336	2.20	0.079	3.214	337
Pan American-Grace Airways	372	1.98	0.038	2.128	829
South African Airways	505	1.94	0.033	2.161	466
Air-India	1,106	1.56	0.024	2.969	1,800
Iberia Airlines of Spain	1,201	2.13	0.034	1.431	371
Canadian Pacific Airlines	1,417	1.77	0.023	2.696	602
Qantas Empire Airways	1,634	1.59	0.020	2.365	1,651
Sabena Belgian World Airlines	1,774	1.90	0.042	2.316	469
Swissair	1,998	1.93	0.027	1.588	481
Trans World Airlines (TWA)	2,454	1.58	0.012	2.298	1,432
Lufthansa German Airlines	2,579	2.13	0.019	1.838	425
British European Airways (BEA)	2,712	2.45	0.032	1.190	295
Alitalia Airlines	2,972	1.94	0.025	1.575	503
Scandinavian Airlines System (SAS)	3,027	1.96	0.023	1.726	412
KLM Royal Dutch Airlines	3,446	1.85	0.031	1.954	655
Air France	5,809	2.16	0.025	0.962	971
British Overseas Airways Corporation (BOAC)	5,827	1.74	0.014	2.351	1,306
Pan American Airways (PAA)	11,395	1.80	0.011	1.635	861
Air Canada	4,342	2.40	0.016	1.986	361
Avianca Airlines	741	2.25	0.066	1.525	219
Ethiopian Airlines	196	2.23	0.103	2.419	276
Thai International	633	1.66	0.063	0.767	4,166
Garuda Indonesian Airways	303	2.25	0.068	1.611	700
Japan Air Lines	1,877	1.95	0.013	1.184	625

Source: International Civil Aviation Organization, *Digest of Statistics, Financial Data, Fleet and Personnel,* and *Traffic Flow* (1962). ICAO carriers that reported incomplete data are excluded.

[a] Cost data are for all operations.

Several issues of ICAO's *Digest of Statistics* were used to compute $AC(d)$. *Fleet and Personnel* gives seat-hours of each plane type, which was converted to seat-miles. *Traffic Flow* provides data for March and September 1962 on stage lengths for each plane type for international operations. Stage lengths for planes used in domestic operations were assumed equal to the mean of all domestic operations.

These data allow estimation of $AC(d)$, a weighted average of plane costs, as a function of stage length. This approximation is best for carriers with most operations international. The costing was confined to firms whose international operations were at least two-thirds of their total.

[b] The ratio n/SM is defined only for international operations, since only international stations were counted.

TABLE B-2. *Average Costs, Thirty-one International Air Carriers, by Components, 1962*

(In cents per seat-mile)

Carrier	Direct Flying[a]	Maintenance and Overhead[b]	Depreciation[c]	Total Station[d]	Other Ground[e]	Passenger Services[f]	Ticketing, Sales, Promotion[g]	General and Administrative[h]	Total Costs per Seat-Mile[i]
Aden Airways	1.227	2.506	0.517	0.862	0.517	0.345	0.690	1.034	8.793
Civil Air Transport (Formosa)	2.324	0.634	0.500	0.915	0.845	0.352	1.408	0.352	5.915
Royal Air Maroc	1.389	1.222	0.500	0.889	0.722	0.333	0.944	0.167	5.444
Tasman Empire Airways	0.858	0.773	0.644	0.515	0.343	0.429	0.687	0.258	4.120
Aer Lingus	1.289	1.080	0.523	1.010	0.592	0.662	1.045	0.488	6.098
Aerlinte Eireann	0.990	0.717	0.410	0.512	0.239	0.478	1.126	0.341	4.573
Finnair	1.226	0.806	0.710	0.871	0.677	0.387	0.581	0.258	4.839
East African Airways	1.667	0.863	0.685	0.565	0.357	0.327	0.506	0.149	4.762
Pan American-Grace Airways	1.237	1.075	0.645	0.726	0.591	0.403	1.048	0.430	5.565
South African Airways	1.129	0.851	0.673	0.436	0.218	0.277	0.653	0.218	4.238
Air-India	0.986	0.570	0.542	0.307	0.036	0.289	1.130	0.163	3.937
Iberia Airlines of Spain	1.107	0.608	0.375	0.391	0.333	0.241	0.508	0.158	3.389
Canadian Pacific Airlines	1.108	0.529	0.176	0.494	0.402	0.282	0.536	0.141	3.260
Qantas Empire Airways	1.126	0.967	0.710	0.588	0.435	0.330	0.747	0.223	4.706
Sabena Belgian World Airlines	1.263	0.631	0.479	0.474	0.327	0.445	0.953	0.118	4.515
Swissair	1.191	0.746	0.606	0.571	0.400	0.320	0.881	0.230	4.540
Trans World Airlines (TWA)	0.856	0.465	0.485	0.509	0.395	0.231	0.762	0.179	3.537
Lufthansa German Airlines	1.229	0.690	0.613	0.675	0.477	0.419	1.291	0.248	5.204
British European Airways (BEA)	1.044	0.822	0.819	1.268	0.929	0.265	0.557	0.380	5.015
Alitalia Airlines	1.104	0.744	0.508	0.404	0.303	0.336	0.929	0.141	4.162
Scandinavian Airlines System (SAS)	1.110	0.796	0.548	0.730	0.565	0.324	0.988	0.218	4.711
KLM Royal Dutch Airlines	1.265	0.615	0.717	0.653	0.502	0.270	1.053	0.398	5.041
Air France	1.480	0.942	0.599	0.792	0.639	0.487	1.109	0.306	5.715
British Overseas Airways Corporation (BOAC)	1.164	0.973	0.541	0.511	0.335	0.369	0.844	0.209	4.613
Pan American Airways (PAA)	0.877	0.813	0.512	0.656	0.550	0.326	0.654	0.186	4.025
Air Canada	0.662	0.738	0.496	0.820	0.675	0.285	0.596	0.163	3.762
Avianca Airlines	0.786	0.461	0.221	0.532	0.324	0.182	0.547	0.312	3.161
Ethiopian Airlines	1.230	0.822	0.582	0.600	0.422	0.163	0.638	0.612	4.647
Thai International	2.262	0.916	0.544	0.659	0.477	0.653	0.415	0.277	5.880
Garuda Indonesian Airways	1.374	1.783	1.342	0.766	0.676	0.542	0.913	0.270	7.185
Japan Air Lines	1.075	0.764	0.638	0.394	0.319	0.342	0.850	0.286	4.352

Source: International Civil Aviation Organization, *Digest of Statistics, Financial Data*, No. 101 (1962).

[a] Direct flying costs: flight crew salaries, fuel and oil, flight equipment insurance and uninsured losses, rental of flight equipment, other.

[b] Maintenance and overhead: parts, engineering labor.

[c] Depreciation: charges for aircraft, and all ground equipment.

[d] Total station: landing and departure fees, and other ground expenses (see note e).

[e] Other ground expenses: hangar charges, station staff for all baggage and passenger handling.

[f] Passenger services: cabin attendants, station staff, passenger meals, and accommodations.

[g] Ticketing, sales, and promotion: sales staff, commissions and agent fees, advertising and publicity.

[h] General and administrative: expenses of general office function.

[i] Components do not add to these totals because of the exclusion of the category "other operating expenses."

TABLE B-3. *Direct Operating Cost and Flight Stage Length of Piston and Turboprop Aircraft, U.S. Domestic Operations, 1962–65*

Model of Aircraft	1962 Cost per Seat-Mile (cents)	1962 Average Flight Stage d (miles)	1963 Cost per Seat-Mile (cents)	1963 Average Flight Stage d (miles)	1964 Cost per Seat-Mile (cents)	1964 Average Flight Stage d (miles)	1965 Cost per Seat-Mile (cents)	1965 Average Flight Stage d (miles)
Domestic Trunkline								
Piston								
Convair 340/440	2.51	127.6	2.50	126.1	2.70	124.8	2.76	128.7
Douglas DC-6/6B	2.55	202.9	2.45	210.3	2.38	202.4	2.53	191.1
Douglas DC-7/7B	2.72	270.1	2.84	254.5	2.50	235.5	2.68	225.4
Lockheed 749	2.89	190.9	2.98	195.5	3.11	198.8	2.99	200.5
Lockheed 1049/1049C/G	3.09	269.1	2.42	246.7	2.35	216.3	2.65	189.5
Douglas DC-3	4.34	95.3	4.59	90.9	....	.....	....	.....
Martin 404	2.60	114.6	....	.....	....	.....	....	.....
Turboprop								
Viscount V-700	2.62	212.6	2.87	199.6	3.06	189.7	3.24	186.8
Viscount V-800	2.62	212.6	2.19	232.8	2.17	237.8	2.21	250.3
Lockheed 188	2.26	260.0	2.29	249.4	2.26	254.7	2.14	241.1
International								
Piston								
Douglas DC-3	....	61.6	4.07	66.9	3.94	65.1	....	68.3
Convair 340/440	....	.....	3.03	105.0	3.38	88.2	3.02	80.5
Douglas DC-6/6B	....	242.8	....	205.6	2.48	179.5	....	188.1
Douglas DC-7/7B	....	715.4	....	689.5	2.93	288.5	3.11	461.1
Lockheed 749	3.41	235.8	3.85	224.5	3.76	223.0	3.61	219.0
Local Service								
Piston								
Douglas DC-3	3.00	81.3	2.96	85.9	2.94	86.5	3.05	87.0
Convair 240	2.55	108.6	2.55	107.8	2.43	117.1	2.40	118.6
Convair 340/440	2.33	126.8	2.43	114.6	2.47	111.4	2.55	100.2
Martin 202	2.84	93.7	2.90	97.4	2.93	103.9	2.74	104.6
Martin 404	2.64	96.6	2.54	99.2	2.58	99.0	2.68	99.-
Turboprop								
Convair 580	....	.....	....	.....	1.49	166.5	1.67	155.1
Fairchild F-27	2.54	120.6	2.55	125.1	2.53	122.3	2.50	125.8
Nord Aviation 262	....	.....	....	.....	....	.....	2.95	80.5

Source: Federal Aviation Agency, *Direct Operating Costs and Other Performance Characteristics of Transport Aircraft in Airline Service,* annual issues.

TABLE B-4. *Direct Operating Cost, Flight Stage Length, and Utilization of Jets, U.S. Domestic Operations, 1961–65*

Make and Model of Aircraft	Aircraft Modification	Carrier	1961 Direct Operating Cost (cents per seat-mile)	1961 Stage Length (miles)	1961 Utilization (hours per day)	1962 Direct Operating Cost (cents per seat-mile)	1962 Stage Length (miles)	1962 Utilization (hours per day)	1963 Direct Operating Cost (cents per seat-mile)	1963 Stage Length (miles)	1963 Utilization (hours per day)	1964 Direct Operating Cost (cents per seat-mile)	1964 Stage Length (miles)	1964 Utilization (hours per day)	1965 Direct Operating Cost (cents per seat-mile)	1965 Stage Length (miles)	1965 Utilization (hours per day)
										Average Flight								
Boeing 707	100	Continental	1.97	954	12.0	1.55	893	11.3	1.28	1,083	10.5	1.4	705	11.3	1.4	687	12.0
	100	Trans World	...	...	...	...	...	...	1.71	691	7.7	1.6	678	8.3	1.6	652	8.7
	100B	American	1.56	1,587	8.5	1.58	1,232	8.2	1.34	1,063	8.7	1.3	1,050	9.0	1.3	1,090	9.0
	100B	Trans World	...	...	...	...	...	...	1.18	1,243	9.4	1.2	1,295	9.7	1.2	1,341	10.1
	131,300	Trans World	...	...	...	...	...	...	1.34	799	7.9	1.5	947	8.6	1.7	841	6.7
	200	Braniff	1.90	702	6.6	1.78	878	7.0	1.70	616	8.0	1.5	619	9.0	1.5	673	9.1
	300B	Trans World	...	...	...	...	...	...	...	...	...	...	...	...	1.4	838	6.9
	300B, C	Northwest	...	...	...	...	...	...	...	...	...	1.4	712	10.5	1.3	734	11.3
Douglas DC-8	10, 20	United	1.59	1,047	8.5	1.44	992	9.1	1.42	952	9.7	1.6	804	9.3	1.3	898	9.3
	20	Eastern	1.75	887	7.5	1.57	757	6.9	1.29	613	10.3	1.6	616	9.3	1.2	801	9.8
	20	National	...	...	...	1.36	987	9.7	1.14	829	9.2	1.2	759	9.8	1.4	705	8.7
	20	United	...	...	...	...	...	...	1.42	952	9.7	1.3	1,134	10.5	1.2	1,219	10.9
	50	Delta	2.01	850	7.8	1.81	599	8.0	1.47	732	8.7	1.4	717	9.2	1.3	690	9.9
	50	National	...	...	...	1.31	791	9.6	1.26	775	10.3	1.2	731	9.8	1.2	799	10.1
	50	United	...	...	...	1.29	1,246	8.2	1.39	1,180	9.7	1.3	1,102	9.9	1.3	1,289	10.6
Convair 880		Delta	2.36	682	6.1	2.03	663	7.5	1.99	597	7.5	1.9	560	7.9	1.8	546	8.5
		Northeast	2.88	797	7.4	2.44	805	7.5	...	...	...	1.8	794	8.1	2.0	823	8.1
		Trans World	2.29	707	6.6	2.22	822	6.9	1.75	842	7.1	2.0	731	7.4	1.9	704	7.7
Convair 990		American	...	...	...	2.16	753	4.4	2.25	890	6.0	2.0	900	6.7	2.0	897	7.2

260

Boeing 720	B	American	1.75	1,099	7.5	1.78	1,023	7.5	1.63	1,039	7.9	1.5	1,055	8.3	1.5	1,122	8.5
		Continental	...	...	...	...	...	...	1.35	627	10.5	1.3	813	11.2	1.3	578	8.2
	B	Northwest	1.64	751	6.4	1.65	789	8.2	1.56	646	9.5	1.5	586	9.5	1.4	586	9.5
	B	Western	1.66	548	6.1	1.52	539	7.7	1.35	509	7.9	1.4	503	7.9	1.4	469	7.4
	B	Braniff	1.60	592	6.5	1.50	611	6.9	1.45	606	8.1	1.4	607	8.2	1.3	578	8.2
		Eastern	1.34	...	4.9	1.83	643	6.5	1.81	563	9.3	1.9	594	8.6	1.7	604	8.4
		United	1.87	622	7.1	1.87	699	7.9	1.36	747	8.8	1.4	787	8.9	1.3	823	9.5
		Trans World	2.45	1,087	5.7	1.94	967	7.3	...	...	...	...	...	...	...	...	...
Boeing 727		American	...	...	...	...	...	...	...	...	...	1.7	608	5.3	1.6	545	6.1
		Eastern	...	...	...	...	...	...	...	...	...	1.5	527	7.1	1.6	479	7.6
		National	...	...	...	...	...	...	...	...	...	...	...	...	1.2	636	8.2
		Northwest	...	...	...	...	...	...	...	...	...	1.7	...	...	1.6	571	6.6
		Trans World	...	...	...	...	...	...	...	...	...	1.7	676	5.3	1.6	603	6.6
		United	2.51	464	3.9	2.99	450	5.1	2.88	417	5.6	1.5	585	5.7	1.6	497	6.8
Sud Caravelle		United	...	...	...	...	...	...	...	...	...	3.1	395	5.7	3.0	389	5.9
British Aircraft Corporation 1-11		Braniff	...	...	...	...	...	...	...	...	...	...	...	...	1.7	243	7.8

Source: *American Aviation* and *Airlift*, summarized from Civil Aeronautics Board Form 41 Reports.

TABLE B-5. *Operating Costs of Jets and Turboprops, British Carriers, Fiscal Years, 1960–63*

(In cents per seat-mile)

Carrier	Make and Model of Aircraft	1960	1961	1962	1963
British Overseas Airways Corporation					
	Boeing 707	2.80	2.44	2.08	1.93
	Comet 4	3.16	3.18	3.50	3.36
	Britannia 312	3.64	3.54	5.16	4.18
	Britannia 102	4.57	4.08	3.28	—
	Douglas DC-7C, 7F	5.38	5.11	4.80	3.65
British European Airways					
	Vanguard		3.31	1.83	2.05
	Comet 4B		2.69	2.42	2.27
	Viscount V-800		2.30	2.21	2.18
	Viscount V-700		3.36	3.68	—
	Herald			4.62	3.70

Source: Annual reports of the carriers, 1960–63.

TABLE B-6. *Operating Costs for DC-9, by Carrier, for Twelve-Month Period, October 1, 1965–September 30, 1966*

Carrier	Daily Utilization (hours: minutes)	Stage Length (miles)	Seats per Plane	Direct Operating Costs (cents per available seat-mile)
Allegheny	7:32	213	75	2.12
Bonanza	7:48	292	72	1.50
Continental	10:03	374	70	1.60
Delta	7:54	270	65	2.02
Eastern	4:45	382	64	2.20
Hawaiian	5:24	131	70	2.40
Ozark	7:00	176	78	1.92
Trans World (TWA)	7:03	260	70	2.36

Source: *Air Transport World*, Vol. 4, No. 1 (January 1967), pp. 34–35.

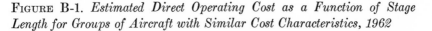

FIGURE B-1. *Estimated Direct Operating Cost as a Function of Stage Length for Groups of Aircraft with Similar Cost Characteristics, 1962*

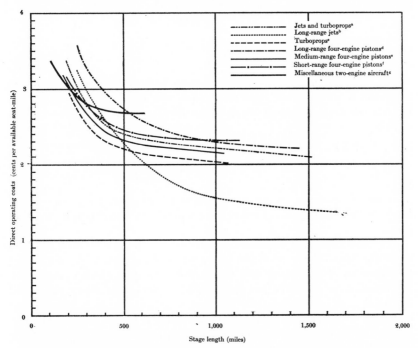

ᵃ Jets include Convair 880 and 990; Comet 4, 4B, and 4C; and Sud Caravelle. Turboprops include Vanguard, Britannia 100 and 300, and Herald.
ᵇ Includes Boeing 707, 727, and 720, and Douglas DC-8.
ᶜ Includes Electra and Viscount.
ᵈ Includes Lockheed 1649, 1649A, 1049, 1049A, 1049D, 1049E, 1049G, and 1049H; Douglas DC-7, DC-7A, DC-7B, DC-7C, and DC-7F; and Brégeut 763.
ᵉ Includes Douglas DC-6, DC-6A, and DC-6B.
ᶠ Includes Lockheed 749, Douglas DC-4, DeHavilland DH-114, Heron, and Curtiss C-54.
ᵍ Includes Douglas DC-3; Curtiss C-46, C-46F, and C-47; Convair 240, 340, and 440; Fairchild F-27; Brégeut 170; and all others with similar cost characteristics.

operating costs for all carriers in this manner would be a considerable data collection and processing task. Aggregation into aircraft groups was necessary to reduce the extent of the computations. Planes with similar cost curves were grouped together, with designed stage length the most important cost-determining characteristic. The Viscount, for example, was grouped with the Electra. While some precision is lost in a grouping procedure of this sort, the approximation apparently is reasonable in view of the significance which the expected cost variable exhibits in the equations.

The labor inputs which appear explicitly in the following equations—both flight crew and nonflight crew labor—will be affected by both the route system and the factor prices. The labor requirements function developed in

Appendix A describes the need for labor inputs as a function of the route system:

(1) $\qquad (L^0/SM) = +0.7885 + 0.5640AC(d) - 91.8(1/d)$
$\qquad\qquad\qquad\qquad (0.2022) \qquad\quad (37.5)$

$\qquad\qquad\qquad + 1,700,000(n/SM) + 50.10(1/W_L)$
$\qquad\qquad\qquad\quad (1,000,000) \qquad\quad (15.80) \qquad\qquad (R^2 = 0.5851)$

Flight crew requirements are derived from plane choice, as described in Appendix A; an empirical approximation of crew requirements can be made by relating crew requirements to stage length, route density, and plane choice:

(2) $\quad (C^0/SM) = 0.3228 + 0.3094AC(d) - 21.8(1/d) + 1,300,000(n/SM)$
$\qquad\qquad\qquad\quad (0.0974) \qquad\quad (18.0) \qquad\quad (500,000)$

$\qquad\qquad\qquad\qquad\qquad\qquad\qquad\qquad\qquad\qquad (R^2 = 0.7538)$

This will be useful as an approximation of the relationships of crew input levels to the route system, facilitating a summary of the complete model of costs.

The most important explanatory variables for direct operating costs involve the actual flying operation—the type of plane chosen, the scheduling or utilization of that plane, and the route system over which it was flown. Equations were estimated for direct flying expenses, for maintenance and overhead, and for depreciation. The direct operating costs of U.S. carriers was used as a basis for representing the effect of plane choice and route system. Labor inputs appear in each equation, weighted by the wage; in the case of direct flying expenses, flight crew labor is the variable used, weighted by the firm's average wage and its flight crew scheduling index. These three equations are as follows:

(3) Direct flying expenses (flight crew, fuel and oil, insurance, uninsured losses, and rental of flight equipment):
$\qquad AC_{DF} = 0.4403 + 68.964(W_P \cdot [C^0/SM] \cdot S_c) + 0.1889S_c + 0.1620AC(d)$
$\qquad\qquad\qquad\qquad (24.447) \qquad\qquad\qquad\qquad\quad (0.0675) \quad (0.1385)$

$\qquad\qquad\qquad\qquad\qquad\qquad\qquad\qquad\qquad\qquad (R^2 = 0.5620)$

(4) Maintenance and overhead:
$\qquad\quad AC_{MO} = 0.5210 + 0.7680AC(d) - 249.5(1/d)$
$\qquad\qquad\qquad\qquad (0.1791) \qquad\quad (30.2)$

$\qquad\qquad\qquad + 3,800,000(n/SM) + 13.42(W_L \cdot [L/SM])$
$\qquad\qquad\qquad + (700,000) \qquad\qquad (5.83) \qquad\qquad (R^2 = 0.8467)$

(5) Depreciation:
$\qquad AC_D = 0.3401 + 0.1599(S_c \cdot K^0/SM) + 12.48(W_L \cdot [L/SM])$
$\qquad\qquad\qquad (0.0977) \qquad\qquad (3.40) \qquad\qquad\qquad (R^2 = 0.3490)$

In equation (3), for direct flying expenses, the variable denoting a firm's flight crew productivity reflects the firm's plane choice, which leads to its pilot requirements, and its scheduling of those pilots. The variable S_c as an index of crew scheduling also appears as an independent variable in the cost equation. In a number of later equations, S_c will appear; apparently S_c acts as a proxy for an effect on costs which was not discovered in the calculation of scheduling differences. The "firm" effect of differing pilot wages has been accounted for by weighting the coefficient of C/SM by the wage.

Direct flying expenses are related to plane choice and stage length by the expected total direct operating cost, $AC(d)$. This variable largely serves as a proxy in this equation for fuel cost, which is a significant part of direct flying expense. Ideally, a fuel requirements variable should be included, along with its price. (The effect of different fuel prices has been omitted for lack of data.) However, $AC(d)$ is not a bad approximation since average fuel requirements per aircraft mile as distance increases is a declining curve and is perhaps the most important determinant of the shape of the $AC(d)$ curves by plane type. Route density has only an indirect effect through the crew requirements variable—denser routes facilitating the use of larger planes, which conserve on crew needs. The high percentage of the variance explained by this equation is encouraging, with an examination of the residuals not suggesting any important omissions.

The fit for equation (4), maintenance and overhead, is excellent. Route density, n/SM, has a substantial coefficient (assuming a fixed charge of $38,000 for the average station). Thin route density thus has a substantial impact on maintenance costs, reflecting the fact that maintenance tends to a considerable extent to be an overhead type of charge. The variable, $AC(d)$, proxies maintenance and overhead requirements, given the choice of planes and stage length, with its coefficient indicating that costs fall as stage length rises. The negative sign of $1/d$, on the other hand, implies that longer stage lengths result in higher cost, a result which seems inconsistent with prior knowledge. These parameter estimates reflect a specification problem, which arises because of high intercorrelation between $AC(d)$ and $1/d$ ($R^2 = 0.8624$). These two terms taken together are a means of representing the nonlinear effect of stage length. The negative sign for $1/d$ serves to lessen the reduction in costs indicated by the $AC(d)$ curves as stage length increases; the two terms simultaneously result in the expected decline in costs as d increases. (For extreme d, beyond the sample range, the $1/d$ term will obviously distort the cost calculation.)

The labor input, L/SM, weighted by labor's wages, equals all labor employed, rather than that portion of labor applied solely to the maintenance and overhead function. No data were available on how much labor was employed in maintenance and how much in other ground and passenger service functions; hence it was assumed that the labor productivity ratio for the firm as a whole was a useful approximation to the various functional labor requirements. Again, the presence of L/SM in the cost equations means that the effect of stage length and route density on costs appears in two stages—the presence of the variable directly in the equation and indirectly via the effect on L/SM.

Equation (5), depreciation, is the least noteworthy of the set. Reported depreciation expenses are largely straight line accounting writeoffs of purchase prices, which, as noted, are a poor approximation to real costs. The labor-productivity term, L/SM, acts as a crude proxy for flight stage and route density in this equation, making depreciation a decreasing function of stage length, as one would expect. The poor empirical fit of real capital consumption per seat-mile in an opportunity sense (based on 1962 market prices) to reported depreciation expenses in the above equation is to be expected in view of the sudden changes in used aircraft prices as jets appeared. (The coefficient for K/SM is significant only at the 10 percent level.) The effect of aircraft scheduling on capital cost per seat-mile is represented by weighting the term by the scheduling index, S_a.

The specification and estimation of equations for indirect expenses is more difficult. There are probably larger firm effects present in indirect costs due to greater heterogeneity in firms' operations, in the services offered, or in ground operations. It is also more difficult to specify the relevant independent variables. The variables used below were largely labor per seat-mile, flight stage length, and passenger trip length. All independent variables used in the equation were weighted by the wage rather than just the labor inputs. This is a crude attempt at adjusting for the differences in factor prices which affect indirect expenses. The presumption was that many of the nonlabor inputs will have input prices which in this cross-section sample will be closely correlated to labor's wage (for example, the relative prices for passenger food and gifts).

The equations representing the different components of indirect costs were as follows:

(6) Other station costs (excluding landing charges):

$$AC_{DS} = \frac{W_L}{10,000} \left[0.1585 + 16,235,000(L/SM) - 0.00034(h) + 1.2447S_c \right]$$
$$(5,697,000) \qquad (0.00014) \qquad (0.2073)$$
$$(R^2 = 0.6679)$$

(7) Passenger services:

$$AC_{PS} = \frac{W_L}{10,000} \left[0.0430 + 17,061,000(L/SM) + 0.000024d + 0.3263S_c \right]$$
$$(3,180,000) \qquad (0.000012) \qquad (0.1161)$$
$$(R^2 = 0.5862)$$

(8) Ticketing, sales, and promotion:

$$AC_{TSP} = \frac{W_L}{10,000} \left[0.5938 + 38,120,000(L/SM) - 1.4406(d/h) + 1.8666S_c \right]$$
$$(9,485,000) \qquad (0.8349) \qquad (0.337)$$
$$(R^2 = 0.5868)$$

(9) General and administrative:

$$AC_{GB} = \frac{W_L}{10,000}\left[-0.4923 + 16,233,000(L/SM) + 1.0893(d/h) + 4,800,000(n/SM)\right]$$
$$(6,815,000) \qquad (0.5837) \qquad (3,600,000)$$

$$(R^2 = 0.4959)$$

The underlying structure of indirect costs is not nearly so obvious as was the case for direct operating costs; the parameterization of the equations for indirect costs is a somewhat less reliable description of the underlying structure of indirect costs. However, the model does represent a first approximation with some interesting interpretations. Labor input appears in each cost component and in each case was the most important variable in the equation. Labor requirements are inversely related to stage length and route density. Thus indirect costs take on the same general downward slope when stage length and density increase (which is the same as in the case of direct operating costs). Flight crew scheduling, S_c, appears in all but the general and administrative category; this variable would appear to serve as a proxy for some sort of labor or other input scheduling or management inefficiency that was not made explicit in the model.

Of note in the equations is the manner in which the stage length and passenger trip length variables appear. In the equation for station costs, passenger trip length appears with a negative sign, implying that station costs (basically the costs of passenger enplaning and deplaning and baggage handling) decline as trip length increases. This suggests that these costs are largely a fixed charge incurred for each aircraft departure. Somewhat surprisingly, in the case of passenger service expenses, the stage length variable (d) has a positive (though small) coefficient. There is some portion of passenger service costs which is a fixed charge that, on a unit cost basis, declines for longer trips. This appears, however, to be more than offset by the greater service competition in long-haul markets, which has typically resulted in fancier, more labor-intensive service. Finally, in the equation for ticketing and sales expenses, a variable representing both passenger trip length and average flight stage (d/h) is significant, with a negative sign. The likely explanation appears to be that when passenger trips are significantly longer than aircraft flight stages, this implies that more passengers are changing planes—necessitating more complicated ticketing procedures (forward reservations and so forth) and thus higher costs, largely in the form of labor. The use of computerized reservation systems undermines such an explanation, of course, but these were not as pervasive in the international airline sample for 1962 (which was used in the costing here) as they are at present.

Summing the equations by cost components yields the entire cost model.[3]

[3] The variety of landing charges in airports made the empirical determination of an equation for landing charges impossible. Though distance is surely relevant, there seemed to be no statistical correlation. The mean level of landing charges, 0.1688 cents per seat-mile, was included in the summary of the complete model.

Assuming that the parameters for a variable in the different equations are independent with zero covariances, the mean and variance of the sum are simply the sums of the individual means and variances. The entire cost model is:

(10) Total costs:

$$AC_T = 0.2398 + 68.964(W_P \cdot [C^o/SM] \cdot S_c) + 0.1889(S_c) + 0.9300 AC(d)$$
$$- 249.5(1/d) + 3{,}800{,}000(n/SM)$$
$$+ 0.1599([K^o/SM] \cdot S_a) + 25.9(W_L \cdot [L^o/SM] \cdot S_l)$$
$$+ \frac{W_L}{10{,}000}(0.2633 + 876{,}400[(L^o/SM) \cdot S_l] + 4{,}800{,}000[n/SM]$$
$$- 0.00034h + 0.000024d + 3.4376 S_c - 0.3513[d/h])$$

Substituting for crew and labor requirements yields the following:

(11) $$AC_T = [0.2838 + 0.00002225(W_P/S_c) - 0.00066684(W_L)]$$
$$+ [0.9310 + 1.00002133(W_P/S_c) + 0.0004958(W_L)]AC(d)$$
$$+ 0.000000024(d)$$
$$- [249.5 + 0.0015029(W_P/S_c) + 0.080699(W_L)](1/d)$$
$$+ 0.1599([K^o/SM] \cdot S_a)$$
$$+ [3{,}800{,}000 + 89.622(W_P/S_c) + 6294(W_L)](n/SM)$$
$$+ [0.1898 + 0.00034376 W_L](S_c)$$
$$- 0.000000034([W_L] \cdot [h]) - 0.00003513([W_L] \cdot [d/h]) \cdot$$

This model is based on data aggregated at the firm level; therefore the underlying structure of costs as they relate to the route structure is represented here in only an approximate fashion. The discussion in the text indicated the effect on costs implied by this aggregate cost model of changes in wages, scheduling, or route system variables. To develop more accurately the details of the cost functions of an airline, especially the way costs relate to particular characteristics of individual city-pair routes, would require more disaggregated data, presumably on a city-pair basis. If cross-section costs for a single firm were available in this detail, the problem of "firm effects" encountered here would not be faced. It would seem fruitful to use this sort of cost data at the city-pair level to develop a simulation model of cost and system operations.

Bayesian Regression Estimation of Airline Demand Functions with Time Series Data

BOTH CROSS-SECTION AND time series data may be used in statistical estimation of demand functions, each having its advantages and disadvantages. In the case of cross-section data (Table C-1) from many countries, the substantial income variation is potentially the basis for estimates of income effects. However, price variables are likely to show little simple variation, making it virtually impossible to estimate price elasticities. On the other hand, with time series data, the variation in both price and income may be such that both price and income elasticities can be estimated if the existence of economic trends over time does not obscure the effects too seriously. The problems and methodology appropriate in time series analysis are discussed in this appendix.[1]

Time Series Data, Multicollinearity, and Ordinary Least Squares

One of the problems in time series analysis is that of obtaining a time series sample in which a single structural model is an appropriate explanation of the

---

[1] The author has discussed the problems and relative advantages and disadvantages of cross-section and time series procedures in transport demand estimation elsewhere (John R. Meyer and others, in a manuscript in preparation on the economics of transport pricing and project evaluation).

TABLE C-1. *Cross-Section Airline Demand Data, to and from Paris, September 1962*

City	Total Traffic (passengers)	Through Traffic as Percent of Total	City Population (thousands)	Per Capita Income of Country (U.S.dollars)	Dummy, 1 = national capital 0 = other	Distance to Paris (kilometers)
Rome	27,306	20.4	2,279	$ 552	1	1,109
Frankfurt	13,549	11.8	692	1,150	0	474
London	88,655	1.8	3,180	1,805	1	365
Milan	16,712	12.8	1,629	552	0	591
Madrid	10,395	6.9	2,443	320	1	1,032
Munich	4,025	13.7	1,125	1,150	0	688
Stuttgart	3,681	15.2	640	1,150	0	501
Lisbon	6,096	10.0	817	249	1	1,441
Montreal	10,428	9.6	1,191	1,460	0	5,525
Athens	3,657	27.1	628	300	1	2,093
Copenhagen	9,316	5.6	713	1,120	1	1,035
Birmingham	2,433	9.4	1,115	1,805	0	486
Chicago	1,310	2.8	3,550	2,270	0	6,674
Tel Aviv	2,399	25.9	392	598	1	3,284
Bristol	335	41.4	434	1,805	0	484
Hamburg	772	5.4	1,843	1,150	0	759
Bournemouth	1,087	7.5	150	1,805	0	377
Venice	1,350	5.0	350	552	0	836
Manchester	2,463	7.2	659	1,805	0	607
Barcelona	5,178	2.2	1,634	320	0	828
Dusseldorf	7,502	15.1	727	1,150	0	422
Palma	3,001	3.7	165	320	0	1,015
Geneva	17,339	12.4	180	1,250	0	394
Zurich	9,742	11.4	441	1,150	0	482
Dakar	2,504	10.8	186	150	1	4,194
Moscow	668	5.0	6,317	400	1	2,469
Warsaw	407	4.1	1,180	250	1	1,365
Douala	1,371	72.2	128	150	0	5,046
Nice	3,641	19.3	293	1,072	0	675
Miami	303	50.5	292	2,270	0	3,943
Bordeaux	1,701	40.2	250	1,072	0	494
New York	36,132	10.0	7,782	2,270	0	5,830
Marseilles	8,161	15.8	778	1,072	0	628
Philadelphia	773	5.0	2,003	2,270	0	5,983
Amsterdam	12,459	4.4	866	992	1	406
Turin	2,402	5.0	1,080	552	0	561
Boston	878	5.0	697	2,270	0	5,547
Tunis	1,673	4.9	410	275	1	1,467

Sources: Cols. 1 and 6—International Civil Aviation Organization, *Digest of Statistics, Traffic Flow*, No. 98(1962). Col. 2—G. Besse, "World Airport Passenger Traffic: A Tentative Analytic Survey," ITA Studies 63/16-E (1963), pp. 8–18. Cols. 3 and 5—United Nations, *Demographic Yearbook, 1963, Population Census Statistics II* (1964), pp. 231–59. Col. 4—estimated from United Nations, *Statistical Yearbook, 1964.*

TABLE C-1—*Continued*

Lyons	146	10.5	529	1,072	0	385
Cologne	1,548	18.4	826	1,150	0	415
Dublin	712	1.0	538	572	1	783
Cork	301	4.8	779	572	0	840
Fort Lamy	451	25.0	90	225	1	4,234
Abidjan	207	2.1	180	150	1	4,872
Brazzaville	513	39.1	134	150	1	6,045
Rabat	1,067	20.0	274	300	1	1,798
Toulouse	437	14.7	324	1,072	0	574
Cairo	1,263	32.5	3,418	200	1	3,202
Perpignan	41	2.4	75	1,072	0	780

underlying behavior. Time series of extended length undermine the premise of structural homogeneity because of the increasing likelihood of changes in technology or tastes which alter the underlying premise of a single model structure. On the other hand, users of time series of short length must face the very practical and serious difficulties in estimation which arise because rather stable trends often characterize many economic time series in the short run. These are such that the available data often exhibit little independent variation in the variables of interest.

The general problem of structural change which must be considered when using time series data is illustrated by the introduction and existence of different classes of airline service over time (see Tables C-2 and C-3). There have been essentially two different markets in the North Atlantic since 1952, business and tourist. Tourist service appeared in almost all other important international aviation markets a year or two later. The demand functions for these two classes of travel are likely to be quite different, a fact which creates problems in specifying demand functions. The use of demand data aggregated over classes of service will yield parameter estimates which are a weighted average of the elasticities of each class of travel. This problem is particularly important in estimating price elasticities, a parameter probably significantly different among classes. The assumption of a constant price elasticity also may be tenuous. Any "price elasticity" estimated from the demand response to the reduction in air fares averaged over all classes of service will reflect the dramatic change in demand resulting from economy fares. Such an estimate of the "price elasticity" for total demand may overstate the elasticity within a class, especially for less dramatic changes in price. Cherington makes such a distinction when examining the U.S. domestic industry and concludes that the market for "new classes" can be substantial, while demand responses within a class, for price changes of 10 percent, for example, are small.[2]

In order to examine these sorts of differences in the demand function for

[2] See Paul Cherington, *Airline Price Policy: A Study of Domestic Airline Passenger Fares* (Harvard University, Division of Research, 1958), p. 439.

TABLE C-2. *Number of Air Passengers, by Class, Fares, and Related Air Demand Data, North Atlantic Market, 1948–64*

| Year | Number of Air Passengers (thousands) | | | Charter | Tourist Sea Fare (Cunard) | Weighted Average, All Fares | U.S. GNP[a] | Consumer Price Index (1957–59 = 100) |
	First Class	Tourist and Economy Class	Total					
1948	240		240	12	$165	$325	259.4	83.8
1949	267		267	6	165	333	258.1	83.0
1950	312		312	6	170	350	284.6	83.8
1951	330		330	12	170	375	329.0	90.5
1952	244	189	432	16	170	361	347.0	92.5
1953	186	321	507	17	170	329	365.4	93.2
1954	170	380	550	31	170	325	363.1	93.6
1955	190	463	652	40	170	323	397.5	93.3
1956	209	576	785	50	187	321	419.2	94.7
1957	229	739	968	51	197	316	442.8	98.0
1958	256	937	1,193	99	197	291	444.5	100.7
1959	294	1,073	1,367	173	207	312	482.7	101.5
1960	306	1,455	1,761	168	222	303	502.6	103.1
1961	245	1,675	1,919	256	222	299	518.2	104.2
1962	208	2,064	2,272	315	226	291	554.9	105.4
1963	193	2,230	2,422	414	231	297	585.0	106.7
1964	236	2,833	3,069	482	—	243	618.0	108.1

Sources: *Economic Report of the President* (1964), pp. 207, 260; various issues of Department of Commerce, *Survey of Current Business*; International Air Transport Association, *World Air Transport Statistics; I.T.A. Bulletin* (Paris: Institut du Transport Aérien); *Official Airline Guide*, World-Wide Timetable Edition; *Official Steamship Guide*.

[a] Gross National Product, in billions of constant 1958 dollars.

economy service in the North Atlantic after 1952, a tourist demand function was estimated as well as a "total" demand function for the post-war period. The parameterization of the tourist demand function will presumably reflect the existence of first class service, but will be independent of the large shifts in demand functions occurring when the new tourist service was first introduced. The tourist class sample data are for 1954 to 1964. An adjustment was made in the data for tourist demand for switching back and forth between classes by first class travelers. As noted in Chapter VI, first class travelers switched to tourist from 1961 to 1963 as a result of the large fare differential. By eliminating the first class travelers who switched into tourist from 1961 to 1963[3] a consistent series of tourist demand data from 1954 to

[3] The amount of the switch can be approximated by extrapolating the 11.05 percent growth rate from 1954–60. This extrapolation shows the amount of first class travel expected after 1960 independent of changes in the price differential.

TABLE C-3. *New York-London Air Fares, by Class, Scheduled Carriers, 1948–64*

(In dollars)

| Date (first of month) | One Way | | | | Round Trip (Icelandic)[a] |
| | First Class | Tourist Class | Economy Class | | |
			Jets	Propeller Planes	
April 1948	325				
April 1949	333				
April 1950	350				
April 1951	375				
May 1952	415	290			
April 1953	395	275			
April 1954	400				
April 1958	435	315		252	469/424
April 1959	440	320	320	252	438/392
May 1960	462	320	320	257	447/401
July 1960	500	tourist	320	250/240[b]	440/405
April 1961	500	class	270	250/240[b]	440/405
May 1963[c]	475	cancelled	270	250	417/388
July 1963[d]	475		263[e]	243	417/388
April 1964	375		210/255[f]	cancelled	440/339

Sources: Various issues of IATA, *World Air Transport Statistics; I.T.A. Bulletin; Official Airline Guide,* World-Wide Timetable Edition; *Official Steamship Guide.*

This table contains only basic fares; a number of special promotional and charter fares have existed.

[a] Round trip fares, on/off season rates.

[b] On/off season rates. Off season, October 1 to March 31.

[c] May 12, 1963.

[d] July 16, 1963.

[e] Customary 10 percent round trip discount reduced to 5 percent.

[f] On/off season rates. On season, eastbound, May 27 to August 3; westbound, July 17 to September 18.

1964 can be obtained; these data are unaffected by changes in the relative prices of first class and economy service. This sort of adjustment creates a more homogeneous sample, with the demand response to fare change reflecting the number of people who are just on the margin of taking an air trip and who in turn respond to the fare changes. (More sophisticated procedures for estimating the effects of fare changes on first class travelers who switch to tourist class proved unsuccessful.)

The more serious problem which must be faced is that of "multicollinearity." The historical time series data available include little independent variation among the variables of interest, which makes the determination of the separate effects of each variable difficult. This estimation problem can be illustrated in terms of a specific model, $Y = X\beta + \varepsilon$, where Y and X are observations, normalized by taking deviations from their means, of dependent and independent variables, respectively; β is a vector of parameters to be estimated; and ε is a vector of error terms. The customary least squares estimate of β (chosen so as to minimize the sum of squared errors, $e^t e$, where $e = Y - Xb$) is $b = (X^t X)^{-1} X^t Y$. (The superscript t's indicate the transpose of a vector or matrix.) In the limiting case where one independent variable is a linear combination of another, the intercorrelation between these variables is one and $(X^t X)$, the correlation matrix, is singular. Least squares estimates are undefined.

In actuality, of course, no such indeterminacy will arise since historical time series data will be highly but not perfectly correlated. However, with the intercorrelations close to one, the $X^t X$ matrix will approach singularity, and the "goodness of fit" of the estimated equation will be dependent upon some number of coefficients less than the full set. The percentage of variance explained by a least squares regression, R^2, will be quite high in these circumstances. The actual parameter estimates will be heavily influenced by or quite sensitive to extreme observations. Moreover, this sensitivity of the estimate to the particular interrelationships of the independent variables which prevailed in the sample period, and to a few extreme observations, implies that the values obtained will not, in general, be reliable structural estimates. The estimates may be useful for predictive purposes, but only if the intercorrelations which generated the sample data continue in the future. Reflecting this sensitivity, the probability distribution of the estimates of β will be diffuse, with the variance of b due primarily to the large diagonal elements of $(X^t X)^{-1}$. The high covariances will reflect the sensitivity of the estimate of one parameter to another.

The multicollinearity problem was severe in the North Atlantic sample data. A very simple airline demand function was specified:

$$(1) \qquad \log x = \beta_0 + \beta_p \log p + \beta_y \log y + \beta_t \cdot t + \epsilon$$

where x is demand, y is real income, p is price in real terms, t is a time trend which assumes the values $0, 1, 2, \ldots$, and the parameters β_p and β_y are price and income elasticities. The time trend represents all factors that would lead to an increase in demand except price and income.

This extremely simplified model was used because of the collinearity problem in the time series data. It will be obvious presently that even the above model stretches the available information to its very limits (some would say beyond!) The product-moment correlations were quite high,[4] essentially the consequence of the persistent high growth in demand which dominates the data. Systematic procedures exist for testing the severity of

[4] The correlation matrix was as follows:

r_{ij}	t	y	p
t (time)	1.000		
y (income)	0.9667	1.000	
p (air fare)	−0.8919	−0.8866	1.000

the multicollinearity problem and locating which variables are sufficiently close to being linearly dependent to cause the difficulty.[5] In this case, it is obvious that all the variables are closely correlated. A single variable fit of demand against a time trend reveals that time alone can explain a very high percentage of the total variance in the dependent variable:

(2) total demand (number of passengers, 1948–64)

$$\log x = 5.2316 + 0.1647(t) \qquad (R^2 = 0.9956)$$
$$(0.0028)$$

(3) adjusted tourist demand (number of passengers, 1954–64)

$$\log x = 6.2077 + 0.1616(t) \qquad (R^2 = 0.9841)$$
$$(0.0068)$$

Addition of other variables to the equation resulted in a seemingly arbitrary set of parameter estimates.

By far the most common reaction to this problem is to simplify the model, usually by omitting variables. Liu has observed that data limitations force most econometricians to underspecify their models.[6] (Given the very simple model stated above, this is a relevant reflection on the demand estimation in this appendix.) This is, however, a rather arbitrary means of model specification and estimation and one which may produce misleading results if important variables are excluded from the equation. The only real solution to the problem of multicollinearity is additional information. Two models are developed below in which information outside of the time series sample, from the cross-section and from case studies, was incorporated into the estimation procedure. This outside information concerning the parameters makes up for the inadequacy of independent variation in the time series data, and yields more reliable structural estimates of the parameters. As will be seen, the means by which outside information is used in the estimation here is a step beyond standard econometric techniques, which customarily are confined to the use of only "objective" sample information.

Constrained Regression

The first procedure used was that of constrained regression.[7] The model chooses estimates of regression parameters, β, subject to specified constraints, so as to minimize the sum of squared errors, that is,

[5] Donald E. Farrar and Robert R. Glauber, "Multicollinearity in Regression Analysis: The Problem Revisited," *Review of Economics and Statistics*, Vol. 49 (February 1967), pp. 92–107.

[6] Ta-Chung Liu, "Underidentification, Structural Estimation and Forecasting," *Econometrica*, Vol. 28 (October 1960), p. 856.

[7] The model was first developed in John Meyer and Robert R. Glauber, *Investment Decisions, Economic Forecasting, and Public Policy* (Harvard University,

$$Y = X\beta + \epsilon$$

choose b to min $e^t e$

subject to $b_l \leq b \leq b_u$

where $e = Y - Xb$ and b_l and b_u are lower and upper bounds on the regression coefficients. Meyer and Glauber have shown that this can be expressed as a quadratic programming problem of the following form:

choose c to min $(X^t X b_l - X^t Y)^t c + \frac{1}{2} c^t X^t X c$

subject to $c \leq b_u - b_l$

$c \geq 0$.

This format is identical to that of the general quadratic programming problem formulated and solved by Wolfe,[8] for which programming logarithms are available. The procedure for introducing constraints has subsequently been generalized so that a set of linear inequalities on the parameter estimates, of the form $Ax \leq r$, can be specified.[9]

Determining the statistical significance of constrained regression estimates is complicated because the distribution properties generally can be expressed only numerically. Zellner has shown that in a single-variable model, with a single inequality constraint on the parameter estimate, the distribution of the constrained estimate will be nonsymmetric, usually a truncated continuous distribution with some nonzero probability assigned to the value of the constraint itself. In the case of normally distributed errors, the continuous portion of the distribution will be a truncated normal. The closer the true parameter value is to the value of the constraint, the greater effect the constraint has on the distribution of the constrained regression estimator; bias in the estimator tends to increase sharply as the constraint is set closer and closer to the true β.[10]

In the general case of many variables and inequality constraints, the distribution of the estimates is even more complex. Whereas in ordinary least squares the estimate b is a linear combination of all the random variables comprising the sample, in the constrained regression case only some subset of the constraint set affects the estimates, a subset which is sample dependent. As

Graduate School of Business Administration, 1964), pp. 181–85. For a subsequent application to intercity passenger demand forecasting, see Systems Analysis and Research Corporation, "Demand for Intercity Passenger Travel in the Washington-Boston Corridor" (processed; prepared for U.S. Department of Commerce, Office of the Under Secretary of Commerce for Transportation, 1965).

[8] Philip Wolfe, "The Simplex Method for Quadratic Programming," *Econometrica*, Vol. 27 (July 1959), pp. 382–98.

[9] George G. Judge and Takashi Takayama, "Inequality Restriction in Regression Analysis," *Journal of the American Statistical Association*, Vol. 6 (March 1966), pp. 166–79.

[10] Arnold Zellner, "Linear Regression with Inequality Constraints on the Coefficients: An Application of Quadratic Programming and Linear Decision Rules," Report 6109 (MS No. 9), Rotterdam: International Center for Management Science, 1961.

in most programming problems, solution requires searching the feasible region defined by the constraints, and hence no single analytic statement of the distribution of the resulting estimates is usually possible. Machine simulation procedures will be necessary to approximate the distribution in each particular application.[11]

A number of sets of constraints are used in the estimation. The price elasticity is constrained to be negative and specifically to have a lower bound of −4.0 and upper bounds of 0, −1.0, and −1.5 on successive trials of the model. These ranges constraining the price elasticity include the value of the price elasticity estimated in the cross-section and in case studies. The income elasticity is constrained to be positive, with upper bound of 2.0 and lower bound of 0.35 or 0.85, estimates based on the cross-section and case studies. The time trend is constrained to be positive.

The constraints employed and the results appear in Table C-4. In each case the estimates of the income and price elasticity assume values at the lower and upper constraints, respectively, and the time trend assumes an intermediate value and one lower than in the unconstrained estimation. Since the unconstrained estimates of the price and income parameters lie outside the constrained region, the constraints force the estimates to a boundary point. The tendency for a parameter estimate to assume a value of one of the constraints is a characteristic of this sort of model. If the constraints are to be effective, that is, are to produce estimates different from the customary least squares estimates, at least one parameter estimate must take on such a value. Since both income and price elasticities assume the value of a constraint boundary, the model is not useful for determining these key parameters.

The statistical properties of the estimates were not derived because of the difficulty of specifying their sampling distributions noted above. One measure of the "goodness of fit" of the estimated equations is given by R^2, a measure analogous to that used in customary regression analysis, where R^2 is the percent of total variance of y explained by the equation. Unconstrained least squares regression estimates are chosen to maximize R^2, and therefore constrained regression estimation with effective constraints necessarily reduces R^2. The reduction in this case is small. This does not verify that the estimates are true structural ones, but rather indicates that the collinearity problem is serious. A variety of constraints on the parameters yields a variety of estimates, including what appear to be reasonable structural ones. In these models the time trend is the key variable which determines the goodness of fit. The presence of other variables is of little importance. The conclusion is that reasonable structural estimates, as well as other estimates, are consistent with the data.

Interpretation of the constraints as a means of including additional information in the model structure would appear consistent with classical econometric estimation techniques. The sampling distributions are, however,

---

[11] See Judge and Takayama, *op. cit.*

TABLE C-4. *Constrained Regression Estimates of Demand Function for North Atlantic Air Market, 1948–64*

Constraints	Regression Estimate, b	R^2
Total demand, 1948–64		
$-4.0 \leq \beta_p \leq -1.0$	-1.0	
$0.35 \leq \beta_y \leq 2.0$	0.35	0.9949
$0.0 \leq \beta_t$	0.1201	
$-4.0 \leq \beta_p \leq -1.0$	-1.0	
$0.85 \leq \beta_y \leq 2.0$	0.85	0.9937
$0.0 \leq \beta_t$	0.1050	
$-4.0 \leq \beta_p \leq -1.5$	-1.5	
$0.35 \leq \beta_y \leq 2.0$	0.35	0.9906
$0.0 \leq \beta_t$	0.1092	
Unconstrained	-0.3157	
	-0.7613	0.9971
	0.1825	
Adjusted tourist demand, 1954–64		
$-4.0 \leq \beta_p \leq -1.0$	-1.0	
$0.35 \leq \beta_y \leq 2.0$	0.35	0.9664
$0.0 \leq \beta_t$	0.1660	
$-4.0 \leq \beta_p \leq 1.5$	-1.5	
$0.35 \leq \beta_y \leq 2.0$	0.35	0.9518
$0.0 \leq \beta_t$	0.1551	
$-4.0 \leq \beta_p \leq 0.0$	-0.5408	
$0.35 \leq \beta_y \leq 2.0$	0.35	0.9785
$0.0 \leq \beta_t$	0.1559	
Unconstrained	-0.9074	
	-0.0026	0.9861
	0.1933	

Source: See text for explanation. The equation is $\log x = \beta_0 + \beta_p \log p + \beta_y \log y + \beta_t \cdot t + \epsilon$. β's are elasticities

greatly complicated by the constraints; in this sense, the constrained regression model appears to be a fairly inflexible means of introducing outside information into the estimation and hence in a sort of undesirable middle ground between ordinary classical regression and more full-fledged decision-theory estimation. It seems more fruitful to regard the additional information in a subjective sense as one's best judgment about the range of the parameter values.[12]

[12] Meyer and Glauber, *op. cit.*, pp. 194–205.

"Subjective" Estimation and Bayesian Procedures

The basis for a decision theory approach to parameter estimation and the ways in which that approach and customary econometric estimation procedures differ have been developed elsewhere and will not be reviewed here;[13] however, the major difference can be quickly summarized. Classical statistical estimation chooses that estimate of some unknown parameter Θ on the basis of sample data so that the estimate maximizes the utility, or minimizes the "loss," of decisions associated with that estimate. (In its most common form the decision in question entails the acceptance or rejection of a null hypothesis, based on an evaluation of various probabilities of making certain types of errors.) In general, the parameter estimate and the appropriate decision rule will be conditional on the true and unknown value of the parameter. When choosing an appropriate estimate or decision rule, statisticians are therefore often implicitly forced to weight the possible choices by their own subjective judgments about what Θ really is. A complete decision theory format simply introduces prior or outside information about Θ explicitly into the analysis. By including a subjective weighting of all possible values of Θ in the analysis, the optimal estimate of Θ or any associated decisions can be made which are no longer conditional on Θ. Raiffa and Schlaifer have identified this subjective weighting of Θ as the "prior" distribution, and defined it so that it conforms to the customary rules of probability. Such a subjective probability on a parameter Θ can be interpreted as the betting odds upon which the decision-maker would place bets, where the outcomes are dependent upon the value which Θ actually assumes. This derivation of a subjective probability distribution, such that probability statements can be made about Θ, is central to the difference between Bayesian and classical procedures.[14]

Of particular interest here is the means by which sample data and other information are employed in obtaining this probability distribution of Θ. The Bayesian model begins with the formulation of an initial or "prior" distribution on a parameter in question, reflecting all information available to date; the distribution is then continually updated and revised as more information (sample data) becomes available. It can be shown that this

[13] Howard Raiffa and Robert Schlaifer, *Applied Statistical Decision Theory* (Harvard University, Graduate School of Business Administration, Division of Research, 1961).

[14] A familiar example, the interpretation of a confidence interval around some estimated value of an unknown parameter, illustrates this orientation of classical statistics. When asked about the true value of Θ, the classical statistician should reply somewhat as follows, "I do not know what the true value is. My procedure, when applied in a large number of situations like this one, will yield a 95 percent confidence interval whose limits will include the true value of Θ 95 percent of the time. In any particular instance, including this one, Θ may or may not fall within the interval I have designated. So make your own decision."

posterior distribution is given by the product of the prior density function, the likelihood function of the sample, and a suitable normalizing constant so that the posterior density integrates to one.[15] The likelihood function is the conditional distribution of the sample given Θ. This revised estimate of the distribution of that parameter, a conditional distribution of the parameter given the sample and the prior, is called the posterior distribution. The posterior distribution is used in choosing the appropriate decision dependent on the estimate of the unknown parameter.

Bayesian estimation can be based on any sort of prior distribution judged appropriate. A sufficiently precise prior distribution can produce any posterior distribution desired, regardless of the sample data; and, conversely, a very diffuse prior distribution will mean that the sample data will bear the most weight in the resulting estimates. This influence of the prior on the posterior distribution is often used as a criticism of Bayesian procedures. Obviously, such analysts are rejecting a decision-theory format. If outside information is to be brought to bear along with sample data, the "prior" distribution obviously must have some effect.

A complete decision-theory format is not the focus of this appendix, although both airline management and public officials engaged in regulation or control over the industry in some phase or other might properly consider this orientation in their sampling, estimation, and decision-making. Only the Bayesian procedure for estimating the posterior distribution on Θ will be discussed below, since what is of interest here is a flexible format for weighting prior information and sample data. The Bayesian procedure has that flexibility.

The Bayesian Regression Model

Bayesian estimation and the Bayesian regression model are described in detail by Raiffa and Schlaifer and will only be summarized here. The demand equation specified above is assumed to be $Y = X\beta + \varepsilon$, where Y is a column vector $(n \times l)$, X is a matrix $(n \times r)$, β is a column vector $(r \times l)$, and ε signifies independent random variables with a normal density $(0, 1/h)$. The quantity h, the inverse of the variance of the distribution of ε, is labeled by Raiffa and Schlaifer the "precision" of the process. While the Bayesian estimation procedure permits the use of any sort of prior distribution, a multi-normal prior distribution was assigned to the parameter β in

---

[15] The Bayesian model is based on Bayes's Rule. If Θ is the parameter and a is sample information, Bayes's Rule can be written as follows:

$$P(\Theta) \cdot P(a/\Theta) = P(a) \cdot P(\Theta/a)$$
$$P(\Theta/a) = (P[\Theta] \cdot P[a/\Theta])/P(a)$$

where $P(\Theta)$ is the prior distribution on Θ, $P(a)$ is the marginal probability, and $P(\Theta/a)$ is the posterior distribution. Bayesian analysis is essentially a creation of this conditional distribution of Θ from the observations a. For a discussion of the procedure for deriving posterior distributions based on Bayes's Rule, see Raiffa and Schlaifer, *op. cit.*, pp. 28–31.

the model estimated here. In addition to being a flexible way of expressing outside information, normal priors are analytically convenient. As will be seen below, if the time series data represent an independent normal process and normal priors are used, the posterior distribution of β will be multivariate-normal.

As noted, for any specified prior distribution assumed for the parameter estimates b, the posterior distribution will be the product of the likelihood function and the prior distribution. The likelihood function is

(4) $f_N(Y/X\beta, hI) = (2\pi)^{-\frac{1}{2}n} \cdot \exp\left(-\frac{1}{2}[Y - X\beta]^t h[Y - X\beta]\right) \cdot h^{\frac{1}{2}n}$

which can be expressed in terms of β and b, where $b = (X^tX)^{-1}X^tY$, the customary least squares estimates, by completing the square in the exponent as follows:

(5) $f_N(Y/X\beta, hI) = (2\pi)^{-\frac{1}{2}n} \cdot \exp\left(-\frac{1}{2}[\beta - b]^t X^t X[\beta - b]h\right)$
        $\cdot \exp\left(-\frac{1}{2}[Y^tY - Y^tX(X^tX)X^tY]h\right) \cdot h^{\frac{1}{2}n}.$

The part of the likelihood function which depends on β is only:

(6) $\exp\left(-\frac{1}{2}[\beta - b]^t X^t X[\beta - b]h\right).$

If the prior distribution is informationless, that is, the prior density of β is a constant, the kernel of the posterior distribution of β is simply expression (6), which produces a normal posterior. A suitable constant can be chosen to make this density integrate to one; the mean is b and the variance is $\sigma^2(X^tX)^{-1}$, the customary least squares estimates.

If a normal prior distribution on β is specified with parameters b' and n', where b' is a vector of means and $(hn')^{-1}$ equals the variance-covariance matrix, a normal posterior is the result. The kernel of this prior distribution is given by:

(7) $\exp\left[-\frac{1}{2}h(\beta - b')^t n'(\beta - b')\right].$

Multiplying the kernel of this prior normal on β with the kernel of the likelihood function yields:

(8) $\exp\left\{-\frac{1}{2}h[(Y - X\beta)^t(Y - X\beta) + (\beta - b')^t n'(\beta - b')]\right\}.$

Expression (8) can be written as $\exp\left[-\frac{1}{2}h(T_1 + T_2)\right]$, where

$$T_1 = (\beta - b'')^t n''(\beta - b'')$$
$$T_2 = b'^t n'b' + Y^tY - b''^t n''b''$$
$$b'' = (n'')^{-1}(n'b' + X^tY) = (n'')^{-1}(n'b' + nb)$$
$$n'' = n' + X^tX = n' + n.$$

Since β appears only in T_1, the kernel of the conditional distribution of β is $\exp\left(-\frac{1}{2}h \cdot T_1\right)$. The posterior distribution of b is normal[16] with parameters b'' and n'', the mean equal to b'' and variance equal to $(hn'')^{-1}$. It

[16] This distribution will be nondegenerate normal if $n'' = (n' + X^tX)$ is positive definite. Since X^tX is positive semidefinite, n'' will be positive definite if n' is

should be noted that with no prior distribution this becomes the customary least squares regression estimate. Similarly, a sufficiently diffuse prior distribution approaches the least squares estimates in the limit.

The above formulation assumes that the precision h is known. A more complete model treats both β and h as unknown and starts with prior information on each, in the form of a joint distribution.[17] While somewhat more complex, the essentials of the model remain unchanged. Assuming a normal prior distribution on β, given h, leads to a posterior marginal distribution of β which is Student t, with b'' and variance $(n - r/n - r - 2)$ $s^2 \cdot (n'')^{-1}$ where b'' and n'' are as defined above, and s^2 is an estimate of the process variance $(1/n - r)(X - Xb)^t (X - Xb)$. As the sample size increases, this Student-t distribution tends toward normality. The parameterization of the distribution of h and its posterior will not be discussed here since the primary emphasis of this appendix is on β.

This Bayesian normal model with both mean and variance unknown was used to estimate a demand function for total demand and adjusted tourist demand. The price elasticity was assumed to have a mean of -2.0 and standard deviation of 1.0, and the income elasticity a mean of 1.75 and standard deviation of 0.585. The prior estimate for the unknown process variance, σ^2, was 0.16. Zero covariances were assumed in the prior distribution. The resultant price and income elasticities are shown in Table C-5. The estimate for the income elasticity was 2.04, the price elasticity for total demand -1.50, and the price elasticity for tourist demand -1.42.

Given the considerable collinearity in the sample data, the choice of the prior distribution affects the results considerably.[18] For example, specification

---

positive definite; that is, if a proper prior is specified, or if X is of rank r, meaning the number of observations of y is enough to allow an estimate to be made of b, namely when $n > r$.

[17] When both β and h are unknown, the kernel of the likelihood function must include all of expression (5). The most convenient means of representing prior information on both these parameters is suggested by examination of the complete likelihood function. It can be seen that the likelihood function is the product of a normal conditional density of β given h and a gamma-2 marginal density of h. It will be useful to express the likelihood in terms of a fourth parameter, v, equal to n-1; v and h are now parameters of the gamma density on h, and β and n parameters of the normal density on β. Analytically the most convenient way of expressing prior information on β and h is that of a normal prior distribution on β with mean b' and variance $(hn')^{-1}$ and a gamma-2 distribution on the precision, h. The posterior distribution of β and h will then be "normal-gamma" as labeled by Raiffa and Schlaifer, op. cit., Chap. 13.

[18] Theil has suggested one means of measuring relative effects of the prior and the sample. Letting the variance of the posterior estimate b'' be $(1/s^2)(X^tX) + A^{-1}$ (where X^tX is the sample moment matrix, A the variance-covariance matrix of the prior, and s^2 the estimate of the variance of the error term), Theil shows that $[1/(n-r)] \ tr \ \{[(1/s^2)(X^tX)][(1/s^2)(X^tX) + A^{-1}]\}$ (where tr means "trace of" the matrix) defines a scale which ranges from zero to one, with values approaching unity mean-

TABLE C-5. *Bayesian Estimates of Demand Function for North Atlantic Air Market and Sensitivity Check on Prior Distribution, 1948–65*

Types of Demand and Elasticity, and Time Trend	Elasticities of Variables and Time Trends			
	Prior Distribution Assumed for Elasticities		Posterior Distribution	
	Mean	Standard Deviation	Mean	Standard Deviation
Total demand, 1948–65				
Income elasticity	1.75	0.585	2.0440	0.517
Price elasticity	−2.00	1.000	−1.5041	0.894
Time trend	0.10	0.050	0.0557	0.043
Adjusted tourist demand, 1954–65				
Income elasticity	1.75	0.585	1.8192	0.522
Price elasticity	−2.00	1.000	−1.4223	0.818
Time trend	0.10	0.050	0.0620	0.046
Sensitivity checks on prior distribution, total demand, 1948–65				
Price elasticity	−2.00	1.000	−1.6170	0.894
Income elasticity	1.17	0.585	1.7150	0.517
Time trend	0.10	0.100	0.0630	0.043
Price elasticity	−1.00	1.000	−0.6280	0.894
Income elasticity	1.17	0.585	1.3870	0.517
Time trend	0.10	0.100	0.0980	0.043
Price elasticity	−3.00	1.000	−2.3030	0.894
Income elasticity	1.17	0.585	1.5760	0.517
Time trend	0.10	0.100	0.0490	0.043
Price elasticity	−2.00	2.250	−1.0840	1.234
Income elasticity	1.17	1.170	1.5860	1.046
Time trend	0.10	0.100	0.0810	0.058

of nonzero covariance between the price and income elasticity estimates raised the absolute value of the posterior estimates and reduced their standard errors.[19] Nonzero covariances essentially amount to the inclusion of "more" information in the prior. To illustrate this sensitivity to the prior, estimates were derived based on several priors. These are shown in Table C-5. The most noteworthy result is the reduction in the price and income

ing increasing weight in the estimates by the sample. See Henri Theil, "On the Use of Incomplete Prior Information in Regression Analysis," *Journal of the American Statistical Association*, Vol. 58 (June 1963), pp. 401–14.

[19] This is illustrated in Mahlon R. Straszheim, "Efficiency in the International Airline Industry" (Ph.D. thesis, Harvard University, 1965).

elasticity estimates when a more "diffuse" prior distribution is used (one with larger variances). The sample is having a greater effect in this instance; as noted, the ordinary regression estimates generated by the sample are not reasonable structural estimates.

The "subjectivity" in the estimation procedure is dramatized by these comparisons. In retrospect, however, it is only the use of outside information which will solve the severe multicollinearity problem of estimation with time series data. The constrained regression model can be interpreted in a subjective estimation context, as presuming a uniform prior over the range of the constraint, and the posterior distribution determined numerically. This is, however, an unusual sort of prior distribution under most circumstances. The Bayesian model with normal priors enjoys much additional flexibility and computational ease in incorporating prior information. The more "reasonable" results, however, can be attributed primarily to the fact that a much "tighter" prior is being employed in the Bayesian estimation above than is implicit in the constraints used in the regression.[20]

Bayesian Estimates in Selected City-Pairs

Bayesian estimation procedures were also applied to selected individual city-pair routes to and from the United States. Individual markets are more amenable to a precise determination of the price or service changes which occurred, though netting out the effects of special circumstances affecting particular markets may be a problem. This is a problem largely mitigated, of course, by market aggregation, for example, as in examination of the North Atlantic market as a whole. The sample data had as observations two one-month periods (March and September) each year, from the earliest date of service after World War II to 1965. (In most cases service began in the late 1940s.) A prior distribution was specified with a price elasticity of −2.0 and income elasticity of 1.17.

The resulting estimates and their comparison to ordinary least squares regression estimates appear in Table C-6. The Caribbean markets, largely tourist-oriented, exhibit a significant price elasticity, as one would expect. In the Canadian and Pacific markets, the Bayesian priors yield reasonable income elasticities and residual time trends, but no significant price effects. Price effects seem to be relatively insignificant in the very long and expensive routes in the Pacific over the sample period; however, one would expect

---

[20] This is evidenced by examining the Bayesian estimates based on a prior distribution specified so that its mean values and "approximate range" (the range of a normal distribution which permits a variable to take on any value over the real line is not strictly defined) closely resembled the "outside information" used in the constrained regression model. (The value of 1.17 was picked since it is a midpoint between the constraints of 0.35 and 2.0 used in the constrained regression model.) While the mean and range of this prior distribution approximate that used in the constrained regression estimation, the assumption of a normal prior is a much "tighter" prior distribution, so that the prior information has a more marked effect on the estimation result as is revealed in Table C-5.

TABLE C-6. *Ordinary Least Squares and Bayesian Estimates of Demand Function, Selected Air Market City-Pair Routes, Late 1940s–1965*

City-Pair Routes	Type of Elasticity and Time Trend	Ordinary Least Squares Regression Estimates		Bayesian Regression Estimates, Posterior Distribution[a]	
		Mean	Variance	Mean	Variance
New York–San Juan	Price elasticity	0.2081	0.3661	−1.7504	0.6211
	Income elasticity	3.6099	1.6773	2.3177	0.9803
	Time trend	0.1223	0.0097	0.0862	0.0021
Miami–San Juan	Price elasticity	0.1665	0.3551	−1.7355	0.6682
	Income elasticity	3.5218	0.4996	1.6507	0.2717
	Time trend	0.1204	0.0212	0.1610	0.0032
Miami–Port au Prince	Price elasticity	0.3370	0.6110	−1.4629	0.8223
	Income elasticity	−0.0301	0.7042	0.8920	0.3120
	Time trend	0.1862	0.0123	0.1139	0.0021
Anchorage–Tokyo	Price elasticity	−0.0635	0.8646	−0.4339	0.3263
	Income elasticity	1.6882	2.0481	2.0841	0.1067
	Time trend	0.1486	0.0809	0.1258	0.0019
Sydney–San Francisco[b]	Price elasticity	3.1285	1.3306	−0.8367	0.3123
	Income elasticity	−0.1500	0.2295	1.8621	0.1030
	Time trend	0.1426	0.0128	0.0808	0.0021
Tokyo–Wake–Honolulu[c]	Price elasticity	−1.7868	1.3421	−0.3965	0.3440
	Income elasticity	5.2646	2.6659	2.1052	0.1127
	Time trend	0.0102	0.1075	0.1444	0.0019
Los Angeles–Honolulu	Price elasticity	−0.3119	0.6211	−0.4144	0.4234
	Income elasticity	3.5034	1.7032	2.0950	0.1409
	Time trend	0.0802	0.0127	0.1302	0.0021
New York–Montreal	Price elasticity	−0.8613	0.0962	−0.8370	0.5322
	Income elasticity	0.3915	2.6923	1.8483	0.1774
	Time trend	0.1153	0.0036	0.0783	0.0030
Chicago–Toronto	Price elasticity	−0.7601	1.0026	−0.7119	0.5510
	Income elasticity	5.3873	6.2530	1.9210	0.1839
	Time trend	−0.0175	0.0081	0.1126	0.0024
New York–Toronto	Price elasticity	0.0554	0.4991	−1.2230	0.6883
	Income elasticity	0.1620	0.1223	0.8395	0.3777
	Time trend	0.1101	0.0092	0.0822	0.0062

[a] Prior distribution assumed:

	Mean	Variance
Price elasticity	−2.00	1.00
Income elasticity	1.17	0.3364
Time trend	0.10	0.01

[b] Passenger travel via Qantas Empire Airlines only.
[c] Includes both traffic stopping at Wake and nonstop Tokyo-Honolulu traffic.

price effects to show up in the West Coast-Honolulu route, especially in more recent years. As before, they are largely concealed in the data by the very rapid growth in demand which has occurred.

These city-pair market comparisons are generally more amenable to interpretation than the North Atlantic case since the multicollinearity is not so severe. In the city-pair markets, the sample data have a greater influence in the estimation. Bayesian priors in this circumstance applied to many such city-pairs may be a useful means of sorting out fairly broad differences among markets. Aside from the weight which one might be willing to attribute to the prior, a single prior applied to many samples amounts to an implicit "analysis of variance" test on some very broad market differences.

Index

Index

Aden Airways, 21, 28n, 167, 245, 257, 258

Aer Lingus, 21, 29, 52, 53, 167, 174, 238, 239, 243, 245, 257, 258; personnel arrangements of, 63; scheduling costs of, 169

Aerlinte Eireann, 21, 49, 52, 54, 70, 167, 175, 238, 239, 243, 245, 257, 258; group fare rates of, 137; personnel arrangements of, 63; scheduling costs of, 169

Aeroflot, 1n

Aerolineas Argentinas, 21, 49, 70, 174, 237, 239, 242

Aeronaves de Mexico, 49

Aerotransportes del Litoral Argentino, 238, 239, 243

Aerovias Venezolanas, 21, 29n

Africa: airline mergers in, 201–02; airline ownership in, 20; airline subsidies in, 26; PAA route grants in, 41; space leasing by airlines in, 63

Agency for International Development, 28

Air Afrique, 21, 49; consolidation of airlines into, 201–02; route grants to, 41; space leasing by, 63

Air Algerie, 21, 28n, 52

Air Canada, 21, 49, 52, 70, 174, 237, 239, 242, 245, 257, 258; and economy fare, 136; operating costs of, 167, 168; proposed merger of, with Canadian Pacific Air Lines, 200

Air Ceylon, 21

Air Congo, 21, 52

Air France, 21, 28n, 49, 52, 53, 54, 70,

71, 167, 237, 239, 242, 245, 257, 258; as member of proposed "Air Union," 200, 201, 202; operating efficiency of, 174, 177; and spare parts pool, 60, 61

Air-India, 21, 49, 54, 167, 174, 245, 257, 258; captive market of, 134

Air Laos, 21

Air Madagascar, 28n

Air Research Bureau, 123

Air Transport Association, 86

"Air Union," 200–02

Air Vietnam, 21, 28n

Aircraft: airport charges for, 64–65; choice of, 20–23, 72, 77–80; direct versus capital costs of, 77–81; new versus used market for, 65, 67–69; productivity of, 75–76; stage length of, 78–79, 85, 88, 97, 98, 99, 146–47, 166; see also Jet aircraft; Piston aircraft; Supersonic aircraft

Alitalia Airlines, 12, 21, 29, 40, 53, 54, 70, 175, 237, 238, 239, 242, 245, 257, 258; cost efficiency of, 167, 168; international market share of, 48, 49; as member of proposed "Air Union," 200; and spare parts pool, 60n

Allegheny Airlines, 262

American Airlines, 52, 260

Argentina, 27, 46n; and use of foreign exchange rate in cost comparisons, 152n

Argonaut, 240

Armstrong-Whitworth 650, 240

Arnoult, R., 108n

Australia: attitude of, toward airline

289